W9-BVX-480

# CARLOS CASTANEDA,

ACADEMIC OPPORTUNISM

PSYCHEDELIC SIXTIES

# CARLOS CASTANEDA,
## ACADEMIC OPPORTUNISM
### AND THE
# PSYCHEDELIC SIXTIES

## JAY COURTNEY FIKES, Ph.D.

Foreword by
**Professor Phil C. Weigand**

**MILLENIA PRESS**
Victoria, B.C.
Canada

1993

Published by Millenia Press
#207-1005 View St.
Victoria, B.C. Canada V8V 3L7

*Layout/Design*: David Christie
*Typeset by*: ElectroPrint Graphics, Inc.
cover design: David Christie
cover photo (drawn by Dick Oden - erased by Carlos Castaneda) courtesy of Dick Oden Drawings

First edition.
Printed in Canada.

To order this book from the publisher, use the order form at back of book.

Library of Congress Cataloging-in-Publication Data

Includes bibliographical references and index
ISBN 0-9696960-0-0 (paper)

1. Castaneda, Carlos, 1925 — Criticism and interpretation. 2. Juan, Don, 1891? 3. Hallucinogenic drugs and religious experience. 4. Hallucinogenic plants—Cross-cultural studies. 5. Huichol Indians. 6. Indians of North America—Religion and mythology. 7. Indians of Mexico—Religion and mythology. 8. New Age 9. Peyotism. 10. Shamanism—North America. 11. Social science research methods.
I. Fikes, Jay Courtney     II. Title

# CONTENTS

# LIST OF ILLUSTRATIONS

**COLOR SECTION**          between xxiv to xxv

**Figure 1:** *Chapalagana Huichol Homeland*

# FOREWORD

I first met Jay Fikes in the mid-1970s, when he was a student who had just initiated his Huichol studies. He came recommended by the late Dr. Betty Bell, who had insisted that he attend a lecture of mine about the Huichols, given to the University of Arizona's Guadalajara Summer School. After that lecture, he introduced himself and told me of his first field experiences among the Huichols of the *comunidad indígena* (indigenous community) of Santa Catarina, Jalisco. I remember that meeting as being full of perceptive questions, many of which I could not begin to answer, concerning his interest in comparative information based on the field work that my wife, Celia García, and I were carrying out in San Sebastián, a neighboring *comunidad indígena*. At that early time, he was expressing already doubts about the accuracy of Peter Furst's and Barbara Myerhoff's work among the Huichols, saying that he found too many contradictions and much that seemed inexplicable because it seemed so unique. However, at that time, he did not want to think that an anthropological colleague in our study area would sensationalize or misconstrue data, and I did not encourage him then to think so. I did explain to him that the work by Furst and Barbara Myerhoff was based on the use of urban-oriented Huichols that did not live in the *comunidades,* and did come from a composite and highly acculturated background. At that point, I believe that he thought that that was a reasonable enough answer for his misgivings.

Throughout the period of the preparation of his doctoral dissertation, which was awarded in 1985, I answered to the best of my abilities his letters containing many

ix

questions concerning our field data and interpretations thereof. On occasions, we sent him unpublished manuscripts and data so that he could form his own opinions about our materials. Fikes never misused these confidences, and that fact, plus his obvious control over the data, engendered a real and lasting respect that I have for him. During the period of his thesis writing, the issue of the veracity of the Furst and Myerhoff material continued to surface. It was this student's interest in these issues, plus the questions from several other students and colleagues, who were asking similar questions about these same works, that stimulated me to include my first critiques of their works in several ethnohistorically oriented publications (1978, 1979b, 1985).

After his doctoral dissertation was completed, he decided to turn to the issue of accuracy in the Furst/Myerhoff corpus, in the context of Castaneda's works. I warned him at the time about the negative impact that this might have on his career, especially as far as a career in academia was involved. We discussed at length the low esteem in which whistle-blowers are held in our society at large, and in our profession in particular. I even sent him many clippings on what had happened to whistle-blowers, my purpose being not so much to discourage his study, but to make sure that he understood what would happen to him as a young professional. We discussed in detail the downside to the type of research that he was initiating. While I told him that I would support his inquiry in any reasonable way, I never suggested to him the course that his inquiry should take. The logistics of his study were his alone, and the findings that he came up with are his discoveries.

Periodically, he informed me of his progress, developments which progressively disheartened and discouraged me more and more as the study began to assume the shape of this book. There was something deep within me that did not want to believe the extent of misinterpretation and sensationalism in the works of Furst and Myerhoff. We felt obliged to cross-check many of his findings, which we did with our own interviews (some of which are taped) and the re-study of the corpus of ethnography under consideration. In addition, I read several articles by Furst and Myerhoff for the first time. I had stopped systematically reading their material after the publication of Myerhoff's 1974 book, because so little of it seemed replicable in our own field work; because it was so completely decontextualized; and because it appeared to have an agenda that was not anthropological in nature. I felt what was worthwhile in their works was simply rehashing of materials that had already been published, especially Lumholtz and Zingg. In my cross-checking of many of Fikes's findings, I never found any inaccuracies on his part. I had simply no idea how deeply the ethnographic errors and misinterpretations had penetrated the Furst/Myerhoff works on the Huichols. By 1985, I had become convinced on my own that these works did not have real ethnographic value, but following Fikes's investigation, I suspected that we may be faced with what deMille might recognize as *prima facie* evidence of fraud (see page 72).

As mentioned, Fikes quite by himself developed his own misgivings with a series of interviews (most of which are taped), letter inquiries, archival searches, comparative textual analysis of the works in question, and comparisons of that corpus with the field data that he had generated from his own work. His persistence and rigor is admirable, and certainly was inspired greatly by Richard deMille's debunking of Carlos Castaneda's writings as inauthentic ethnography. His work, however, is different from deMille's critique, which was done largely from a literary perspective. Lacking field experience among the Huichol, deMille concluded that Castaneda's reports about Mexican Indian shamans were valid, largely because they corresponded to the ethnographic reports on the Huichol provided by Furst and Myerhoff. But Fikes has shown that much of what Furst and Myerhoff attributed to the Huichol is anomalous and unverified. The validity deMille attributes to Castaneda's model of Mexican Indian shamanism is, therefore, illusory. As Fikes notes, Castaneda's work is as invalid as Erich von Däniken's extraterrestrial archaeology. In addition, Fikes discusses the moral sensibilities and issues revolving around the misuse and misrepresentation of ethnographic material as it affects Native Americans per se. Bias, misrepresentation, and sensationalism may infect the cultural life and self-images of the Huichol and other Native Americans. When this happens, their human rights and dignity are endangered. Clearly, as anthropologists, we do not have now nor never have had the right to distort, for our own or any agenda, the heritage of any of the peoples that we have chosen to study. Fikes also addresses the fact that New Age believers have rights, too, though clearly this is of secondary importance to the primary rights that Native Americans have to be portrayed accurately, for posterity, in the anthropological literature. For New Age consumers of non-Western religions, informed consent to products promoted by their spiritual advisors, gurus, and shamans can be based only in accurate ethnography, work which is free of sensationalism and distortion.

Another issue that needs to be discussed directly is that of misconduct in science (both social and physical), and its corollary, the issue of truth. Obviously, this is an issue not just for anthropology, but for all science and our society at large. If we as academics cannot trust ourselves to be truthful about our ethnographic data, then the entire discipline loses its credibility and its raison d'etre. We lose self-respect among ourselves, with our granting agencies, with our students, with our public, and, more importantly, among the very peoples that we purport to study. In addition, as we all know, it is important to be able to rely upon the ethnographic corpus because this is the data that are the building blocks of all theory in our discipline. The historiographic note by Shelby Foote seems entirely appropriate as a guide to ethnographic studies:

> I have tried for accuracy because I have never known a modern historical instance where the truth was not superior to distortion, by any standard and in every way. Whenever the choice lay between soundness and "color," soundness had it every time (Foote 1990: 815-16).

Foote's standard for historical writing is not too high for anthropology; indeed, it is absolutely essential. Choosing "color" when soundness is the necessary and recognized standard, violates the norms of intellectual inquiry.

If we represent ourselves to the people that we study as the preservers, for posterity, of their rites, customs, languages, cultures, and institutions, then we indeed have a very special obligation to do just that. That obligation includes reporting *prima facie* evidence of fraud when and where it can be identified and documented. Misconduct in science is too serious to be ignored or covered up. To do so is to become a collaborator in that original misconduct.

When we find fraud in science that medically affects people, it is widely regarded as reprehensible behavior. To me, ethnographic misrepresentation and embellishment of data is just as reprehensible as it infects our historical record, our perception of human-kind through time, our

images of other cultures. The American Association for the
Advancement of Science's *Science*, the New York Academy of Science's *The Sciences*, the *Skeptical Inquirer*,
among other publications, recently have devoted space to
the issue of fraud in science and the complementary topic,
pseudo-science. A recent interview between Laurie Garrett, Barbara Mishkin, and Patricia Woolf in the *A.A.A.S.
Observer* (#7, 1989) explored the question of what impels
individuals to cheat in their research. They suggested a
variety of themes; charlatanism, negligence followed by
cover-up, desperation, impending deadlines, "competing
goods," faking for personal and professional profits, and so
on. The reasons are complex and multifaceted. Fikes
mentions several possible motives for the popularizing of
inaccurate images of Mexican Indian shamans but allows
readers to reach their own conclusions. The problems that
whistle-blowers have was examined also by Woolf:

> People defending their colleagues is entirely to be
> expected. If you've worked with somebody for 25
> years . . . then when somebody comes along and
> says that the work of your colleague is full of
> holes, you are likely to examine that person rather
> than the accused. But clearly all of us have been
> put on the alert that we can't do that in a way that's
> facile or defensive or demeaning to the accuser. This
> defensiveness has to be examined too (Garrett,
> Mishkin, and Woolf 1989: 9).

Robert Root-Bernstein is concerned with the interpersonal
context in which fraud in science occurs. His generalizations about the gullibility of the audience may apply to
Fikes's study of ethnographic anomalies and misrepresentations in the works of Castaneda, Delgado, Furst, and

Myerhoff in the ambience of the 1960s and 1970s psychedelic movement:

> All frauds, scientific or otherwise, have one thing in
> common: The perpetrators pander to the expecta-
> tions of their audiences.... Fraudulent individuals
> usually deceive only those whose expectations are
> known – those who have subordinated their skepti-
> cism to their desires. In any fraud, the gullibility of
> the audience is as much to blame as the dishonesty of
> the deceiver (Root-Bernstein 1989: 9).

We, the audience of professional anthropologists, must be
especially receptive to a basic and important component of
anthropological inquiry: we must insist on documentation
which is verifiable and contextualized, and we must be increasingly skeptical of the work of those individuals, like
Castaneda, Delgado, Furst, and Myerhoff, who refuse to
discuss that contextualization openly and honestly. As
Root-Bernstein said, we are the audience; and we are
responsible for the health of our discipline. To preserve and
protect our discipline's well-being we must examine impartially all singular and unverified data. With an activist
stance for responsibility, the charlatans and deceivers will
not prosper. Concomitantly, the whistle-blowers need to be
received as contributors to serious forums concerning anthropological ethics. The "knee-jerk defense" discussed by
Woolf, without examining the cases of offenders, for
whatever reasons, has to give way to this forum. In this
fashion, the self-correction that impartial investigation of
previous research automatically brings about in the experimental sciences can take place in the social sciences.

This study is timely, too, from another perspective; in
the anti-intellectual climate in which so much pseudo-

science assumes cult status, it is opportune to root out the worthless from the worthwhile ethnographic efforts. The shameless and sensationalistic exploitation of Huichol and other Native American religious practices by anthropologists and cult-seekers alike has to be confronted directly within this profession. It is an ethical issue of the most serious proportions. To some, UFOs, pyramid power, channeling, horoscopes, subliminal stimulation, water witching, ESP, etc. may be slightly funny or harmless. But fabricating shamans and sensationalizing Native American religious practices is vicious and exploitative.

We all know that honest ethnography often contains errors. These errors are corrected and correctable in most cases by the normal processes of the development of our inquiries. The investigator responsible for the error most frequently appreciates or tolerates the correction as much as his/her colleagues, however embarrassing. Such correction is a routine feature of the human endeavor and its inquiry into the cultural systems of others. It is cumulative but as accurate as possible from the outset. But misconduct, or failure to abide by scholarly standards, requires another step, unpopular as that step may be with the don't-rock-the-boat crowd; it requires a contextualized exposé, as deMille performed on Carlos Castaneda's corpus, and as Fikes offers in this book on Castaneda's colleagues, Delgado, Furst, and Myerhoff. This contextualized exposé is necessary so that we may re-examine the affected ethnographic literature, as well as to remind us to remain alert for the activities of opportunists who care only for their careers and images, and who would misuse and hence destroy the credibility of our discipline. Fikes is cautious about concluding that ethnographic data were intentionally misrepresented or fabricated. He believes that most of the mutations he has identified can be interpreted as a manifestation of a cavalier neglect of the canons of ethnographic research (see pages 96-100). His research suggests that an intolerable level of indifference to ethnographic truth may have caused problems I regarded as a product of fabrication (1985: 151-52, 1989b: 148). One of these problems, turning an acculturated Huichol into something he was not, i.e., a Huichol singing shaman, could be a consequence of Furst and Myerhoff having failed to discriminate between Huichol religious types such as healer, singer, and *cahuitero* (see page 11). Regardless of whether one decides that fraud, as I have defined it, or indifference to ethnographic truth, as Fikes defines it, best explains a specific ethnographic anomaly, all scholars must agree that maintaining the credibility of our discipline depends on our willingness to comply with standards of honest ethnography.

Professor Phil C. Weigand

# Acknowledgements

This book is dedicated to my father, Dr. J.C. Fikes. He inspired my commitment to the "Socratic method," demonstrated the virtue of having integrity in the midst of hardship, and fostered my faith in the power of truth. My intellectual debt to Professor Phil C. Weigand can never be repaid. He approximates the ideal mentor junior scholars dream of finding. Without his support my research might never have been completed. His study of the Chapalagana Huichol represents the best of what I take to be the Boasian tradition. I am grateful to his wife, Celia, for her unequivocal support of my investigative research. She kindly loaned me a copy of her taped interview with Dr. Marie Areti Hers, identified several errors and anomalies in Furst's and Myerhoff's publications, and showed keen interest in my interviews with Guadalupe de la Cruz Rios.

My heartfelt thanks go to James David. He did much of the preliminary research on Aldous Huxley, Timothy Leary, Gordon Wasson, and the most memorable events of the 1960s.

I have benefited enormously from my friendship with Juan and Yvonne Negrín. Since we met in 1976 Juan has been an unflinching ally and a trusted companion. He understands better than any non-Huichol the innermost realm of Huichol religion.

I am grateful for the encouragement John and Colette Lilly gave me during a difficult period of my investigative research. I am especially appreciative of their thorough analysis of Peter Furst's film, "To Find Our Life," for information about Carlos Castaneda, and for putting me in touch with David Christie.

David Christie's faith in the accuracy and importance of my research helped see me through its final phase. He provided numerous leads, sent me several published references (including those of Margaret Castaneda, Ray Clare, and Joseph Campbell), and pointed out numerous omissions in my manuscript. He also typeset the book.

I am most grateful to Dave Robbins, Susan Lobo, Eric Sterling, and James Botsford for their suggestions on improving my manuscript. Thanks are due to Dr. Weston LaBarre and Dr. Carroll Riley for commenting on portions of the manuscript, and to Nelleke Nix and Elizabeth Thornton for listening attentively while I began making sense of data acquired during the first phase of this research. Rex Wilson encouraged me during times of doubt and provided invaluable advice on investigative reporting.

Before her untimely death in 1986, Dr. Betty Bell gave me numerous leads, introduced me to several Mexican government officials, and speculated about how collaboration between Castaneda, Delgado, Furst, and Myerhoff might have occurred. Our conversations about obtaining accurate ethnographic data, dangers archaeologists face from "pot-hunters," and the exigencies of "show business" and U.S. intelligence agencies did much to set the initial course of my research.

Last but not least, I am deeply appreciative of my wife and daughter. They listened to me talk at extraordinary length about Huichol Indians and ethnographic anomalies. I hope they will not have to endure again the hardships entailed by completing this sort of investigative research.

# INTRODUCTION

After passionately absorbing the nuances in Carlos Castaneda's first four books I decided to become a professional anthropologist and study the ritual cycle of the Huichol Indians of Mexico. I heard nothing but praise for Castaneda's first four books, even in graduate courses in anthropology I attended in 1975 at the University of Michigan. The acclaim for Castaneda and my lack of first-hand experience with Mexican Indian shamans led me to believe that Castaneda's work was entirely authentic. When I first made contact with Huichol Indians inhabiting the region around the aboriginal temple at Santa Catarina, in July of 1976, I imagined that I might even become a shaman while simultaneously obtaining a doctoral degree in anthropology at the University of Michigan. Castaneda's strategy of disclosing his own uncanny experiences, and implying that they were integral to correct interpretation of the "Yaqui way of knowledge" he was learning under the tutelage of the Yaqui sorcerer, don Juan Matus, motivated me to supplement orthodox anthropological research methods. His captivating accounts of his extraordinary experiences as an "apprentice" to a Yaqui Indian sorcerer convinced me that to comprehend fully the meaning of Huichol rituals I should participate in them and make pilgrimages to sacred sites, just as aspiring Huichol shamans do. Following Castaneda's example significantly influenced the scope of my Huichol research. Although I was willing to undergo uncommon experiences in the pursuit of increased understanding of Huichol rituals and shamans, I found no justification for discarding the "old-fashioned" research strat-

xxi

egy associated with the Boasian tradition in anthropology. My first flight into Chapalagana Huichol territory was arranged by a Mexican government official named Alfonso Manzanilla (Fikes 1985: 1). When I told him I wanted to study Huichol language and religion in the most conservative region of their mountainous homeland he arranged for a guide to take me to the ceremonial center of Santa Catarina. During this first visit to Santa Catarina I was adopted by a renowned Huichol healer and singer. When I returned to his house in the summer of 1977 he began explaining some of the significance of temple rituals I had observed and told me about a particularly unpleasant encounter he had with a drug-intoxicated foreigner. This foreigner had nearly killed my adopted father. The hazards of dramatizing marvelous customs of other cultures, in this case the Huichol peyote hunt, began to dawn on me.

Living with my adopted father, Jerónimo Bonales, allowed me to observe him healing patients, to observe numerous rituals, and to tape record songs and ritual texts he recited. By 1981, when I observed Bonales performing his final ritual, I was on the verge of accepting the meaning Huichols ascribed to certain amazing experiences I had while participating in several rituals and visiting some of their sacred sites. Shortly before dawn on a cold January morning in 1981 I stopped tape recording the funeral ritual song Bonales had been singing. I felt compelled to join the relatives who were preparing to bid farewell to the deceased woman for whom the ritual was being performed. I was astonished when a small, blue fly (which for traditional Huichols represents the deceased person) suddenly appeared. The blue fly was hovering near her human relatives who were standing outside their village god-house in front of a wooden platform on which sacred paraphernalia had been placed. I offered the blue fly the same beverages and foods her relatives were offering. While the fly hovered in our midst both her grieving relatives and I wept profusely. They cried, convinced that this was the last time they would communicate with their departing loved one. I cried because I knew I was crossing a mental frontier, embracing emotionally a world-view I had been taught to consider only intellectually plausible and symbolic. After this funeral ritual I was plagued by the suspicion that this great healer and singer who had adopted me as his son might be merely a virtuoso con-artist or a master hypnotist. Had he been hiding the fly somewhere until the right moment arrived? Was he merely a clever magician who had fooled me as well as his audience? If his performance was not fraudulent, how on earth had he summoned the deceased in the form of a fly? Eventually I decided to accept the orthodox Huichol explanation of his conduct. This meant honoring the Huichol belief in the immortality of the soul, and the possibility of its transformation. This leap of faith allowed me to reconcile my trust in Bonales with the profoundly moving encounter I had at the funeral ritual he performed. Acceptance was a catalyst which allowed me to digest my previous metaphysical experiences. It also bolstered my belief in the capacity of bona fide shamans like Bonales.

My admiration for authentic Huichol shamans increased steadily not simply as a result of having numerous mystical experiences, but also because of what I was learning about the sacrifices aspiring Huichol singers are expected to make, including serving for ten years as aboriginal temple officers (Fikes 1985: 71-78). In 1986, I made a pilgrimage to a Huichol sacred site hidden deep within the mountains. The extraordinary experiences I had there during my all-night vision quest were almost as unsettling and vivid as anything ever reported in

Castaneda's first four books (the only Castaneda books I have read). When I discussed this occurence with Fernando Serratos (whose account of how maize was acquired is contained in Appendix B) he hinted that many more such pilgrimages were needed if I were ever to acquire the skills of a bona fide Huichol healer or singer. Serratos suggested that because I did not live permanently among the Huichol it would be virtually impossible to become an effective healer or singer. I gradually realized that my unspoken dream of becoming a shaman was an illusion.

Admitting my limitations did nothing to alter my assumption that authentic Huichol shamans have access to a world which transcends but remains connected to the symbolic realm in which conventional anthropological analysis operates. I remain convinced that we who are only dilettantes in their world should not deceive ourselves or others about the hardships required of those aspiring to serve their people as healers and singers. Bonales and other Huichol singers insisted that their ritual songs were revealed to them by the ancestor-deities. They taught me that because such songs are sacred and acquired by profound personal sacrifices they cannot simply be sold. My personal experiences and study of Huichol ritual increased my skepticism about certain claims made by Castaneda and predisposed me to distrust non-Indians who sell shamanic techniques.

After reading Richard deMille's denunciation of Castaneda and his books, and acquiring considerable first-hand experience with traditional Huichol healers and singers, I was certain that scholars such as Carlos Castaneda, Peter Furst, Barbara Myerhoff, and Diego Delgado had missed the mark on Mexican Indian shamanism. In 1981, when I first wrote Richard deMille, I hoped he would want to do the investigative research I have now completed. It

**Guadalupe Rios displays a yarn painting**

Temple officers collect yellow root for face painting

Photo: Juan Negrín

**Temple officer leaves offerings at *Tatei Matinyeri***

Peyote dancers circle patio at aboriginal Huichol temple

Photo: Juan Negrín

Photo: Juan Negrín

**Peyote dance leader with plumed serpent staff confers
with three singing shamans**

**Huichol men singing at village harvest ritual**

Photo: Juan Negrín

Photo: Juan Negrín

**Huichol singer and son conduct harvest ritual at village**

**Huichol singer beats drum at harvest ritual**

Photo: Juan Negrín

was only after my doctoral dissertation, *Huichol Indian Identity and Adaptation*, was approved, and only because I failed to entice Richard deMille to investigate, that I began the research which culminated in this book.

My ethnographic research on aboriginal Huichol ritual, and study of the "ethnographic" anomalies infecting the work of Castaneda, Delgado, Furst, and Myerhoff prompted me to conclude that their "findings" are best interpreted as a manifestation of the American popular culture of the 1960s. Accordingly, the highlights of the 1960s psychedelic movement are summarized in Chapter 1. The scope and significance of the collaboration between Furst, Myerhoff, Delgado, and Castaneda is evaluated in Chapter 2. All available evidence suggests that Castaneda's connection with Huichol Indians, and with three colleagues from the University of California, Los Angeles who studied Huichol religion (Furst, Myerhoff, and Delgado), helped prepare professional anthropologists and receptive members of the American public to buy his books as if they were an orthodox ethnography. In evaluating this formative period in Castaneda's literary career we must re-examine the central issue of our political era, false consensus and the "credibility gap." Chapter 3 shows how misinformation about Huichol Indian shamans has been accepted by several entrepreneurs dedicated to marketing a distorted version of Huichol religion to consumers. Some of the problems the psychedelic movement has presented to Huichol Indians and to the Native American Church are also indicated. Chapter 4 contrasts the Huichol Indian use of "defensive lies" with the caricatures of other cultures circulated by professional anthropologists. To help set the ethnographic record straight, descriptions of the Huichol Indian first fruits ritual and peyote hunt are presented in Chapter 5. A Huichol glossary is included to facilitate understanding

Huichol words and names.

I hope this book helps advance several goals, the foremost being to revive the essence of the Boasian tradition in anthropology. If professional anthropologists learn anything from the Castaneda controversy it should be to place a greater premium on scrupulous recording of ethnographic details. Like Franz Boas, the founding father of American anthropology, I believe theory-building should always be subordinated to doing meticulous research. Emphasizing accuracy in ethnographic investigations will in turn promote greater respect for Huichol and Native American religions. Most ethnographers who care enough about other people to record details of their religious life will learn to appreciate the elaborate symbolism, the beauty and profound meaning of the rituals, and the dedication exemplified by the finest of traditional religious practitioners. Such researchers will also be better equipped to debunk spurious and sensational accounts of Native American religions. Disseminating sensitive and authentic reports about Native American religions may also enable consumers to identify the more astounding (and inaccurate) claims circulating about Native American religions.

By 1985 I had become distressed about the threat non-Indian peyote seekers posed to the continuity of ancient Huichol peyote rituals. When the U.S. Supreme Court ruled by a six to three vote on April 17, 1990 that there was no constitutional protection for the religious rituals of the Native American Church, whose members reverently ingest peyote during all-night rituals, I suspected that media coverage of non-Indian experimentation with psychedelic drugs and pseudo-religious use of peyote had helped cloud the Supreme Court's judgment. Research completed since then confirmed that sensational accounts of peyote use published by academics such as Castaneda, Furst, and

Myerhoff, in conjunction with lavish publicity accorded to Aldous Huxley, Timothy Leary, Gordon Wasson and other psychedelic celebrities (see Chapter 1), helped enhance the appeal of psychedelic experimentation to non-Indians. Dread about psychedelic drug use among non-Indians is widespread in America. Fear of recreational drug use is an obstacle which hampers passage of national legislation needed to protect the solemn religious practices of the Native American Church. The legal precedent set in this landmark Supreme Court ruling jeopardizes the religious freedom of all Americans. It has already caused the religiously motivated conduct of Jews, Quakers, Amish, and others to be abridged or prohibited.

Today, even ordinary Americans must learn the truth about Native American Church rituals. Because this 1990 Supreme Court ruling (described in Appendix A) gives voters extraordinary power to decide matters of religious freedom, non-Indians must have accurate information about Native American religions. In particular, the dignified and sacramental use of peyote among the Huichol, and members of the Native American Church, must be accurately distinguished from recreational drug use advocated by psychedelic partisans.

The concerns mentioned above might never have been so compelling had I not learned so much from certain Huichol friends and teachers. The Huichol healers and singers I have known best worship a Creator who takes the form of a child in order to instruct them. Some of my readers will identify their child-deity as symbolic of our species' perennial quest for enlightenment. One of Aldous Huxley's favorite excerpts illustrates the essence of the pursuit of truth common to science, Christianity, Huichol Indian and other religions:

Science seems to me to teach, in the highest and strongest manner, the great truth which is embodied in the Christian concept of the entire surrender to the will of God. Sit down before fact like a little child, and be prepared to give up every preconceived notion, follow humbly wherever and to whatever abysses Nature leads or you shall learn nothing. I have only begun to learn content and peace of mind since I have resolved at all risks to do this (L. Huxley 1968: 330).

The information I obtained from my Huichol teachers and friends, combined with data derived later from investigative research, should help unravel misconceptions stimulated by Castaneda's writing about an allegedly Yaqui Indian "way of knowledge," and misinterpretations of Huichol Indian religion circulated by Furst, Myerhoff, and Delgado. I have concluded that the caricature of Huichol religion circulated by these three UCLA graduates was compounded by copious misinformation contained in Castaneda's first few books. Yet my research into Castaneda's Huichol connection yielded no evidence of any all-encompassing conspiracy between Furst, Myerhoff, Delgado, and Castaneda. All available evidence indicates that the primary problem each of these four UCLA graduates exhibited, in varying degrees, was a lack of concern for ethnographic truth (see page 97).

# Prologue

## *The Murder of Ramón Medina Silva*

When Ramón Medina Silva was murdered on June 23, 1971 he was almost as famous as Carlos Castaneda's teacher, don Juan Matus. Reports from Barbara Myerhoff and Ramón Medina's widow (cited in Chapter 2) indicate that Castaneda's character, don Juan Matus, closely resembled Ramón Medina. Although Ramón Medina was a Huichol Indian, two anthropologists, Peter Furst and Barbara Myerhoff, turned him into a Huichol *mara'acame* and full-fledged singer, which he was not. "He (Medina) was cynically exploited, even after his tragic murder, and turned into something he was not" (Weigand 1985: 151).

Ramón Medina's family, like hundreds of other Huichol Indian refugees, left the aboriginal Huichol homeland, whose title had been recognized by the Spanish Crown in 1722, to escape the violence of the Mexican revolution, which began in 1910. The revolution prompted some Huichol to migrate to Mexican cities. Others founded enclaves on land controlled by Mexicans. Such refugee Huichol settlements have, for the last 80 years, been subject to greater acculturation than more isolated regions within the traditional Chapalagana Huichol homeland (Benítez 1968a; Weigand 1981, 1985). As a result, most traditional Huichol social, economic, and political forms have disappeared in refugee Huichol enclaves. Also absent among the refugee Huichol are the ceremonial centers where aboriginal rituals are performed. The collapse of this particular social institution is particularly crucial because Huichol temple officers form the backbone of traditional Huichol

1

religion and facilitate the education of aspiring Huichol healers and singers. The higher proportion of female healers and singers, most notably Ramón Medina's mother and older sister, which Benítez observed among refugee Huichol (1968a: 355-56), may be a concomitant of their having abandoned the aboriginal ritual cycle still performed at various Huichol ceremonial centers in the Chapalagana Huichol homeland. Inasmuch as refugee Huichol are more acculturated than Chapalagana Huichol who have remained within aboriginal territory (Benítez 1968a: 353-54; Weigand 1979a, 1979b, 1981, 1985), they are typically less well informed about aboriginal Huichol rituals, and about sacred sites located within Chapalagana Huichol territory.

Today most professional anthropologists lacking research experience among the traditional Chapalagana Huichol still have the mistaken impression that Ramón Medina was a Huichol "shaman," and a well-qualified representative of traditional Chapalagana Huichol culture. But Ramón Medina's popularizers, Furst and Myerhoff, did not conduct ethnographic research among the traditional Huichol. Nor did they use traditional Huichol singers (shamans) as informants. Nor did they provide candid reports about Ramón Medina and his relatives, accounts comparable to those published in Spanish by the Mexican writer and journalist, Fernando Benítez (1968a). Accordingly, Ramón Medina and his relatives appear to inhabit a touching and colorful fantasy land. The best way to begin unmasking this charming but "separate reality" is to summarize the events surrounding Ramón Medina's tragic murder, as told by his widow, Guadalupe de la Cruz Rios.

In an interview taped on March 23, 1991, I asked Guadalupe Rios (**GR**) to explain how Ramón Medina was murdered. Who murdered him and for what motive? She dictated this story without prodding. My questions, indicated by putting my initials inside parenthesis (**JF**), were meant only to clarify her narrative.

(**GR**) We also had a house there in El Colorín. I had a house there with my father, José Rios. I had requested that people build a house for me there (at El Colorín). Ramón (Medina Silva) was here in Tepíc. He had another woman. A sister (of his) had given him this woman. It wasn't desirable for me to stay with him so I separated myself from him. He went there (to El Colorín). I didn't want to follow him, but he insisted and said, "How am I going to leave you? It was my wish (to marry you) and when I acquired you it was with work." That is what Ramón said. "That is why I don't want to leave you," he said. "What I am going to do is to abandon this woman they gave me because she doesn't serve me. She has already been sexually involved with a brother of mine. That is why I don't really want her anymore. I would prefer to get back together with you. So I am going to send that woman back to her father."

(**JF**) What was the woman's name?

(**GR**) Her name was Leuteria. Leuteria Gonzales was her name (For more about Leuteria see Benitez 1968a: 354, 358-363).

(**JF**) Was she from El Colorín?

(**GR**) She was from the Mesa de Caballo (The Plateau of the Horse). She was from somewhere else. And then they separated. Ramón went to leave her with her father, but they already had a child. She had a little boy. And then he went to leave her and then he came back to me. When we got back together again Ramón told me that, "We are going to go because I have a lot of work in Tepíc. So you must help do the work. From now on we will live very well." So I told him, "Look, if you don't do the same thing you did to me again (commit adultery) then I am willing. But if you persist in doing the same thing, then I do not want to (get back together). I have recovered from what you did to me. "But no," he said, "I am going to change." "All right then, if that is the way it is I'll come back to you," I told him. So we came to Tepíc and we started to work.

Sometime later, it was a female cousin (named Mariana) who arrived with us. They suspected that a robbery had taken place. She asked Ramón if he could help her (to investigate the robbery). So Ramón said that he could help her. I didn't imagine that this cousin of mine was going to deceive me. So they came back to organize everything well so that nothing would happen to her. I think she had promised him she would be his (woman). That is how it was when she came. But that woman, my cousin, already had a husband. They (Ramón and Mariana) surely had an agreement. Finally they came back. My cousin arrived very late one night. They must have had sex. I still didn't know anything. I thought, well it is my cousin. Why should I be angry? But that is what happened. And then she left.

Then a week passed and then Ramón said (something), because a sister of his had sent him a letter. That sister had been saying to that woman (Mariana), that she liked Ramón. Because I couldn't have children and she (Ramón's sister) wanted Ramón to have a child. That is what my sister-in-law said to her. It must have convinced him. So she got involved.

The woman left. Everything had been arranged. A week later Ramón said, "My sister has sent me a letter (requesting) that I go (to see her)." So I told him, because they were going to begin planting, "Look, it will be the same if I go instead of you. You have a lot of work to do. It will be better if you stay here to work and I go. I am going to go and take care of this matter. Anyway, with money everything can be accomplished. So I am going to go." But then he told me, "No, I must go personally to see why they sent me this letter. I am going to learn why." "All right then, if that is how it is, you go ahead. I will remain here working." So then he left. He left on a Sunday. On Monday they were performing a ritual (or having a party) there at El Colorín. (**JF**) Which ritual were they performing? (**GR**) They were performing a ritual at El Colorín in order to plant (corn). So they arrived Monday up above on the plateau overlooking El Colorín. Then my father, José Rios, said to Ramón, "Now that you have come, I am invited to attend a ritual – why don't you come too?" "Very well then. I am going too because I have been longing for some corn beer."

So they went that afternoon to El Colorín. They arrived in the afternoon, but the singer (shaman) who was to sing there hadn't arrived yet. So Ramón spoke to my cousins, because they are musicians. He said, "Why don't you play us some music? It is very quiet and we need to liven things up. Why don't you do me the favor of playing for a couple of hours?" "No, but our instruments are up above there at the Mesita (the plateau)." "But I will pay for everything," Ramón said. "Why don't you send a boy there to bring back your instruments?" So they sent somebody there to bring back the instruments. So they started to play their music and while they were playing the singer arrived. But the singer was already drunk when he arrived. The singer was a friend of Ramón's. His name was Pablo. Ramón and Pablo the singer were friends. They approached each other and hugged each other there. The singer took out a gourd container full of corn beer and gave it to Ramón. He drank it. So Ramón told him, "We are having a great time here. Doesn't that please you?" "Yes, of course."

A little while later they spoke to Alejandro, a man who has died since then, and who had a daughter that was an "old maid." Ramón asked him for permission to dance with his daughter. The father said he didn't know (about that), only his daughter could decide if she would dance or not. "Ask her if she wants to dance." So Ramón went over to the woman to ask her if she would dance and the woman said yes. So he helped her stand up and they began dancing (in the way Mexicans do). Nothing had happened yet when Ramón danced. Ramón had a friend with him and they said that while they were dancing the singer started shooting bullets at them because the woman was, I believe, a lover of the singer. Because of that (shooting) they stopped playing the music. The singer didn't say anything. He only shot. The bullets passed by the dancers but they didn't hit him.

A little while later Ramón said, "Well I have to go relieve myself." So he went behind the house and another man was over there. He began a conversation with the other man when he felt the bullets coming from behind him. When he turned around the bullets hit him. He was hit by six bullets. One here, one in his arm, six bullets. My cousins were there too and two of them were hit with bullets.

Why did this happen? Then they said that the wrong-doer (the singer) started running away. He didn't sing anymore after shooting. He started to flee. It was nighttime. There was a small pool of water below a tiny waterfall and they said he fell down there into the pool. The youngest cousin of mine asked Ramón, "My brother-in-law, you have a gun, why don't you shoot too." No, said Ramón "I don't want to stain my hands. Despite what has happened, I still don't want to lift a finger against the singer." Another cousin asked to borrow the gun and he took it from Ramón. He went after the singer and they said that the singer fell. They were shooting bullets but they could not hit him. So the youngest cousin took a knife from Ramón and he stabbed the singer. He stabbed him here and another one about here (she points to her abdomen). The singer fell into the pool of water. Later everybody was gathered around to lift him out of there. He was badly wounded too. He was (wounded) over there and Ramón was writhing around. After that the brawl was over. So they decided it would be best to take Ramón up to the Mesita with my father don José. They arrived up there and bound up Ramón's wounds very well. A bullet had passed through his arm but the other ones in his stomach were still in there. That's what happened.

It was Tuesday morning when they sent a messenger to Tepíc, telling me to get a helicopter, because Ramón wanted to return and he had a friend who owned a helicopter . . . . It was Wednesday and we left. We had already sent the messenger (to tell them) where we would meet each other because they urged him to hurry. Dr. Campos had all the medical supplies with him to give him (Ramón). We were approaching the river. It was already late. The sun was setting. The doctor said, "I think they are coming on foot." I said, "No, they are not coming on foot. They are coming by river," I told him. "But, they aren't bringing him alive?" I said to him. "How do you know?" he asked. "Because," I said, "I have a premonition. We will find out whether it is true," I said to him.

Then when they left (the scene of the crime), Ramón's beloved was already dressed in black, and (so was) his sister. They were coming (dressed) that way. "I told you, didn't I, that they wouldn't be bringing him alive. At that moment when I was telling you I believe that was when Ramón died." So that was the way they brought him. Then it began pouring rain . . .

So we transported him in that Tropical truck. All of us went (to the hospital). They charged me 200 (pesos) and I paid it, to carry him in that Tropical truck. I paid. The driver said, "It is nighttime, so I must charge that much." It doesn't matter we must take him. So we went at night and arrived there at the central hospital (in Tepíc). So they removed him and put him in there. I didn't want to go near there. I was in a rage. His lover was there, seated by his side. (**JF**) What was her name? (**GR**) Her name was Mariana. The lover of the singer (who shot Ramón) was the one dancing with Ramón. (**JF**) She was the lover of the singer who killed Ramón. Right? (**GR**) No, the lover of the singer (who shot Ramón) was named Juana. She was named Juana, and Ramón's lover was Mariana, who is my cousin. She was the one (inside the hospital). I was outside. I was in a rage. But then I thought, well, what am I going to do out here? There are a lot of people but I thought that I should kick her, Mariana my cousin. . . . But I had to endure it.

A lot of people came, friends and relatives of Ramón's. They were all outside there. They were drinking and they invited me. I didn't want to drink because I was so angry. I didn't want to drink. The next day they did the *histocia* (**JF**: I infer from the context that this non-Spanish word means deposition or autopsy) there. After that I came in but to scold him (Ramón). Three times I hit him. He was laying there in bed (and I said) "Look, Ramón I was telling you. I was telling you, do you remember?" Three times I spoke: "You wanted to end up this way," I told him. "That is why I wanted to go (to El Colorín instead of Ramón), but you wanted it that way. And now I guess you are satisfied with how things are." On the third time when I hit him on top of his head, then it was as if he moved, and he stretched out. That is all I had to say.

Then I left, and went outside. The woman (Mariana) was there crying and screaming. That woman, my cousin. I was still extremely angry with her (my cousin).

(JF) Was Juana there?

(GR) No, she didn't come.... All the brothers and sisters were there but the injured ones, my cousins, were already in jail, because the wrongdoer had still not died. They said he had blamed them. The singer alleged that they had attacked him and stabbed him. They brought him back wounded to the hospital. They had him there healing him.

The next day we went to bury him (Ramón)... There he remains. I told him, "Now truly you are all satisfied." Then I was (so upset) that I got very drunk. Dr. Campos and José Benitez took me to my house. They took me home but I didn't know it. It wasn't until the next morning that I woke up and wondered what had happened. Then I remembered that it was because of that woman (Mariana) that this had happened, that Ramón had died.

(JF) Guadalupe, do you think that they set up a trap to trick Ramón?

(GR) I thought it was that way, that it was a trap because Ramón was earning a lot of money and because of envy I believe that this had happened I thought. That cousin Mariana had another lover, and I believe that her lover had ordered the murder of Ramón. The singer (the one who had shot Ramón), was the godfather of this lover of my cousin. I think he ordered him (the singer) to kill Ramón.

(JF) Then the singer didn't know that Ramón was going to dance with his lover? They also fooled him, the singer who killed Ramón, right?

(GR) Yes, he found out. As I say, they (the singer and Ramón) were good friends, but the singer was very drunk. Ramón was not drunk. The singer was drunk, and perhaps to trick him this happened too I thought. But later, when the singer had recuperated they put him in prison too. My cousins were in jail over there too. So when I saw the singer I asked him why he had done it. And he told me, while crying, "I didn't know anything. We were such good friends. I don't know what came over me. It is only now that I realize I did wrong," the singer told me.

A sister of Ramón's went there (to the prison) too. She told him a lot of things, and really scolded him a lot. She said, "Anyway you will have to leave prison someday and we will see you then." "Yes, I owe you," he said. "I already owe you. Anyway, I wasn't planning to do it," he said. But I think they had already paid him. They had already told him to do it (murder Ramón). The singer never changed his story (by admitting the murder was premeditated). So we were just waiting to see when he would be released. But I think Ramón himself had bewitched the singer as he (Ramón) was dying. Because the singer was not eating anything, or drinking, even water. So Ramón had set a trap (bewitched) for the singer, to kill him after he (Ramón) had died. That is what happened.

So when he was in jail they sent him to clean up down below. As he was climbing up he slipped and fell down and hit himself exactly where he had been injured. Because of that he was vomiting up mouthfuls of blood and he died there in jail. Well now we are even. So I was more content. That is how it happened. That is all.

Guadalupe's narration corroborates Negrín's information, that Ramón Medina was fatally shot "in a drunken brawl over a woman" (1975: 26), supplements data supplied by Fernando Benítez, and fills in much of the void about Ramón Medina's background that Furst and Myerhoff may have camouflaged. If Furst and Myerhoff had candidly and completely described the social matrix which shaped Ramón's life and death, people such as the psychiatrist, Arnold Mandell, would not have been so dismayed about the motive for Ramón Medina's murder.

I simply could not imagine that (Ramón's murder) happening after reading their material about him and his life. It was as though his head had been invaded by a force not manifested anywhere else in their ethnographies (Mandell 1978: 81).

It appears undeniable that Furst and Myerhoff were able to aggrandize Ramón Medina's achievements by evading explanation of the context in which he lived and died. The witchcraft, envy, adultery, and abuse of alcohol Guadalupe tells of in recounting how her husband was murdered clearly illuminates a way of life more wretched than romantic. Moreover, Guadalupe's testimony about Ramón Medina's fathering a child with Leuteria, whom Benítez described as Ramón Medina's mistress (1968a: 358-363), contradicts the claim that Ramón Medina Silva became an authentic Huichol singer (see Chapter 2).

Although Professor Weigand concluded (1985: 152) that Furst and Myerhoff "fabricated a *mara'acame*", they may simply have rushed to publish their findings without recognizing that Huichols make distinctions between healers, singers, and *cahuiteros* (see page 206). Their over-use of the term *mara'acame*, which my informants apply to animals, plants, or persons credited with "supernatural" power, may be a concomitant of indifference or imperviousness to how things really are among Chapalagana Huichols. Such profound indifference to ethnographic truth epitomizes Castaneda's writing and exemplifies a kind of misrepresentation distinguishable from disinformation or fabrication (see pages 96-98). Myerhoff's admission, that for Huichols aspiring to become healers and singers "there is no apprenticeship as such" (1974: 99), suggests she overcame such imperviousness to ethnographic truth.

The extraordinary portrait of Ramón Medina has, for the past 25 years, complemented the titillating tales about don Juan Matus popularized by Carlos Castaneda. Furst and Myerhoff's depiction of Ramón Medina is sensational and misleading because, with minor exceptions, it avoids meaningful discussion of the alcoholism, adultery, and political powerlessness endemic among Huichols living in urban centers and refugee settlements, and glosses over the collapse of traditional Huichol religion and social organization in such enclaves. Their hyperselective focus has obscured both traditional Huichol culture and Ramón Medina's true status among the refugee Huichol. My research, like that of Fernando Benítez, indicated that Ramón Medina was caught in a conflict between Huichol culture and modern Mexican life (1968a: 381-382). According to Benítez, ranchos in the refugee Huichol region where Ramón Medina lived were not integrated into aboriginal ceremonial centers such as San Andrés, San Sebastían, and Santa Catarina. As a consequence, refugee Huichol ranchos have "improvised shamans deprived of the wisdom and power of the great mara'acames" (1968a: 354). Benítez recorded numerous myths dictated in Spanish by Ramón Medina (1968a: 353, 389), but noted that true shamans spoke only Huichol (1968a: 390). This book explores how and why such charming myths dictated by Mexican Indian "shamans" infatuated anthropologists and other Americans, enhanced the appeal of Castaneda's first three books, and helped pave the way for marketing Huichol and Native American "shamans."

# CHAPTER ONE

## A STROLL THROUGH THE
## PSYCHEDELIC SIXTIES

Carlos Castaneda's first book, *The Teachings of Don Juan*, "initiated a psychic revolution ... His books have led millions of young people into the quest" for a mystical way of life "with the aid of mescaline and peyote" (M. Castaneda 1975: 77-78). Such opinions, expressed by Castaneda's ex-spouse, Margaret Castaneda, are slightly exaggerated. In 1968, the year when Castaneda's first book became an instant best-seller, the psychedelic movement was in full bloom. The formation of an audience ready and willing to be awed by the antics of Castaneda's exotic mentor, don Juan Matus, took fifteen years of super-sensational media coverage of psychedelic superstars and their establishment opponents.

This chapter tells some of the fascinating story behind the public's enthusiastic reception of Castaneda's books. It documents how his three most prominent predecessors, Aldous Huxley, Dr. Timothy Leary, and Gordon Wasson, helped popularize chemical psychedelics, such as mescaline and lysergic acid diethylamide (LSD), and psychedelic plants, such as peyote and psilocybin mushrooms. The media coverage surrounding these and other celebrities, and the media's fascination with the counterculture they represented, helped prepare millions of readers to applaud the appearance of don Juan and Carlos Castaneda. Carlos Castaneda's first book appeared at the right time, and contained exactly the message those in the psychedelic movement yearned to hear.

Infatuation with Carlos Castaneda's "teachings" and experimentation with plant psychedelics such as peyote, jimsonweed, and psilocybin mushrooms has persisted. Among the American public, his fame as an anthropologist is surpassed solely by Margaret Mead. While it is surely wrong to acknowledge Castaneda as the founder of the "New Age" movement, his books have definitely influenced the lives of millions of readers. The total number of Castaneda books sold is over eight million.

## Did Aldous Huxley Open Pandora's Box or the Doors of Perception?

Aldous Huxley, the English author whose numerous works of fiction and nonfiction include *Brave New World* and *Doors of Perception*, is the real pioneer of the psychedelic movement. As an aspiring artist-author, Carlos Castaneda's imagination must have been stretched substantially by reading Huxley's 1954 book, *Doors of Perception*, and Huxley's 1958 essay, "Drugs That Shape Men's Minds". In this 1958 essay, circulated in the *Saturday Evening Post*, Huxley hinted that peyote and LSD could stimulate the caliber of mystical experience required to ignite a religious revolution (Huxley 1958: 113). Ten years later, the "psychic revolution" that Margaret Castaneda claimed Carlos Castaneda's first book had initiated was just reaching its peak. I suspect, as does deMille, that Huxley was one of Carlos Castaneda's favorite writers (deMille 1978: xii). [1]

In the early 1950s, the English psychiatrist Dr. Humphry Osmond and two Canadian colleagues were discreetly using mescaline to treat patients with schizophrenia in a state mental hospital in Saskatchewan, Canada.

Aldous Huxley learned about the results of Dr. Osmond's research in certain medical and scientific journals, and soon invited Osmond to meet him. Dr. Osmond administered mescaline to Aldous Huxley in Los Angeles one bright morning in May 1953. Dr. Osmond and Huxley's wife observed while he had his first mescaline experience. Huxley did not hallucinate. He saw familiar objects in a wonderfully compelling and aesthetic way. He was back in a world where the infinite "Inner Light" shone through furniture . . . where the doors of perception were cleansed enough to allow him a glimpse of a "sacramental vision of reality" (Bedford 1974: 538). Huxley's reflections on this experience were published within a year in *Doors of Perception*. This rather intellectual little book sparked considerable controversy and paved the way for the psychedelic movement. Several other notable anthropologists and scientists, among them James Mooney, Weston LaBarre, and William James, had ingested peyote or mescaline long before Huxley (see Appendix A). But, none of them had Huxley's literary reputation, or his ability to make personal mystical experience attractive to the general public.

Why did this famous writer wish to ingest a "mind-expanding" chemical used in the treatment of mental illness? Huxley evidently believed that mescaline, in addition to mystical enlightenment, emotional shock, aesthetic experience, and disease, could facilitate an expansion of mind beyond the narrow confines of the utilitarian, conventionally real world. He assumed that drug-induced experiences could help attune people to a primordial reality which had been bypassed by focusing on the exigencies of survival. Huxley's "Mind at Large Theory" explained human consciousness from a survival-oriented psychological perspective, one rather unlike the cultural relativism espoused by Castaneda. Believing that psychedelics were one of several ways to satisfy the "universal desire for self-transcendence," Huxley advocated widespread dissemination of a "new drug which will relieve and console our species without doing more harm in the long run than good in the short" (Bedford 1974: 542).

Although Huxley mentioned the limitations and contraindications associated with mescaline use (Bedford 1974: 542-43), he claimed it was almost completely innocuous for most people, and clearly preferable to alcohol, tobacco, marijuana, and barbituates. To his credit, he abstained from the psychedelic sensationalizing so vividly illustrated by Timothy Leary. In 1956, Huxley declined to participate in a series of half-hour television shows to be aired on CBS. He warned Dr. Osmond that television would reveal the most remarkable mysteries of mescaline and the mind to an enormous plebian audience. Huxley's experiences had convinced him that reaction from members of the "lunatic fringe" was excessive "even after . . . a two and a half dollar book." (Bedford 1974: 604).

Even without Huxley having to appear on TV, his book, *Doors of Perception*, contributed significantly to the public's fascination with mind-expanding plants and chemicals. One assumes it was a reader inspired by *Doors of Perception* whose letter to the editor appeared in *Life* magazine in 1957, just after it had published Wasson's extraordinary account of his encounter with María Sabina's magic mushrooms in a Mazatec Indian village in central Mexico.

Sirs: I've been having hallucinatory visions . . . in my New York apartment for the past three years . . . . produced by eating American-grown peyote cactus plants . . . from a company in Texas . . . for $8 per 100 buttons (Stafford 1983: 116).

But by the late 1950s, LSD was already eclipsing peyote and mescaline as America's most preferred psychedelic. Throughout the 1950s, medical and scientific research with LSD generated little publicity. The prominent psychedelic researcher, Dr. Oscar Janiger, believes the research of Dr. Sidney Cohen, a psychiatrist affiliated with the Veterans Hospital at UCLA, stimulated demand for recreational LSD use among the elite of Los Angeles. By the late 1950s Janiger himself was participating in a new institution, social gatherings devoted to recreational use of LSD. [2] These small gatherings held in private homes brought together researchers and celebrities, including Aldous Huxley. LSD-using groups were also being assembled by avant-garde inhabitants of Greenwich Village, New York (Stafford 1983: 42). By 1960, LSD and mescaline had shed their association with insanity and alcoholism. Thanks in part to Huxley and Wasson, LSD had acquired mystical, artistic, and creative connotations among an elite on both coasts.

Huxley's request to be given LSD on his deathbed, in 1963, and his 1959 letter to Father Thomas Merton (Bedford 1974: 713, 740) express the admiration Huxley had for psychedelics. But Huxley popularized psychedelics without becoming a guru or media star. Unlike Leary, Huxley did not exaggerate the extent to which psychedelics might be of benefit to others. Huxley took mescaline and LSD no more than eleven or twelve times during the final eleven years of his life (Bedford 1974: 715). In an interview in London in 1961, Huxley admitted he would like to take LSD or mescaline about once a year, and observed that most people who have taken it, "have no desire to sort of fool with it constantly," they take their experiences too seriously to "wallow in it" (Bedford 1974: 716).

Huxley's positive personal experiences with mind-expanding chemicals were not irresponsibly publicized, although he presumably intended to persuade readers that psychedelics might have social value. If Huxley did favor widespread social use of mind-expanding substances, it was with the caveat that they be used in social circumstances resembling those he imagined in his 1962 novel, *Island*. Two passages in it show inhabitants of Huxley's utopian island using a perfected version of LSD as a sacrament. The characters in *Island* presumably illustrate Huxley's conviction that psychedelics must be taken cautiously, under controlled and congenial circumstances (Bedford 1974: 717). Incidentally, *Island* inspired Dr. Leary's disciples to experiment with communal living (LaBarre 1969: 232).

Given Huxley's cautious approach to psychedelic use, it should come as no surprise that he was concerned about the dangers of commercializing LSD use. By 1960, Los Angeles psychoanalyst Mortimer Hartman had turned on one of Hollywood's brightest stars, Cary Grant (Kobler 1963: 39; LaBarre 1969: 229). *Time* magazine publisher Henry Luce took an LSD trip in the privacy of his Arizona residence. Luce later reported his positive impressions of that journey into inner space (but by the late 1960s *Time* was running exaggerated attacks on LSD). In 1960 Huxley wrote Dr. Osmond:

> What frightful people there are in your profession! We met two Beverly Hills psychiatrists the other day, who specialize in LSD therapy at $100 a shot, and really, I have seldom met people of lower sensibility, more vulgar mind! To think of people made vulnerable by LSD being exposed to such people is

profoundly disturbing (Bedford 1974: 637).

Similarly, despite Huxley's fondness for Timothy Leary, he deplored the provocative style of this Harvard academic who was transformed into the high (some might say hyperbolic) priest of the New Age. In a letter to Osmond written in December of 1962, Huxley declared that Leary's

> nonsense-talking is just another device for annoying people in authority, flouting convention, cocking snooks at the academic world; it is the reaction of a mischievous Irish boy to the headmaster of his school. One of these days the headmaster will lose patience ... why, oh why, does he have to be such an ass? (Bedford 1974: 717)

Huxley's words about the headmaster (Harvard) losing patience with the mischievous Irish boy (Dr. Leary) were prophetic. Dr. Timothy Leary's quasi-religious conversion was theatrical enough to arouse the most hardened of reporters and annoy the Harvard University administration.

### Dr. Leary's Trip: From Harvard Psychologist to the High Priest of LSD

Aldous Huxley was the first writer to popularize psychedelics. But the press coverage of Timothy Leary's adventures, more than anything else (with the possible exception of the numerous experiments funded by intelligence agencies) gave psychedelics the reputation they have today. The contrast between LSD and mescaline is roughly analogous to the vastly different public images associated with Timothy Leary and Aldous Huxley. LSD is 4,000 times more potent than mescaline, and was not intentionally patterned after anything in nature (Stafford 1983: 37-39). Similarly, Leary's zealous promotion of LSD seemed several hundred times more thrilling than Huxley's mild-mannered 1954 book inspired by his mescaline experience, his sober 1958 essay, and his learned college lectures on psychedelics. To appreciate the accuracy of these bold comparisons, one must understand the legendary transformation of Timothy Leary, from Harvard Professor of Psychology into the High Priest of LSD.

Mescaline is a chemical modeled upon the most psychoactive alkaloid found in a small, spineless cactus commonly known as peyote (see Appendix A). LSD was manufactured in 1938 by a Swiss chemist, Dr. Albert Hofmann, looking for a new patent drug, not a mind-expanding one, to sell on the medical market. Dr. Hofmann and his associates at Sandoz pharmaceutical laboratories in Basel, Switzerland abandoned research on LSD in 1938, after experimenting with it on animals. Dr. Hoffman asserts that he discovered the mind-expanding properties of LSD by accident, in 1943. After ingesting a minute quantity of this clear and odorless chemical, Hofmann reported that "Space and time became disorganized and I was overcome with fears that I was going crazy" (Kobler 1963; LaBarre 1969: 220).

Three years later, the first LSD experiments in the U.S.A. were conducted under the direction of Dr. Max Rinkel at the Massachusetts Mental Health Center. Rinkel concluded that, "LSD has no therapeutic value whatsoever" (Kobler 1963). In 1953, the year Huxley first took mescaline, the first public LSD clinic in England was opened. The clinic, in a small English mental hospital, was administered by Dr. Ronald Sandison. And, in April 1953 the United States' Central Intelligence Agency became involved in LSD research.

The CIA had $300,000 to study this new and powerful mind-altering drug. Research was partly motivated by the fear that the Soviet Union might acquire this potential chemical weapon. Dr. Sidney Gottlieb was assigned to direct the MKULTRA research project. The CIA's mission was to determine whether the behavior of an individual secretly dosed with LSD could be changed and directed.

The extent of CIA involvement in early psychedelic experiments may never be known. Army, Air Force, and Naval intelligence were also interested in LSD. LSD tests administered by the U.S. Army alone may have involved 1,500 individuals (Furst 1990: 73). Years passed before Dr. Hofmann admitted that during the 1950s the U.S. Army had been contacting him every two years to request his assistance in military experiments (Stafford 1983: 45). In 1953, CIA agents were sent to Sandoz laboratories to negotiate the purchase of enough LSD to "turn on" 100 million people (Stafford 1983: 45). Sandoz laboratories agreed to supply as much LSD as possible to the CIA, and keep them informed of the identities of all other purchasers.

Sandoz continued marketing LSD to psychiatrists interested in using it to treat schizophrenics. LSD therapy in the late 1950s yielded different results, some of them quite promising. Five hospitals in Saskatchewan, Canada administered LSD to about 500 alcoholics. Follow-up studies indicated that approximately half of them quit drinking, or showed marked improvement. By 1959 sufficient medical research had been done to warrant holding the first international conference on LSD in New York (Grinspoon and Bakalar 1979: 62; Stafford 1977: 28).

In 1960, 44 doctors who had published papers

describing their experiments with either LSD or mescaline responded to a questionnaire sent by Dr. Sidney Cohen. Dr. Cohen, the psychiatrist affiliated with UCLA and the Los Angeles Veterans Hospital, may have stimulated recreational use of LSD among the Los Angeles elite (see above). The results of this first survey of psychedelic research may seem surprising: "not a single physical complication was reported — even when psychedelics were given to alcoholics with generally impaired health" (Stafford 1983: 22). According to Dr. Leuner, a European expert on psychedelic therapy, Cohen's study indicated that the risk of psychedelic therapy is quite low, "if it is carried out responsibly by qualified doctors" (quoted in Stafford 1983: 22).

While Dr. Cohen was preparing the first report to summarize the results of medical research on LSD, Dr. Timothy Leary was taking the first step on the road to becoming the most famous doctor ever to experiment with LSD. During his 1960 summer vacation, Dr. Leary was lounging by a pool in Cuernavaca, Mexico when a German anthropologist and friend named Gerhart Braun gave him seven psychedelic mushrooms. The Harvard professor later proclaimed that "It was above all and without question the deepest religious experience of my life" (Stafford 1983: 239). The stage was being set for this psychedelic evangelist to begin recruiting America's sons and daughters to the New Age movement.

When Dr. Leary returned to Harvard University that fall, he met with Aldous Huxley and Dr. Osmond. Leary then asked Sandoz to supply the psilocybin to be administered to participants in his "creativity studies" (Stafford 1983: 240). Leary, joined by another Harvard psychology professor, Richard Alpert, soon established the Center for Research in Personality. They optimistically announced that "psilocybin would be the solution to the emotional problems of Western man" because "it cuts beyond routine ego and social games" (Weil 1963).

Alpert and Leary began their creativity experiments with 38 volunteers, including such famous personalities as Aldous Huxley, Allen Ginsberg, the beatnik poet (see Appendix A), and William Burroughs (a psychedelic advocate and controversial author). Of the 167 individuals given psilocybin, 95% replied, in a follow-up questionnaire, that "the drug session changed their lives for the better" (Weil 1963). Leary's 1961 study of psilocybin given to 32 Concord State prisoners was equally promising. The results of Leary's psilocybin studies inspired the research of Walter Pahnke in 1962. Pahnke's controlled study of Christian theology students suggested that psilocybin facilitated religious experience (Stafford 1983: 241-44, 272). Pahnke's request for psilocybin and government approval to conduct a follow-up study was denied.

By the time Pahnke's study was finished, the first batch of unauthorized LSD, enough for 62,000 doses, had been manufactured by two unlicensed chemists (Stafford 1983: 22). In 1962, the demand for LSD began exceeding what laboratories like Sandoz could supply. The creed of the emerging psychedelic movement was captured in Leary's declaration that "LSD is more important than Harvard." Leary and his associates were advertising LSD as the key to the "new age" (Stafford 1983: 51). Two foundations for the study of LSD were established in 1962. One, the International Foundation for Advanced Study, opened in Menlo Park, California (near Stanford University). The other, called the Agora Scientific Trust, was opened in Manhattan, New York by Michael Hollingshead.

Hollingshead was an especially well-connected advocate of LSD. After receiving a portion of a gram of Sandoz LSD in the fall of 1960, he started Timothy Leary on his first LSD trip. Hollingshead also turned on a host of luminaries including the Beatles' Paul McCartney, the Rolling Stones' Keith Richards, folksinger Donovan Leitch, psychologists Richard Alpert and Ralph Metzner, and the Zen philosopher Alan Watts (Stafford 1983: 49-50). The psychedelic sixties had begun.

Meanwhile, back at Harvard, Leary and Alpert were avoiding the dreaded "D" word, drugs, by referring to LSD and psilocybin as "consciousness expanding materials." Nevertheless, their experiments at the Center for Research in Personality were becoming an issue of concern to other faculty members. "The work violates the values of the academic community," commented social psychologist, Herbert C. Kelman. Kelman protested: "Its emphasis is on pure experience, not on verbalizing findings. One can hardly fail to infer that one effect of the drug (LSD) is to decrease responsibility" (Kobler 1963; Weil 1963: 44).

A reporter from the Harvard school newspaper who attended, unauthorized, a faculty meeting on March 14, 1962 pertaining to Leary and Alpert's psychedelic research, enlarged the debacle beyond the boundaries of the ivory tower (LaBarre 1969: 232). After this student journalist's story appeared in the *Harvard Crimson*, Harvard Square was suddenly filled with hawkers of sugar cubes laced with LSD. Mescaline, LSD, and marijuana began popping up as mysteriously as psilocybin mushrooms in cow-dung. Inquiring students wanted to know what all the commotion was about.

The unanticipated appeal of psychedelics prompted Harvard University's administration to demand that Leary and Alpert cease involving undergraduates in their experiments. Leary, perhaps feeling that his Harvard days were numbered, started the International Federation for Internal Freedom (IFIF). After admitting that he had violated his pledge not to give drugs to undergraduates, Alpert was dismissed from Harvard, on May 27, 1963 (LaBarre 1969: 233). Dr. Leary transferred the IFIF off-campus to Newton, a Boston suburb. Another IFIF center opened in Los Angeles.

The scandal at Harvard prompted Sandoz to stop selling LSD and psilocybin to researchers. The American Chemical Company, which had been selling mescaline for $4 per dose, suspended sales in February 1963. Residents of Newton passed a petition demanding that the IFIF leave town. Leary was forced to relocate to the La Catalina Hotel in Zihuatenejo, Mexico (LaBarre 1969: 232). It was there that Leary rejected Carlos Castaneda's bid to become his apprentice, in May 1963 (Leary 1983: 167-171 and see below).

Following numerous adventures south of the U.S. border, Leary was rescued by William Hitchcock, a New York millionaire and advocate of psychedelics. Leary and his followers settled down at Hitchcock's 4,000-acre estate in Millbrook, New York. It was at Millbrook that Leary founded a religion, the League for Spiritual Discovery (LSD).

By late 1963 the media had made LSD a highly inflammatory topic (LaBarre 1969: 234). Leary's uncanny ability to make outrageous, highly quotable statements was spectacular. One of these, "Tune in, Turn on, Drop Out," became a buzzword for younger Americans rejecting the materialistic values of their elders, an escalating war in the jungles of Southeast Asia, and a dormant racism about to erupt in flames in several of America's black ghettos. Well-publicized interviews with media-selected authorities on drugs began persuading lawmakers that LSD and other psychedelics should be made illegal.

It was sometime during this period that Castaneda

met Dr. Leary. Although it would have been more convenient for Castaneda to meet Leary at the IFIF center Leary
opened in Los Angeles in 1963 (LaBarre 1969: 232-33),
Castaneda met Leary and other LSD worshippers in 1964 in
New York. In his *Time* magazine interview Castaneda
disparaged them for being

> children indulging in incoherent revelations. A sor-
> cerer takes hallucinogens for a different reason than
> heads do, and after he has gotten where he wants to
> go, he stops taking them (*Time* 1973: 33). [3]

Leary became more notorious in December 1965,
when he was arrested in Laredo, Texas for possession of
half an ounce of marijuana. He was sentenced to 30 years
in prison and a $30,000 fine. While his case languished in
court, Leary returned to Millbrook. Five months later he
was in trouble again, after a minute quantity of marijuana
was found at the mansion. The early morning raid on
Millbrook was led by none other than G. Gordon Liddy,
then assistant district attorney of Dutchess County. Who
could have predicted then that a crime-fighter like Liddy,
the most outspoken of Nixon's Watergate men, would
eventually wind up behind bars too?

Leary's September 1966 interview in *Playboy* magazine was "right on" for some readers. Other readers thought
it preposterous. According to Leary, the psychedelic drug
experience "means ecstasy, sensual unfolding, religious
experience, revelation, illumination, contact with nature."
Moreover, "Sexual ecstasy is the basic reason for the
current LSD boom." Raining on Leary's fire, the inter-
viewer probed Leary about recent reports indicating that
many LSD users had experienced psychotic reactions and
had ended up in hospital emergency rooms. As *Time*

magazine put it, "non-swimmers think they can swim, and others think they can fly" (Leary 1966). Leary responded with the stoicism of an astute statistician: "So one episode out of 10,000 cases is no reason for any kind of hand wringing and grandmotherly panic" (Leary 1966). Leary had plenty of followers who were convinced that whatever the risks might be, they were worth taking.

By 1966, San Francisco's low-rent Haight-Ashbury district had become a Mecca for disenfranchised youth who lived by the mottoes "Peace, Love, and Do Your Own Thing." Shoulder-length hair on men, outlandishly colorful clothes, beads, and incense all became "hippie" gear. LSD-using musical groups, notably the Grateful Dead, were popular. Ken Kesey and his "Merry Pranksters" roamed the land in a garishly painted bus. They "turned on" the willing and dosed the unwilling with "Electric Kool-Aid Acid" (LSD). The media loved this display of colorful eccentricity. Less famous hippie centers appeared in Greenwich Village and elsewhere (Stafford 1983: 53).

LSD use among the counterculture continued to mount. The zenith of the psychedelic movement may have been reached in 1967. It was a "Summer of Love" in San Francisco. The "tribes" gathered in Haight-Ashbury listened to such popular songs as Scott McKenzie's "San Francisco" and "San Francisco Nights" by Eric Burdon and the Animals. Such songs conveyed an image of bliss, peace, and harmony so attractive that hordes of New Age seekers kept coming. It was not long before the "bad vibrations" associated with violent crime, prostitution, heroin, and speed crept into the Haight-Ashbury district.

Although Leary rode the crest of the psychedelic movement's wave by publishing *High Priest* and *The Politics of Ecstasy* in 1968 and by lecturing all over the country, a political tidal wave was about to engulf him. On

October 16, 1966, the state of California made possession
and sale of LSD a crime. The former actor, and then
Democrat named Ronald Reagan won the nomination for
governor of California in part because he called for tougher
federal legislation on drugs. Shortly after LSD became
illegal, the National Institute of Mental Health reduced
research programs using psychedelics from more than 100
to six (Stafford 1983: 23). The rampant unauthorized use
of LSD was regarded as a sure sign of decadence by most
political leaders. President Lyndon Johnson, in his 1968
State of the Union Address to Congress, promised to combat the rising tide of drug-induced rebellion:

> This year I will propose a Drug Control Act to
> provide stricter penalties for those who traffic in LSD
> and other dangerous drugs with our people. I will ask
> for more vigorous enforcement of all of our drug
> laws by increasing the number of Federal drug and
> narcotics control officials by more than 30 percent.
> The time has come to stop the sale of slavery to the
> young.

The most effective propaganda pieces in what was becoming an undeclared war on drugs came when scientists
announced that LSD caused chromosome damage. The
first study, published in 1967 in *Science* magazine by a New
York geneticist, was immediately dramatized by journalists eager for a hot story. Shortly thereafter, another report
implicating LSD in chromosome breakage was released by
two medical doctors from Portland, Oregon (Stafford 1983:
60-61). Once again the media circulated stories speculating
about how LSD-using couples will be cursed with two-
headed babies that have too many or too few fingers and
toes. Scientists soon pointed out that the people profiled in

these studies had abused other proven chromosome-damaging drugs in tandem with LSD. The media took little if any notice of saner, scientific questions about the allegations it had already popularized. Scientific skepticism about the accuracy of the horror stories the media had lent credence to surely lacked sufficient sex appeal to rekindle public interest in yesterday's headlines.

Psychedelic advocates felt that the evidence of LSD's culpability was inconclusive. Nevertheless, LSD's tarnished reputation mitigated against funding for the medical and scientific research required to yield conclusive knowledge about the risks and benefits of psychedelics. Whatever the truth may be, the public perception of psychedelics was that they had no redeeming medical or social value. Media-induced hysteria had turned even legitimate scientific research with psychedelics into a forbidden subject. Ironically, by broadcasting the controversy, journalists may have unintentionally increased psychedelic use.

Art Linkletter, the beloved television star, became a high-profile anti-LSD crusader following the death of his daughter Diane. In the fall of 1969, Diane, then twenty years old, leaped to her death from her sixth floor apartment while under the influence of LSD (Linkletter 1973). By the time Linkletter's daughter died, most Americans viewed taking LSD as an American equivalent of Russian Roulette. Linkletter's national crusade helped mobilize support for national legislation to prohibit anybody from using any psychedelics.

It was not until President Richard Nixon's administration that Johnson's federal drug ban law was enacted. The Comprehensive Drug Abuse Prevention and Control Act of 1970 includes the Controlled Substances Act. Under this provision, drugs are classified and placed on one of five different schedules. Criteria used for placement include the potential for abuse, accepted medical uses, safety, and potential for physical or psychological dependence. LSD, psilocybin, mescaline, and peyote are treated as equivalents in the Controlled Substances Act. They are classified as hallucinogens, and placed on Schedule 1, which means they have no redeeming medical value. The penalty for trafficking with these substances is harsh: a term of imprisonment of not more than 15 years, a fine of not more than $25,000, or both (Anderson 1980: 208; Grinspoon and Bakalar 1979: 310). Less severe penalties are imposed for simple possession (Anderson 1980: 209). The only persons other than an infinitesimal number of certified medical researchers who are exempted from this law are approximately 250,000 card-carrying members of the Native American Church who eat peyote as a sacrament in bona fide religious rituals (see Appendix A).

Of all these Schedule One substances, LSD is clearly the most potent. And of all the advocates of LSD use, Timothy Leary was the most outspoken and controversial. However much reporters may have helped, it is Leary more than anyone else who best represented the enemy Congress wanted to banish in 1970 when it passed the Controlled Substances Act. Leary's capers contributed much to the emergence of America's drug-war mentality. Those who realize that the psychedelic movement was also nurtured, albeit less visibly by Huxley, Wasson, and certain members of the intelligence community, will identify Leary as simply the tip of the psychedelic movement's iceberg.

More than ten years passed before Leary repented. In his essay entitled "After the Sober, Serious, Safe and Sane '70's, Let Us Welcome the Return of LSD," Leary admits that LSD is not for "every brain" and that his energetic proselytizing for it was "naively democratic." He warned certain people to abstain from taking it, and affirmed the wisdom of Huxley's "elitist position" on LSD use (Stafford 1983: 25-26). The 1960s are generally regarded as the "high point" in psychedelic drug use. Although cocaine use has captured the headlines in recent years, today psychedelic use continues, perhaps unabated. The consensus among certain experts attending an international drug conference in Washington, D.C. in 1990 is that LSD use by young Americans is increasing. [4]

*Wasson's Wondrous Mazatec Mushrooms*

Until 1927, the only time R. Gordon Wasson ever paid attention to mushrooms was when they were floating in beef gravy atop mashed potatoes. That was the year the ex-business reporter turned New York banker was walking in the Catskill Mountains when his new bride, Valentina, a Russian pediatrician, told him she was going to eat the wild mushrooms she had discovered (Wasson 1957: 113). Their conflicting attitudes toward mushrooms sparked unprecedented research which culminated in publication of several books and won international acclaim for the Wassons.

During the course of their investigations the Wassons learned from the famous Harvard ethnobotanist Richard Evan Schultes of a place in southern Mexico where mind-expanding mushrooms were still ingested by Indians. Schultes told them about Plasius Paul Reko, an Austrian physician living in Mexico. Reko was convinced that Indians still used mushrooms to induce altered states of consciousness. The Wassons were heartened after viewing stone carvings portraying mushrooms being prepared for ceremonial ingestion (Wasson 1957: 101, 114; Stafford

1983: 231). Similar mushroom stones, as well as mushrooms depicted in pottery, first appear about 1650 B.C. in the Maya Indian territory (Borhegyi 1961, 1963, 1965). The linguistic clues the Wassons gained from Eunice Pike, a Protestant missionary to the Mazatec Indians, also proved tantalizing. The fact that the Mazatecs called the mushrooms, "the dear little ones that leap forth" suggested reverence.

The Wassons searched for the elusive mushroom eaters in the mountains of Oaxaca, a state in southern Mexico, during three consecutive summers. In June 1955, Wasson and his companion, Allan Richardson (a New York socialite photographer) struck pay dirt in the Mazatec Indian village of Huatla de Jiménez. They were introduced to María Sabina, a Mazatec Indian woman esteemed as a healer. Wasson experienced pleasant visions, and saw the walls in María Sabina's house dissolve, after ingesting twelve acrid-tasting psilocybin mushrooms (Wasson 1957: 102).

Wasson disclosed to millions of readers of *Life* magazine that he and Richardson were the first non-Indians to eat mushrooms revered by Mazatecs as "the divine flesh of the gods." "Seeking the Magic Mushroom," the *Life* article Wasson published on May 13, 1957, was sensational. In it, Wasson described Sabina's virtuoso all-night performance, which included ventriloquism and chanting. Acknowledging the need to protect the privacy of his informant, Wasson gave María Sabina a pseudonym, Eva Mendez, and concealed her identity as a Mazatec Indian by calling her a Mixteco. Nevertheless, the *Life* magazine story advertised the exotic and promoted the Wasson's new book, *Mushrooms, Russia, and History*. Only 512 copies of this book were published. At $125 per copy, it was read only by elite intellectuals, psychedelic seekers, and probably Carlos Castaneda (deMille 1978: 60-61).

However much they differed in style, both Huxley and Leary were primarily psychologically oriented popularizers of psychedelics. However much they differed, both Wasson and Castaneda were anthropologically oriented enthusiasts of Mexican Indian mysticism. Gordon Wasson's reports on Mexican Indian psychedelic mushroom rituals were a major influence on Castaneda's incredible accounts of a Yaqui Indian's use of psychedelic plants. As we shall see, after publication of Carlos Castaneda's first two books, the Mazatec Indians the Wassons had introduced to the world in 1957 were inundated by irreverent psychedelic seekers.

The story behind the psychedelic mushroom discovery is full of intrigue. In early 1953, just before the Wassons' first trip in search of the mushrooms, CIA scientists began searching too, fascinated by stories that mushrooms could be used "to produce confessions or to locate stolen objects or to predict the future" (Stafford 1983: 233). One of Wasson's friends, Andrija Puharich, casually comments in his book, *The Sacred Mushroom* (1959), that he informed the U.S. Army about Wasson's activities.

> I did feel that it was my duty to pass on to the military the knowledge that Mr. Wasson had given me of the mushroom used in Middle America to enhance or fortify telepathic powers. I asked Mr. Wasson's permission to do this, which he granted.

Whether or not Puharich was the initial source, a botanist informant for the CIA, then stationed in Mexico City, filed a report on Wasson's discovery of María Sabina's mushroom rituals shortly after it occurred (Stafford 1983: 233). On Wasson's next trip, in the summer of 1956, he was accompanied by Dr. James Moore, a CIA chemist employed by the University of Delaware. Moore was an "expert at synthesizing psychoactive and chemical weapons for the CIA on short notice, he was known as the CIA's 'short-order cook'" (Stafford 1983: 234). Dr. Moore brought back Mazatec mushrooms, but was unable to isolate the psychoactive component. Meanwhile, a French scientist who had also accompanied Wasson sent some mushrooms to Albert Hofmann. Hofmann's team, working for Sandoz Inc., beat Moore and the CIA to the psychedelic punch. Hofmann labeled the chemical compound derived from the magic mushrooms psilocybin. Wasson altered the Mazatec world forever by introducing this chemical psychedelic to María Sabina. Unlike the mushrooms, which grow only in the rainy season, psilocybin may be purchased anytime. María Sabina would thereafter be able to "serve people even when no mushrooms were available" (quoted in Stafford 1983: 239).

A brief excursion into the world of the enigmatic and influential parapsychologist, Andrija Puharich, only increases one's sense of mystery about how and why the magic mushrooms were uncovered. In 1954, Puharich was conducting ESP experiments in his laboratory in Maine. One of his research subjects, a Dutch sculptor named Harry Stone, would go into a trance and assume an ancient Egyptian Ra Ho Tep personality (Puharich 1959). Readers should not confuse this with the Ra Me Tep murderers pursued by a young Sherlock Holmes in Stephen Spielberg's movie. Aldous Huxley witnessed performances by Harry Stone, and several other remarkable characters sponsored by Puharich's Round Table Foundation. Huxley was evidently favorably disposed toward the parapsychological gatherings held at Dr. Henry Puharich's house. Huxley believed Puharich's mission was

> to reproduce by modern pharmacological, electronic and physical methods the conditions used by the shamans for getting into a state of traveling clairvoyance and then, if he succeeds, to send people to explore systematically "the Other World" (Bedford 1974: 581).

During one of these trance-channeling sessions, Stone scrawled hieroglyphics and pictures of mushrooms. This inspired Puharich enough that he met Gordon Wasson twice in New York City. Despite his keen interest in mushrooms, Puharich's schedule prevented him from accepting Wasson's invitation to go to Mexico that very summer when Wasson's quest for the long, lost mushrooms ended successfully. Nevertheless, Wasson and Puharich agreed to set up ESP experiments between Mexico and Maine. When Wasson ate the mushrooms offered by María Sabina, he soon decided that his "bemushroomed" faculties were in no condition to participate in the ESP experiment with Puharich.

Castaneda's ex-spouse, Margaret, acknowledged that Puharich's book influenced them both. Perhaps so. But, when Puharich's book, *The Sacred Mushroom*, appeared in 1959, Castaneda may already have entered the brave, new psychedelic world sketched by Huxley and Wasson. According to Margaret, some persons suspected that Castaneda had already tried the magic mushrooms by the time they finished reading the Puharich book – in December 1959 (M. Castaneda 1975: 76). It is intriguing that Margaret's claim that she and Carlos were married in Tijuana, Mexico (M. Castaneda 1975: 75), a city only a few hours by car from Los Angeles, is contradicted by the data entered on their marriage contract. Their marriage contract indicates, in Spanish, that they were married on January 27, 1960 in Tlaquiltenango, Morelos (M. Castaneda 1975: 73). This town in Morelos is conveniently located only a few hours away from the site of the Mazatec mushroom ceremonies celebrated by Wasson.

Except for a few enterprising experimenters such as Timothy Leary and Carlos Castaneda, the psychedelic mushrooms remained beyond the boundaries of most New Age seekers. Chemical psychedelics such as psilocybin, mescaline, and LSD were much easier to locate. By 1968, such chemicals were illegal in many states and the psychedelic movement was beginning to stall. A growing number of psychedelic users were wary of chemicals manufactured in underground laboratories, and worried about the legal penalties associated with their use. The stage was set for a wave of experimentation with the psychedelic plants that would be enticingly peddled by a young graduate student from UCLA. The timing for that UCLA student's first book, *The Teachings of Don Juan: A Yaqui Way of Knowledge*, could not have been better.

### Flying High with Don Juan as Co-Pilot

The behavior encouraged by reading Castaneda's books and the influence the books have had on his readers (including their disruption of certain Native American societies Castaneda's books sensationalized), are issues which have been almost completely overlooked. Most commentary on Castaneda (especially that written before 1976) lavished the books with praise. Since then most critics have been concerned with the question of whether or not the books are fiction. The extent of their authenticity is an issue which will be thoroughly examined in the next chapter. Here we will briefly examine what some of Castaneda's fans have done with jimsonweed (or various species of the genus *Datura*) and psilocybin mushrooms, two of the three plant psychedelics popularized by Castaneda. Experimentation with peyote, the third plant used by don Juan, merits special treatment (see Appendix A).

In his first book, Castaneda explained how he became an apprentice to the Yaqui Indian shaman, don Juan Matus. Don Juan taught Castaneda to fly under the influence of jimsonweed and to smoke a magical blend consisting of psilocybin mushrooms and other plants. Because his book didn't provide detailed road maps, readers were obliged to look for don Juan and search for the source of the magic mushrooms he gave Castaneda. Inasmuch as Wasson's *Life* magazine account of the Mazatec mushroom ceremonies was easily available (and since the mushrooms are unavailable in the Yaqui Indian homeland) thousands of readers seeking an alternative to chemical psychedelics headed for the hills of southern Mexico.

A Reuters news wire story published July 23, 1970, in the *New York Times* reported that hundreds of hippies were risking imprisonment and fines to ingest the magic mushrooms growing in the state of Oaxaca, Mexico (Pollack 1975). The *New York Times* article unintentionally added to the romance about psychedelic plants by quoting "David," a veteran of the decaying San Francisco psychedelic scene. David offered an all-American analogy about what compelled him to undertake such a long and risky pilgrimage: "The difference between LSD and the magic mushroom is the same difference between a stale hamburger and a T-bone steak."

The local Indians were overwhelmed by the sheer numbers of hippies and appalled by their manners. Comparing foreign mushroom consumers with themselves, one Mazatec Indian declared: "We eat them in small numbers. We dream but we eat them only when we need to and then with the right ritual." A local law enforcement official warned that: "We can not allow the vice to spread. The mushrooms are a great medicine. Taken in right quantities they can do miracles." It would not be long before the Mexican army moved in to make arrests. The Indians must have been relieved. New Age seekers would have to do their seeking elsewhere. And that is precisely what they did.

After Gordon Wasson's *Life* magazine article appeared, Carlos Castaneda's books sensationalized magic mushrooms. Thereafter they became illegal in Mexico and the United States. However, various types of psilocybin mushrooms have been discovered throughout the earth. They are particularly plentiful in the Pacific Northwest region of North America. Although eating psilocybin mushrooms is relatively safe from a physical perspective, in 1981 two deaths resulted when members of a poisonous species were eaten after being mistaken for psilocybin mushrooms (Stafford 1983: 262). Books useful in differentiating poisonous from psychedelic mushrooms abound (Furst 1986; and see Stafford 1983: 245, 249 for other mushroom guides). Psychedelic mushrooms have become second only to marijuana as America's most popular homegrown plant psychedelic (Siegel 1989: 283).

Jimsonweed (a species in the genus *Datura*) is infinitely more dangerous than mushrooms. It is such a toxic plant that even among Native Americans who use it fatalities occur. [5] By branding it "devil's weed," Castaneda was borrowing a European term (Duerr 1985: 81) and accentuating the dangerous connotations implied by its Spanish-English nickname, locoweed (*loco* means crazy in Spanish). Dr. Weil, in his essay "Some Notes on Datura," mentions that the *Datura* experience commonly produces delirium and disorientation. Throughout history, Weil finds that it has been associated with "poisoners, criminals, and black magicians." The effect that jimsonweed had on members of the first English colony in America was memorable. According to historians, jimson is a corruption of Jamestown. English settlers at Jamestown were given *Datura* by the local Indians (Weil 1977). Whether the Indians were trying to poison people they regarded as intruders, or initiate them into the mysteries of sorcery is unclear.

Weil notes that Castaneda's description of activities triggered by "devil's weed" parallels accounts of its use among Medieval European witches. German anthropologist Hans Peter Duerr notes that flying is an activity typically attributed to European witches but cites some evidence suggesting that *Datura* use may have persisted among conservative Yaquis (see note 5 and Duerr 1985: 81-82, 297). Jimsonweed is still used by members of several southern California tribes located within a few hours of Los Angeles (Applegate 1975; Gayton 1928; LaBarre 1969).

One of the most common reactions to *Datura* is a burning thirst, fever, and the sensation of the skin being on fire. It is not uncommon for *Datura* eaters to make a beeline for the nearest water. The outcome is often death by drowning, even in shallow depths.

In the 1970s some young midwestern Indians began mixing jimsonweed with alcohol and inhalants. A significant number of overdoses and deaths have been reported. Authorities infer that Castaneda's account of flying on the devil's weed (1969: 127-28) motivated many of them to try

*Datura*, much to their detriment. Dr. Ronald Siegel, author of *Intoxication*, notes that many adults have taken fatal overdoses of *Datura* since 1980.

## Covert Psychedelic Experiments

To be fair to Castaneda, whose influence on young mystics anxious to enter the arcane world of psychedelic plants was indirect, we must review the dirty tricks of certain elements in the establishment, and of some of those who rebelled against it. The extent to which U.S. intelligence agencies and some of the psychedelic zealots originally incited by experiments funded by the intelligence agencies augmented the size and intensity of the psychedelic movement is debatable. The murky water left behind by the various U.S. intelligence agencies involved in the psychedelic movement makes seeing through to a "bottom line" impossible.

What little is known about the experiments of intelligence agents and psychedelic research funded by various intelligence agencies suggests they played a far more significant role in promoting the development of the psychedelic movement than was known at the time. The experiments they funded and conducted did much, unintentionally of course, to prepare an audience for Castaneda's books. The scope of CIA-funded experiments is astonishing (see John Mark's 1979 book, *The Search for the Manchurian Candidate* and Weinstein's 1990 book, *Psychiatry and the CIA*). The drug experiments conducted by the CIA and other intelligence agencies produced two diametrically opposed responses. Many were unwitting victims. Others became psychedelic advocates.

Members of the intelligence community pursued

psychedelic research for essentially two reasons: 1. for use as a possible truth serum, or for mind-control, and 2. as a chemical weapon for incapacitating the enemy. Their research took place on army bases, in university hospitals, and in private "safehouses" in Greenwich Village and San Francisco. Individuals who were given LSD without their knowledge at the safehouses were hustled by prostitutes to determine if they would "disclose closely-held secrets" (Stafford 1983: 47). The U.S. Army conducted "field operations" overseas, hotly interrogating "foreign nationals" who were under the influence of LSD (Stafford 1983: 48). The CIA even funded research to determine how much LSD was needed to kill a bull elephant (Anonymous 1990). But the most atrocious of all this covert research was done as part of the CIA's MKULTRA project.

Harvey Weinstein, psychiatrist and author of *Psychiatry and the CIA*, notes that civilians were given LSD unwittingly by 185 different researchers in 80 different institutions. Many of these victims of the CIA's MKULTRA experiments in mind-control were hospital patients. The covert MKULTRA mind-bending experiments took an especially tragic turn when Dr. Frank Olson leapt to his death from the tenth-story window of New York's Statler-Hilton Hotel. At the time he took his life, Olson was suffering from severe depression, reportedly induced by accepting a glass of liquor from the project's director, Dr. Gottleib. What Olson wasn't told then, in November 1953, was that the liquor he drank contained LSD. Olson, a specialist in the airborne delivery of chemical weapons, believed he had given away classified information while under the influence of LSD. Olson's family would have to wait more than twenty years to learn the truth about his suicide. In 1977 Congress awarded the Olsons $750,000 in compensation (Stafford 1983: 47-48).

Another Army man, James Thornwell, was suspected of stealing classified documents in 1961 while stationed in France. In attempting to determine what, if anything Thornwell had leaked, he was given LSD without his knowledge. His Army interrogators threatened "to extend (his shattered) state indefinitely . . . even to a permanent condition of insanity" (Stafford 1983: 49). In 1980 Thornwell received $650,000 in compensation. In 1958, James Stanley, a former sergent in the Army was given LSD unwittingly four times by an Army psychiatrist as part of a mind-control experiment. He hopes a bill introduced by Rep. Harry Johnston of Florida will bring him $650,000 in damages (Stanley 1990).

By 1959, the U.S. military was employing civilian guinea pigs for their LSD experiments. Abbie Hoffman, the most famous radical political activist of the 1960s, first heard about LSD from Aldous Huxley in 1957. Two years later, Herb Caen, the *San Francisco Chronicle* columnist, wrote that volunteers participating in LSD-25 experiments would be paid $150. According to Hoffman, "That emptied Berkeley." The line of people hoping to get paid for going on a trip was so long that Hoffman didn't get any. He had to wait until 1965 (Stafford 1983: 44).

Another military-sponsored research program was housed at Stanford. It was there that Margaret Mead's ex-spouse, anthropologist Gregory Bateson, arranged for Allen Ginsberg to take LSD. Bateson's own LSD trips were evidently pleasant and illuminating (1972: 463). Bateson had been given LSD by Dr. Harold Abramson, a CIA operative who delighted in "turning on" intellectuals (Stafford 1983: 46-47). Another literary light who got LSD at Stanford was Ken Kesey. Kesey's novel, *One Flew Over the Cuckoo's Nest* was a relatively restrained attack on the establishment compared to the pranks he pulled in the Bay

Area. He and his Merry Pranksters slipped so much LSD into the punch of the unsuspecting that they became infamous. Those "good old days" of the psychedelic movement are celebrated by Tom Wolfe in his book, *The Electric Kool-Aid Acid Test.* Media coverage of Ken Kesey and his Merry Pranksters increased the national panic about drugs. The Pranksters' tactics matched those of intelligence agents such as Dr. Gottlieb. Those reckless extremists, affiliated with both the establishment and the counterculture, who failed to obtain the informed consent of those to whom they gave LSD, helped endow psychedelics with their evil image. One consequence of this widespread non-Indian experimentation and abuse of chemical psychedelics is that the religious freedom of the Native American Church is imperiled (see Appendix A).

*Target Marketing of Mexican Indian Shamans*

The counterculture or New Age movement which developed during the 1960s made the taking of psychedelics almost an oath of allegiance, a political symbol or statement that one was defecting from the Establishment (Linkletter 1973: 98-99).

> Experimenting with marijuana, for instance, was a statement that the government's case against it was exaggerated. Benevolent experiences with marijuana led many users to question authority in other areas as well; if the government misinformed people about marijuana, what about our role in the Vietnam war? (Stafford 1983: 20).

Others may have had misgivings about the Vietnam war before they sampled marijuana or other psychedelics. Many of those who decided marijuana was benign graduated to more potent psychedelics. Islands of non-conformists, epitomized by the Haight-Ashbury community in San Francisco, must have been somewhat threatening to the Establishment. Leaders of both sides frequently overstated their cases (Grinspoon and Bakalar 1979: 68-69). A war of words preceded the declaration of a war on drugs. After 1965, tales of terror about the dangers of LSD began pervading America's consciousness. A crescendo of national hysteria was amplified by the 1967 horror stories about chromosome damage. A 1977 study suggests that LSD usage reached its peak between 1965 and 1968, the first year when a dramatic decline in LSD use appeared. "Many were frightened by the chromosome damage charge, others by the fact it was illegal" (Stafford 1983: 62). In 1968, this nation's stage was set for something less frightening and more exotic than LSD. Don Juan, Castaneda's essentially fictional guru of plant psychedelics (Castaneda 1969, 1971, 1972, 1973), Ramón Medina Silva, the Huichol Indian "shaman" made into a spectacle by Peter Furst (1969, 1972a, 1973, 1974, 1975, 1978), Barbara Myerhoff (1968, 1974, 1976, 1978), Furst and Myerhoff (1966), and María Sabina, a real Mazatec Indian mushroom specialist uncovered by Gordon Wasson (1957, 1972, 1980) were bound for glory.

What was most seductive about Castaneda's psychedelic story was that his guru, or teacher, don Juan did more than merely instruct the UCLA graduate, Castaneda, in a systematic body of knowledge in which psychedelic plants played a prominent part. Castaneda "transcended" (or breached) the boundaries of routine anthropological research by becoming, he says, a sorcerer's apprentice. Don

Juan, and his Huichol Indian counterpart, Ramón Medina Silva, were the first of many so-called "shamans" to be marketed to the counterculture. The idolization of Mexican Indian "shamans" and Far Eastern gurus was a logical concomitant of the scarcity of reliable guides to the altered states of consciousness New Age seekers yearned to explore.

# Notes

1.    Castaneda began taking creative writing classes at Los Angeles City College by the time he first visited Margaret at her apartment, on June 2, 1956 (*Time* 1973: 33; M. Castaneda 1975: 74). On his first visit to Margaret he brought several of his paintings (M. Castaneda 1975: 74). But don Juan's separate reality was so thrilling he abandoned painting in favor of writing (Castaneda and Roszak 1968). By May 24, 1965, Alberta Greenfield, Castaneda's co-author, and he had completed a book manuscript titled *"The Whole World Sounds Strange, Don't You Think?"* (deMille 1990: 484).

2.    Psychiatrist Oscar Janiger first tried LSD in 1954. He soon began giving it to artists. Between 1955 and 1962, Dr. Janiger "had given several thousand administrations of LSD to 875 individuals, many from the creative community in Los Angeles, as well as plumbers, carpenters, and housewives" (Stafford 1983: 42).

3.    DeMille questions whether this and other reports Castaneda provides about meetings with Leary and/or his followers are entirely accurate. He interprets them as symbolic of Castaneda's attempt to best Leary, "a fellow Catholic apostate and charismatic adversary" (deMille 1990: 314).

4.    All estimates of past or present LSD use are imprecise because it is an illegal drug. In 1977, the National Institute on Drug Abuse (NIDA) estimated that 10 million Americans, six percent of all Americans over age 12, had taken a strong psychedelic, primarily LSD. The most recent data available from the National Clearinghouse for

Alcohol and Drug Information indicates that in 1988 there were 1,317 emergency room medical exams attributed to bad LSD trips. Four persons, three in Boston, one in Baltimore, were counted as casualties of LSD. Some experts would question the accuracy of such statistics, pointing out that many of the chemicals being sold as LSD are in fact other compounds. Others would argue that even if they are relatively accurate, there is ample evidence indicating that LSD may be useful in reducing pain, preparing people for death, treating alcoholism, and motivating some neurotics to get well (see Stafford 1983: 74-81). Some of those who are fighting our nation's drug war might claim that LSD use is declining.

5.     The most famous jimsonweed fatality is Abraham Lincoln's mother. After drinking the milk of a cow that had eaten locoweed, she contracted a "milk sickness" which slowly killed her (Weil 1977). Aboriginal American use of *Datura* has been studied by several scholars (La Barre 1969; Applegate 1975; Duerr 1985: 76, 294; Gayton 1928; Safford 1920).

There is some evidence which lends credence to Castaneda's claims about don Juan teaching him to fly with jimsonweed. Robert Bye (1987: 121) cites Maximino Martínez (whose books are cited in Weston LaBarre's *The Peyote Cult* bibliography), who described how the Yaqui and other northern Mexican tribes used an ointment of *Datura* to become intoxicated and see visions. Rosalio Moisés, a Yaqui Indian, admitted that Yaqui witches use *Datura* in potions designed to kill or harm their victims (Moisés, Kelley, and Holden 1971: 20, 192). Moisés also mentioned that leaves from the "Don Juan plant" are used in this witches' brew.

My Huichol informants do not use *Datura* for visions or witchcraft. Robert Zingg (1938) misidentified *quieri*, a powerful plant in the genus *Solandra*, as *Datura*. Although this plant is native to Huichol territory, and thus could easily have been seen, Zingg's error was repeated by Furst and Myerhoff (1966 and 1972). Similarly, J. Alden Mason's report (1918: 138-140, 143-44), that the Tepecano Indians (who live just east of the Huichol) venerated the *Datura* or *toloache* plant, should be tested against ethnographic and botanical evidence about *quieri* (Knab 1977). The Tepecano may have venerated the same plant species, in the *Solandra* genus, that Huichols do.

# CHAPTER TWO

## *TO FIND DON JUAN: INVESTIGATING CASTANEDA'S HUICHOL WAY OF KNOWLEDGE*

"Carlos Castaneda is the greatest psychic fraud of the 20th century," insisted Jane Rush, one of his friends at UCLA (quoted in M. Castaneda 1975: 73). A comparable conclusion was reached by the son of moviemaker Cecil B. deMille. Richard deMille, a psychologist who became Castaneda's greatest critic, denounced the Castaneda books as a "transparent fraud" (1990: 354). Until deMille's first exposé appeared in 1976, almost all professional anthropologists were celebrating Castaneda's books as illustrative of a new paradigm. Even anthropologists specializing in the study of Native American religions praised it. "An overwhelming majority of Americanists thought Castaneda's first book was authentic ethnography" (Jason Green, personal communication: 1988).

The purpose of my study was to uncover how and why Carlos Castaneda could successfully sell as authentic ethnography a pseudo-ethnography about a "Yaqui Indian" way of knowledge he allegedly learned from don Juan Matus. The proficient marketing of this self-proclaimed sorcerer's apprentice and his books, among anthropologists and American consumers alike, was predicated upon several factors: a) On the demand side there was an audience disenchanted with orthodox anthropology and "establishment" religion. The formation of this counterculture (Roszak 1969), or psychedelic movement, has been discussed in the previous chapter, "Strolling Through the

Psychedelic Sixties." b) Viewed from a marketing angle there was enthusiastic endorsement of his books by several prominent professional anthropologists. This is briefly discussed in "Canonization of Dr. Castaneda's Literary Corpus." c) Viewed from the supply side there was Castaneda's collaboration with three other University of California at Los Angeles (UCLA) anthropologists professing expertise on Huichol Indian shamanism. Of these, the most critical but least obvious component in the Castaneda success story is his Huichol connection.

Castaneda's Huichol Indian connection played a crucial role in launching him on the course to stardom, yet it remained totally obscure before 1978. Examining Castaneda's connection with refugee Huichols, and with other UCLA scholars studying those Huichols, led me to consider the significance of certain strikingly similar ethnographic anomalies in their reports. That so many academic experts were seduced by Castaneda's books is primarily a result of Castaneda's ability to disguise his first-hand experiences with Huichol Indians, and to benefit from his association with three UCLA students of Huichol culture. Castaneda's collaboration with these three UCLA colleagues, in addition to book endorsements from weighty anthropologists, made it difficult for most professional anthropologists to discredit Castaneda's books as quickly and completely as they did those of the infamous exponent of extraterrestrial archaeology, Erich von Däniken. [6]

My interviews with Guadalupe Rios, widow of Ramón Medina Silva (the famous Huichol Indian "shaman"), contain data which casts new light on the controversy surrounding the authenticity of Castaneda's writings. Data from these interviews, and from several other sources, suggest that: a) Carlos Castaneda's early writing was considerably influenced by his connection with certain

Huichol Indians, and by three UCLA students of Huichol culture: Diego Delgado, Peter Furst, and Barbara Myerhoff; and b) that collaboration between Castaneda and his academic allies, including Delgado, Furst, and Myerhoff, made it more difficult to detect spurious elements in Castaneda's books and mutations in the Huichol Indian literature. Because Castaneda has not documented his contacts with Yaquis, but was directly involved with Huichols and Huichol experts, deMille's judgment, that his work is a "transparent fraud" (1990: 354) seems sound.

## Richard deMille's Journey and Beyond

In 1981, after residing almost a year in the Huichol community of Santa Catarina (Fikes 1985), I read *Castaneda's Journey* and *The Don Juan Papers*. I agreed then with Richard deMille's bold deduction: that Castaneda had perpetrated a "transparent fraud" (deMille 1990: 354). To show Castaneda's statements were improbable, Dr. deMille repeatedly demonstrated how events in the real world were contradicted by events in the chronology Castaneda provided for readers. For instance, on September 6, 1968, the same day Castaneda mailed his letter to Gordon Wasson from Los Angeles (see below) he was allegedly hunting jackrabbits with Yaquis in the desert of Sonora (deMille 1990: 322). DeMille, citing evidence from independent experts, contradicted Castaneda's claims about various details of life in the Sonoran desert, how psychedelic mushrooms were eaten rather than smoked, etc. Dr. deMille's documentation of alleged "ethnographic plagiarism," especially his identification of some 37 ethnographic passages Castaneda allegedly "borrowed" from Furst and Myerhoff, aroused my curiosity. [7]

Clues connecting Castaneda with Ramón Medina Silva were manifested in excerpts from deMille's two 1978 interviews with Barbara Myerhoff. Scrutinizing deMille's interviews with Myerhoff, I wondered whether Castaneda could actually have collaborated with Delgado, Furst, Myerhoff, and Ramón Medina. I wrote to deMille, expecting to meet with him and furnish leads vital for further investigation. I hoped that by explaining leads implicit in the Myerhoff interview, providing circumstantial evidence of collaboration between Delgado and Castaneda, and testimony from other Huichol scholars (Professor Phil Weigand and Juan Negrín) and from Dr. Betty Bell (a UCLA archaeologist who was a friend and colleague of Peter Furst), I could induce him to continue investigating. I had no desire then to do the research I have done now.

Because deMille had some reservations about his conclusion that Castaneda had acted alone in fabricating don Juan and his supporting cast of literary characters (1978: x, 78-80; 1990: 347), I thought that the leads I could provide would compel him to investigate the scope and significance of Castaneda's involvement with Furst, Myerhoff, Delgado, and the Huichol. He declined at least two invitations to conduct further research. My investigation didn't begin in earnest until five years after I first wrote deMille. Until June 1989, deMille encouraged my research and supplied many leads.

It is possible that most of the 37 entries deMille (1990: Alleglossary) credited to Furst and Myerhoff (see note 7) came to Castaneda directly from Ramón Medina Silva and perhaps another person associated with him (see note 14). How much more information Carlos Castaneda obtained directly from Ramón Medina may never be known. Intrigued by Myerhoff's statements that she had given Castaneda "a costume that had belonged to Ramón

. . . after Ramón had been murdered" (deMille 1990: 348), and that Carlos had visited Ramón's widow, Guadalupe, in Mexico after Ramón's death (deMille 1990: 344), I began my research. After learning from a University of Southern California colleague of Myerhoff's that Barbara Myerhoff had regretfully admitted to him that don Juan was essentially modeled after her informant, Ramón Medina Silva, [8] I decided to locate Ramón Medina's widow.

I found Guadalupe de la Cruz Rios living in a shack on the outskirts of Tepíc, Nayarit on May 3, 1988. During this and a subsequent interview (on May 14, 1988), both of which were taped, she confirmed the fact that Carlos Castaneda had come to visit her after hearing of Ramón Medina's murder. She then asserted that Carlos had given her some money during that visit. She also mentioned that Carlos Castaneda had met Ramón Medina in Mexico a few years before his death. Carlos and Ramón became friends after being introduced to each other *in Mexico* by Myerhoff. Castaneda had even taken peyote. But, Guadalupe emphasized in response to my question, Castaneda had learned nothing significant about Huichol culture. According to her, Castaneda, unlike Furst and Myerhoff, had not done any interviews.

> Barbara Myerhoff brought Carlos Castaneda to meet Ramón Medina Silva and I. Carlos became a friend of Ramón's. Carlos went to eat peyote. He was going. He ate a little. Carlos didn't go with us to gather peyote. After Ramón died, Carlos came to see me. He helped me by giving me some money. Carlos didn't learn anything important from Ramón; they were just friends. Carlos was entertained (Guadalupe Rios interviews of 3 and 14 May, 1988).

My interviews with Guadalupe Rios indicated that although Castaneda has yet to prove that he studied with a Yaqui sorcerer named don Juan, he did have direct access to Huichol informants, and to those UCLA colleagues of his who popularized Ramón. Evidently the conclusion reached by the Yaqui Indian specialist, Professor Jane Kelley (in the Archaeology Department at the University of Calgary), is correct: "Castaneda did not invent [don Juan] out of whole cloth" (20 May 1988 letter). In addition to his Huichol connection, Castaneda may well have contacted Maria Sabina, Wasson's Mazatec Indian informant.

In May 1963 Carlos Castaneda attempted to persuade Dr. Leary to accept him into the circle of IFIF disciples gathered at Zihuatenejo, Mexico. After giving Leary some candles and copal incense, allegedly from María Sabina, Castaneda told Leary that María Sabina "asked me to share some of her secrets with you" (Leary 1983: 168). When Leary asked Castaneda what he wanted Castaneda replied:

> To share your knowledge. I want to follow in your footsteps. I have learned much from the Indians of Oaxaca and Peru and northern Mexico. I can share their magic with you. We can both become stronger (Leary 1983: 169).

Statements offered by Timothy Leary and Guadalupe de la Cruz Rios imply that Castaneda had almost as much field experience as some travel writers. Castaneda's books are, therefore, somewhat less fabricated than deMille was able to recognize. Although deMille's portrayal of Castaneda's "ethnography" as "transparent fraud" (deMille 1990: 354) may be slightly exaggerated, those few kernels of truth Castaneda's books contain are dissolved inside a concoction full of spurious ingredients. Finding ethnographic truth in Castaneda's books is almost as laborious as panning for gold. Several scholars, including Colin Wilson, have noted that Castaneda's more recent books have less authentic elements than did the first three. My experiences with Huichol shamans, observations of Huichol ritual, consultation with Huichol scholars such as Weigand, Negrín, Lilly, and Bauml, interviews with Guadalupe Rios, and analysis of clues Myerhoff provided to deMille make it obvious that Castaneda's work is somewhat less inauthentic than deMille asserted, but vastly less valid. Even the first three of Castaneda's books are far less valid than deMille could recognize (deMille 1990: 49, 1990b: 227-253).

Most anthropologists are dedicated to the pursuit of theory, and its ally, validity, which deMille defines as the "correspondence between the content of a scientific report and some established background of theory and recorded observation" (1990: 44). Despite his predilection for debunking, deMille assumed that reports about the Huichol provided by Furst and Myerhoff were entirely reliable. He reasoned that even if Castaneda had invented certain things, which coincidentally happened to correspond to purportedly Huichol events, Castaneda's reports about Mexican Indian shamans were still valid. But, if much of what is attributed to the Huichol is anomalous and unverified, most of the validity of Castaneda's reports suddenly vanishes.

Richard deMille's chief contributions are the evidence he uncovered about Castaneda's Huichol connection, and the rigorous analytic framework he used to unmask Castaneda's ethnography as spurious.

To show that Castaneda's purported accounts are fiction I presented three kinds of evidence, textual inconsistency, contradiction of independent knowledge (as of the nature of the desert environment or of the psychopharmacological effects of drugs), and examples of apparent ethnographic plagiarism, stating that the first of these kinds of evidence has the greatest weight, while the third has the least (deMille 1984: 223, 1976: 166, 1990: 392).

DeMille's "three kinds of evidence" were indispensable in defining my criticism of anomalous Huichol ethnography. My research taught me that investigating anomalies is as vital to insuring accurate ethnography as it is to unmasking invalid or unauthentic ethnographic reports. Kuhn's recognition that "Discovery commences with the awareness of anomaly" led Werner and Schoepfle (1987: 60-61) to conclude that maximum ethnographic insights result from searching for, and resolving, all possible sources of anomaly.

*Where is Don Juan, the Yaqui Sorcerer?*

Neither Professor Jane Kelley, nor Mr. John Dedrick, a Protestant missionary who lived among the Yaqui Indians of Vicam, Sonora from 1940 to 1979, are persuaded that anybody like don Juan exists among the Yaquis. Nor can Dedrick find any evidence justifying Castaneda's use of the word *apprentice* to describe the way Yaquis acquire religious instruction. Spicer's description of the Yaqui ceremonial system (Spicer 1940) and a Yaqui Indian's account of his participation in it (Kelley, Holden, and Moisés 1971) make it obvious that Castaneda's use of the term *apprentice* is out of place (see note 20). The shortage of authentic Yaqui elements led Dedrick to conclude, in his May 23, 1989 letter:

I only read Castaneda's "Teachings of Don Juan" and before I was a third of the way through the book, I knew he was not talking about Yaquis and had not been in Yaqui territory. There is no terminology in Yaqui language for any of the instructions and explanations "Don Juan" was giving him.

Nor was UCLA's own Yaqui specialist, Professor Ralph Beals, convinced that Castaneda had found a Yaqui sorcerer or shaman. When Beals asked to see the self-proclaimed apprentice's fieldnotes, Castaneda never replied (Beals 1978: 357). Four other UCLA professors were less inclined to demand verification. They included Professors Walter Goldschmidt, Pedro Carrasco, William Edgerton, and Bill Bright, each of whom recommended publication of the manuscript that later became Castaneda's book. UCLA Professor Johannes Wilbert, who mentored Furst, Myerhoff, and Delgado, was also favorably impressed by Castaneda. [9] Judging from all correspondence available to me, it seems reasonable to conclude that Bright, Carrasco, and possibly Wilbert were simply fooled by Castaneda. Further research is needed to determine why Goldschmidt and Edgerton supported Castaneda.

After reading Castaneda's manuscript, Professor Pedro Carrasco spoke with Castaneda in late May 1967 (before *The Teachings of Don Juan* was first published). At that meeting, Carrasco told Castaneda his material did not resemble Yaqui but it

rather looked like southern Mexico, especially the mushrooms, and I told him that since some Yaqui had been removed to Valle Nacionál that might have been the way someone could have learned about them

(Carrasco March 3, 1989 letter).

It appears that Castaneda quickly incorporated the core of Carrasco's comments in his first book, without acknowledging the conversation with Carrasco. Describing don Juan, Castaneda noted (1969: 6) that

> in 1900 his family was exiled by the Mexican government to central Mexico along with thousands of other Sonoran Indians; and that he had lived in central and southern Mexico until 1940.

Noting Castaneda's disclaimer about don Juan, that "it is not my intention here to determine his precise cultural milieu" (1969: 6), and recognizing several implausible or contradictory assertions, Dedrick deduced that the profile of don Juan presented in *The Teachings* invalidates Castaneda's claim that it is "a Yaqui way of knowledge." Dedrick's letter of January 17, 1990 highlights several mutually exclusive, or highly improbable propositions, which "totally invalidate" the claim that don Juan's teachings represent a "Yaqui way of knowledge."

*Profile of don Juan (Castaneda 1969: 6)*

a)  Born in Southwest (U.S. ?) in 1891
b)  Spent nearly all his life in Mexico
c)  In 1900 family exiled to Central Mexico along with thousands of other Sonoran (?) Indians
d)  Lived in central and southern Mexico until 1940
e)  Had traveled a great deal
f)  His knowledge may have been the product of many influences
g)  Regarded himself as an Indian (?) from Sonora

Anthropologists eager to accept Castaneda's claim that don Juan "regarded himself as an Indian from Sonora" (1969:6) overlooked the contrived complexity of don Juan's cultural provenience. Although Yaqui Indian specialist Ed Spicer did not believe that Castaneda's first book was about Yaqui culture, he and most other anthropologists specializing in American Indian studies spared it the degree of stinging criticism articulated by Edmund Leach in 1969 (in deMille 1990: 107), Weston LaBarre in 1972 (in Noel: 1976 and deMille 1990: 105-07), Beals (1978), Wasson, and others (in deMille 1990: 120).

Gordon Wasson, perhaps the only serious scholar to receive a written response from Castaneda, asked, in his August 26, 1968 letter to Castaneda, how the Yaqui Indian, don Juan, could have learned how to use the psychedelic mushrooms which grow only in the wetter southern portion of Mexico. To counteract the marked skepticism permeating Wasson's letter, Castaneda embellished upon the lead from Carrasco, i.e., the story that don Juan had been deported to the Valle Nacionál area of Oaxaca. Castaneda's September 6, 1968 letter to Gordon Wasson, paraphrased by deMille (1990: 323-324), suggested that don Juan's teacher must have been Mazatec, and that don Juan spoke the Mazatec language (deMille 1990: 324, 327). Thus the stage was set for don Genaro, the Mazatec waterfall performer, to make a grand entrance in *A Separate Reality*, Castaneda's second book.

But why would an exiled Yaqui from Sonora want to learn about psychedelic mushrooms from a Mazatec Indian in Oaxaca? Dedrick's extensive experience with Yaquis who returned to the Yaqui river area in Sonora after exile in the Valle Nacionál persuaded him that such Yaquis "had maintained both the language and cultural patterns with little modification" (letter of January 17, 1990). The inconsistency, if not deliberate vagueness in claims about don Juan's cultural provenience can only be stretched so far before credulity snaps. But Castaneda knew how to reassure Wasson and others who suspected he was fudging. When Wasson asked Castaneda if he had ever gathered the psilocybin mushrooms, Castaneda claimed he had indeed, but that he was not at liberty to describe don Juan's mushroom collecting ritual because it was a closely guarded secret (deMille 1990: 323). Castaneda's rejoinder to Wasson's question about which species of mushrooms don Juan had used divulged just enough of don Juan's mushroom collecting techniques to satisfy Wasson's curiosity. In pacifying Wasson, Castaneda tacitly violated his previous assertion that total secrecy about mushroom collecting was a rule don Juan had imposed (deMille 1990: 324). Castaneda's suggestion, that verification is impossible because don Juan wouldn't allow it, does little to inspire confidence.

Eliciting sympathy from his critics is another strategy mastered by Castaneda. When Wasson inquired about don Juan's cultural provenience, Castaneda made the University of California Press into a scapegoat or villain, and thereby misled Wasson about who (Castaneda) was responsible for providing the subtitle, "A Yaqui Way of Knowledge," for his first book, *The Teachings of don Juan.* According to an editor at the University of California Press, "The title of Castaneda's book and the entire text are the work of the author" (deMille 1990: 324-325).

In order to divert debunkers, Castaneda embellished upon the alleged complexity of don Juan's cultural provenience. Even those unaware of Castaneda's contact with Huichols have concluded that don Juan's character was too eclectic to be believable (Bharati in deMille 1990: 148-49). Superimposed on the pseudo-Huichol model was a combination of shreds and patches Castaneda gleaned from various sources and cultures. Improvising to recycle objections implicit in Wasson's questions was a strategy Castaneda continued using to deflect deMille's criticisms, albeit indirectly (1990: 378-79). The improvised alterations have accumulated to the point where Castaneda's don Juan appears as a composite character reminiscent of Frankenstein, or a cheap version of the archetypical trickster. [10] As we shall see, the vagueness, "textual inconsistency" (deMille), slurred reporting, or "fudging" evident in Castaneda's portrait of don Juan has its parallel among his Huichol collaborators. Readers who like the flavor of their fudge have rarely bothered to inquire about its ingredients. Analysis of key ingredients in Castaneda's concocted or improvised ethnography, e.g., the Mazatec teacher's waterfall jumping, suggests that far too much artificial flavoring was used.

*Evaluating Huichol Shamans and Stunts*

Yaqui specialists such as Kelley and Spicer have suggested that Castaneda's version of Yaqui culture is anomalous (deMille 1990: 33, 119-120). This conclusion is equally true about Castaneda's camouflaged version of Huichol culture. No Yaquis in Sonora that Dedrick, Kelley, or Spicer know of use peyote. Guadalupe Rios's testimony suggests that Huichols may have imparted something about peyote to Castaneda. Yet his report that while under the influence of peyote he played with a black dog, and that don Juan interpreted this as an omen is bizarre (Castaneda 1969: 33-41; Castaneda and Roszak 1968). His vague or obfuscating description of the peyote "deity," Mescalito, as a humanoid cricket (1969: 97-98; Castaneda and Roszak

1968; deMille 1990: 418) bears no resemblance whatsoever to Huichol ancestors associated with peyote (Benítez 1968b; Lumholtz 1900, 1902; Zingg 1938). [11] I believe that Jiminy Cricket, Walt Disney's cartoon character, stimulated Castaneda's image of Mescalito.

The Yaqui female who could change herself into a black dog (Castaneda 1969: 5) recalls an episode of Huichol mythology. [12] But having her get shot for stealing cheese from a white man effectively trivializes both nahualism, i.e., transformation into animal form (Eliade 1964: 94, 385, 459-461; Hultkrantz 1953: 372-73, 1979: 71-75; Clastres 1977: 126-27; Furst 1968a; Zerries 1968: 267-68, 272; Santoscoy 1899: xlii; McCarty and Matson 1975: 203-04; Dibble and Anderson 1961: 31; Foster 1944; Krickeberg 1961: 127, 173-74; Leon-Portilla 1963: 108-110; Fikes 1985), and the horrible history of Spanish, then Mexican violence against Yaquis (see Spicer 1962).

Although Castaneda's concocted episodes often have something authentic about them, they trivialize Huichol, Yaqui, or any Native American culture by masking or ignoring its true genius. They substitute sets, complete with colorful props, rather than describing the reality of everyday life. These and numerous other examples common in Castaneda's books, many of which are identified in deMille's Alleglossary, lend support to Guadalupe Rios's conclusion that Carlos Castaneda had learned nothing significant about Huichol culture. Some of the ethnographic "reality" readers find in Castaneda's books is simulated. Most is of negligible value, and could just as easily have been acquired by reading Lumholtz or Zingg. The books are superficially authentic and seemingly valid. They are comparable to books of von Däniken (see note 6).

Those more charitably inclined than I toward Carlos Castaneda are free to believe that if Castaneda did not go peyote hunting with Ramón Medina and Guadalupe Rios, but did take peyote (as she claims), his (as yet unknown other) Huichol mentor may have taught him secrets about which even Guadalupe was ignorant. [13] If Carlos Castaneda had a Huichol mentor other than Ramón Medina, it must have been don José Rios (Matsuwa). [14] David Christie and Phil Weigand speculate that Castaneda deliberately used don José Matsuwa's initials, DJM, to refer to don Juan Matus.

Further research pertaining to Castaneda's access to refugee Huichols, those dwelling outside the traditional *comunidades* (communities) originally given charters by the Spanish Crown in 1722, might be worthwhile (see Benítez 1968a: 353-380, 489; Fikes 1985: 44, 48, 63; Weigand 1978, 1979b, 1981, 1985 for distinctions between refugee/urban and traditional Chapalagana Huichols). My intent here is to correct a few of the numerous and wide-spread misconceptions about Chapalagana Huichol culture popularized for the last twenty-five years by Delgado, Furst, and Myerhoff. I have already identified and inter-preted numerous errors, omissions, misconceptions, and anomalies in Furst's and Myerhoff's published accounts of Huichol culture. [15] Here I shall comment on several glaring misrepresentations of Huichol culture endorsed by Delgado, and two of the most famous anomalies popular-ized by Furst and Myerhoff: Ramón's waterfall jumping and the highly abbreviated peyote hunts he led.

According to Delgado (Morotti 1970), the first Huichol shaman, *Makiritare*, met, seduced, and killed four evil sisters. After seducing the fifth and youngest sister, he spared her life because she promised to assist him whenever he needed her. [16] Despite reports that Huichol shamans face east when performing rituals, Delgado claimed they always face their left, a direction Western culture defines as evil or sinister. [17] Evil is simply accepted by Huichols. [18] Huichol women can not become full-fledged shamans because they have only four souls (rather than five as men do). [19] If traditional Huichols could read, such caricatures of their culture would be condemned as defamatory.

If anthropologists read "between the lines" they will recognize a "textual inconsistency" in Delgado's claims. By stating that the youngest sister promised to assist *Makiritare*, who is allegedly the first Huichol shaman, Delgado seems to contradict his assertion that Huichol women can not become full-fledged shamans. If she weren't a powerful shaman why would *Makiritare* need her aid? Incidently, Delgado hijacked the name *Makiritare* from a South American tribe described in the same issue of *Anthropologica* in which Furst's 1965 essay on West Mexican tomb sculpture was published.

Delgado's far-fetched, if not defamatory, version of Huichol culture was publicized in lectures given in 1969 and 1970 to Lowell Bean's classes on shamanism. Professor Bean, at California State University, Hayward, is an expert on California Indians, and was an acquaintance of Castaneda's at UCLA. Delgado also disseminated his version of Huichol "shamanism" to his own students at California State University, Sacramento from 1969-1972, and at the United States International University at San Diego in 1972. He claimed his knowledge was the product of a three-year "apprenticeship" to a Huichol shaman. [20] According to Guadalupe Rios (3 and 14 May 1988 interviews):

> Diego was a friend of Peter Furst and Ramón. Delgado and Furst came together the first time they met Ramón at Zapopan. Delgado went on both peyote hunts with us, but was afraid to eat much peyote.

He was reluctant to confess his sexual sins [as Huichols must do before eating peyote]. He didn't learn very much about how to become a *mara'acame* because he was too interested in women. He ate peyote.

Among the most spectacular claims made by Delgado are: a) that he introduced don Juan to Carlos Castaneda; b) that he had become a greater shaman than don Juan; c) that Carlos Castaneda was a pupil of his; and d) that he talked Castaneda out of his fears about publishing his experiences among the Yaquis (Morotti 1970; Hernandez 1972). Although Delgado's claims about the Huichol, don Juan, and Castaneda are apparently exaggerated, at the time they were made (1969-1972), they effectively enhanced credibility for Castaneda and his books, and advertised Delgado's own super "shamanic powers." [21] Both Castaneda and Delgado proclaimed they were sorcerer's apprentices to maximize the mystique about themselves. Their acquaintance, Ramón Medina Silva, was also accorded such undeserved status.

Professor Phil C. Weigand's research among Huichols residing in the community of San Sebastián has resulted in numerous scholarly publications on Huichol ethnohistory and culture. Weigand has concluded that the anomalies inserted into the Huichol ethnographic record by Furst and Myerhoff may never be corrected.

He (Medina) was cynically exploited, even after his tragic murder, and turned into something he was not. ... It continues to puzzle the anthropologists that have worked in the *comunidades* among traditional Huichols, as it puzzles the Huichols themselves, why Furst and Myerhoff fabricated a *mara'acame* out of that small minority of citified and nonpracticing Huichols, instead of doing reliable fieldwork in the traditional settings (Weigand 1979b, 1985: 151-152).

Furst's comments (in his letter of July 25, 1981) on Weigand's accusation (1979b) that he and Myerhoff "fabricated a *mara'acame*" were unconvincing. His use of the term "mara'akame" to describe Huichols who have completed five peyote pilgrimages did not recognize distinctions the Huichol make between healers, singers, and ritual specialists known as *cahuiteros* (Weigand 1978; Negrín 1975, 1977, 1985; Zingg 1938; Fabila 1959; Fikes 1985). Myerhoff declined to comment publicly on either Weigand's allegation (which she received via deMille in 1981) or on Furst's July 25, 1981 letter to Weigand (which she received from Furst).

The Huichol belief that sexual abstinence or fidelity to one's spouse is required of aspiring healers and singers is widely documented (Fikes 1985: 54; Benítez 1968a: 330, 449-451; Furst 1968: 165; Lumholtz 1902: 236-37; Myerhoff 1974: 100, 134-135; Zingg 1938: 138-140, 207-209, 236; Eger 1978: 45-46; Mata Torres 1974: 13, 18). According to Lumholtz (1902: 236),

> a man who wants to become a shaman must be faithful to his wife for five years. If he violates this rule, he is sure to be taken ill, and will lose the power of curing.

Myerhoff reported that Ramón Medina confessed his sexual infractions during the December 1966 peyote pilgrimage without acknowledging that they would nullify his endeavor to become a shaman (Myerhoff 1974: 100, 134-

135). Furst (1968a: 165, Furst 1972a: 155; Furst in Halifax 1979: 249-250) knew that the Huichol believe sexual misconduct violates the ethical code imposed on those aspiring to become healers and singers, yet neglected to mention what he knew from witnessing Ramón's confessions in 1966 and 1968, i.e., that Ramón Medina was not faithful to Guadalupe.

In addition to abrogating his quest to become a "shaman" (Fikes 1985: 40, 54), Ramon's sexual promiscuity disrupted his marriage with Guadalupe, and was, according to her, the cause of his murder. The well-known Mexican writer, Fernando Benítez, learned in November 1967 that Ramón Medina had enjoyed sexual congress with his concubine, Leuteria (1968a: 358-363). Benítez regarded Ramón as a good informant (1968a: 353), but did not camouflage the reason, attempted bigamy, for his flagrant marital conflict with Guadalupe Rios. Unlike Furst and Myerhoff, Benítez' accounts about his key informants, and his relationship with them, are unequivocal and complete. As we shall see, disclosing such information is as indispensable to ethnographers as detailed accounts of excavation are to archaeologists.

Ramón Medina's sexual infidelity to Guadalupe, evident in his affairs with Leuteria, and later with Mariana (who was Guadalupe's cousin), undermines Furst's claim that Ramón became a full-fledged Huichol singer (Furst 1989: 34). Furst reported that Ramón Medina's murderer was consumed by jealousy, but professed ignorance about the motive (Furst and Anguiano 1977: 171). Guadalupe Rios is convinced that Ramón's illicit liason with Mariana provoked Mariana's jealous lover to have Ramón murdered.

In addition to being disqualified due to sexual misconduct, Ramón had never completed the ten years of service and informal training as a temple officer (in two terms of five consecutive years each) required to qualify as an authentic Huichol singer. Ramón Medina couldn't complete these two terms of service because he did not live in a traditional Huichol temple district but rather in an urban environment. Inexplicably, Furst and Myerhoff have glorified Ramón Medina as a true *mara'acame* (Myerhoff 1974: 46; Furst 1974: 58-60, Furst 1989: 34; Furst and Anguiano 1977: 135), while inserting inconspicuous disclaimers about his status (Myerhoff 1974: 101; Furst and Anguiano 1977: 175).

Ramón's status was allegedly that of "apprentice-shaman" when he was photographed at the waterfall, and in 1966 and 1968, when he led the two abbreviated peyote hunts described by Furst and Myerhoff. By introducing Ramón as an apprentice-shaman, Furst and Myerhoff tacitly disclosed that Ramón was poorly qualified to clarify the meaning of ritual. But their use of the term *apprentice* was grossly misleading because it ignored the learning process embedded in the Huichol temple ritual system. Despite the fact that Castaneda, Furst, Myerhoff, and Delgado all used the term, there is no justification for using "apprentice" or "apprentice-shaman" in either the Yaqui or Huichol context. But, for non-Indians who proclaim that they have become "apprentices" of shamans or sorcerers, it would be convenient if native apprentices really did exist in Yaqui and Huichol cultures.

The four UCLA graduates didn't document the obligations associated with participation in Huichol aboriginal temple rituals, much less attend the rituals. These rituals are cooperatively performed public events directed by singers who are merely part-time ritual practitioners. Those who aspire to become "singers" (Fikes 1985: 336) learn how to perform rituals by being involved in the temple group processes which replicate rituals originally taught by Huichol ancestors. Huichols acquire religious knowledge without formal instruction or lectures. They learn how to heal, sing, pray, make offerings, and perform rituals while serving various ancestors as temple officers (Lumholtz 1902: 150-151; Negrín 1975: 11-13; Weigand 1978; Zingg 1938: 171-197; Fabila 1959: 100-101), or *huahuahuüte* (Fikes 1985: 71, 336). In helping to perform temple rituals, Huichols have the opportunity to make personal contact with ancestors, and observe healers and singers. Among Chapalagana Huichols the status accorded to part-time religious practitioners depends on acquiring skills through serving the community as temple officers during five consecutive years in office (Fikes 1985: 71-78). Huichol singers must have completed at least two five-year terms as temple officers. Data obtained by Weigand (personal communication: April 9, 1991) and Negrín (personal communication: April 1, 1991) suggest that temple officers do not necessarily make five consecutive peyote pilgrimages as temple officers. However, they must be prepared to make peyote and other pilgrimages each year while serving as temple officers. There are no apprentice Huichol healers or singers.

Apprentices are persons learning a trade, or perhaps students of full-time practitioners, such as Zen masters or Asian gurus. Apart from class-organized societies such as Aztec, Mayan, and Incan, few Native American societies are specialized enough to produce what can be properly defined as apprentices. Navajos have something superficially similar. Among Navajos, "apprentices" are expected to help singers execute elaborate rituals. But these "apprentices" learn and help Navajo singers only when rituals (public events) are performed (Faris 1990). Only Navajos learning the secrets of witchcraft do so in a way characteristic of Castaneda's use of the term *apprentice*. They do not learn such anti-social techniques in public. The anti-social element in sorcery or witchcraft undoubtedly forces sorcerers' apprentices to learn their tricks of the trade underground (see note 20). In the summer of 1966, Ramón Medina Silva was photographed above a waterfall near Guadalajara demonstrating a feat purported to be paradigmatic of "shamanic balance." After Castaneda's second book was published, Furst (1972: 153) and Myerhoff (1974: 44-46) cited Ramón's stunt as "strikingly similar" to the waterfall wonders demonstrated by Castaneda's Mazatec sorcerer, don Genaro (Castaneda 1971). Ironically, don Genaro's daring deed allegedly occurred on the same day Myerhoff defended her dissertation, October 17, 1968 (deMille 1990: 338, 483).

In a 1970 lecture series he organized at UCLA, Furst reported on Ramón's demonstration of shamanic balance while Castaneda publicized don Genaro's somewhat more spectacular demonstration (deMille 1990: 338; Furst 1972: 153). Furst (1974: 59-60) mentioned Ramón's feat again, this time without corroborating it by citing Castaneda. In 1974, Furst noted that it is "very much in accord with shamanic lore about waterfalls as supernatural power sources in South America and elsewhere" (Furst 1974: 60). Some persons will conclude that Furst's and Myerhoff's interpretation of Ramón's stunt was based on a misconceived synthesis, or magical blend, of Eliade's 1964 theory of shamanic balance (a universal theme of shamanism) and Harner's 1962 report about how Jivaro shamans seek souls at sacred waterfalls in South America (a trait of a particular culture). [22]

Whatever the case in South America, showing off at waterfalls to illustrate shamanic balance has never been described by other Yaqui or Mazatec ethnographers. Nowhere else in the literature on Huichol culture is such a bizarre activity reported (Fikes 1985: 50). Recognizing that Ramón's alleged feat was anomalous, I advised that it was premature to assert, as deMille had, that it is a valid, generally recognized fact that "shamans do perform feats of agility atop Mexican waterfalls" (deMille 1978b). Furst's letter of January 30, 1988 called my attention to a disclaimer which he did not originally use (Furst 1972: 153). According to Furst, Ramón decided "to give us a kind of theatrical performance, a literal translation of a metaphysical phenomenon . . . fundamental to what remains of archaic shamanism" (1974: 60). I reminded Furst that Myerhoff had originally fostered the impression that this waterfall stunt was a ritual. "Whether seen as a practice session or as a ritual, the events of the afternoon provided a most demonstrative assertion that Ramón was a true *mara'akame*" (Myerhoff 1974: 46). Furst has yet to explain Myerhoff's equivocation or textual inconsistency.

Suspecting, after my interviews with Ramón Medina's widow, Guadalupe, that the waterfall stunt was best seen as a "theatrical performance" or a "practice session," my April 19, 1989 letter to Furst asked him to explain what he meant by interpreting Ramón's behavior as a "kind of theatrical performance," asked him to provide me with his fieldnotes citing Ramón Medina's explanation of the significance of that particular waterfall, asked for the Huichol name of this waterfall (which Furst alleged was "especially for shamans"), and for an explanation of the "deeper meaning" of "shamanic balance." He has refused to supply fieldnotes and to respond directly to these questions.

Fieldnotes, tape recorded interviews, and photographs are essential ingredients in the ethnographic record

(Spradley 1979: 69-76). Both Richard deMille and Ralph Beals, the UCLA anthropologist who never saw Castaneda again after asking for his fieldnotes, know that requesting fieldnotes to clarify an anomalous event is perfectly reasonable. Beals recommended that an anthropologist should make his "observations available to his colleagues in their original form if demanded, for persons functioning as anthropologists have no vested rights in their data once the results have been reported publicly" (1978: 356). Incidentally, Beals's fieldnotes are on file at the Smithsonian Institution. According to deMille (1990: 61),

> Fieldnotes are the primary data of anthropology. They are part of the scientific record. Refusal to submit them for examination violates the norms of scientific conduct and amounts to *prima facie* evidence of fraud.

In 1992 David Christie carefully read all Myerhoff's fieldnotes on file in Los Angeles. She left no fieldnotes about "shamanic balance" at waterfalls. In 1992 I received written confirmation that Myerhoff did not deposit anything other than the notes Christie had reviewed. Despite Furst's belated disclaimer about Ramón's "theatrical performance" (1974: 60), and Myerhoff's (1974) slurred reporting about the meaning of the event, the impression their writing fostered in readers, deMille included, is that "shamanic balance," as illustrated by Ramón Medina's performance, is an essential facet of Huichol culture. Those starved for metaphysical meaning were so impressed by Ramón's waterfall jumping that disclaimers and proof of ethnographic authenticity became irrelevant. After Ramón and don Genaro were first advertised as waterfall jumpers in 1970 lectures at UCLA by Furst and Castaneda (deMille

1978: 112-13, 1990: 338), Furst published two essays describing it (1972a, 1974). In his opinion, the 1974 essay "has been much-cited and even reprinted in a hard-cover book" (Furst January 30, 1988 letter). The excerpt of Myerhoff's 1974 version of this event, reprinted in a 1976 book, *American Folk Medicine: A Symposium* edited by Wayland D. Hand, includes Myerhoff's fudging or slurred reporting (i.e., calling it either a practice session or ritual). It is followed by this attempt to enhance credibility:

> Those familiar with Castaneda's (1971) work will recall a strikingly similar display of virtuoso balance in one of his books. The description of Don Genaro leaping across rocks and cliffs suggests the same interpretation, a shaman's presentation of credentials as a mediator (Myerhoff in Hand 1976: 101).

The portion of Ramón's stunt reprinted in Joan Halifax's 1979 book, *Shamanic Voices*, includes neither Myerhoff's slurred reporting of the event, nor the additional explanation quoted above. Joan Halifax, a medical anthropologist specializing in shamanism, celebrated Ramón's stunt as a "demonstration of shamanic equilibrium," and evidently of magical flight (Halifax 1979: 19-20). Halifax's appraisal may be regarded as authoritative. It exemplifies the erroneous view typical of anthropologists lacking the perspective shaped by bona fide ethnographic research among Chapalagana Huichols.

Those of us who have lived with traditional Huichols know that waterfall jumping has nothing to do with authentic Huichol ritual. Nor does it train Huichols aspiring to become shamans. Huichols do venerate numerous Rain-Mothers (Fikes 1985: 155-58) and leave offerings at various lakes, year-round springs, and seeps. However, because the amount of rain is erratic and limited to a four-month season, there are no permanent waterfalls in the area surrounding Santa Catarina. Waterfalls visited by Jivaros of South America are presumably permanent. Their permanence is undoubtedly a precondition for their being places of pilgrimage.

The textual inconsistency in Myerhoff's interpretation and ambiguity in Furst's report about shamanic balance are puzzling. Before interviewing Guadalupe, I had assumed that Ramón Medina was solely responsible for this anomaly. After all, comments in Myerhoff's 1978 interviews with deMille imply that Ramón and Carlos Castaneda recognized each other as tricksters. [23] But Guadalupe's testimony will stimulate scholars to rethink who is responsible for the outlandish accounts of Ramón Medina's waterfall jumping.

According to Guadalupe Rios (May 14, 1988 interview), Ramón Medina was peering down into a canyon above a waterfall near Guadalajara, when Myerhoff suddenly had the idea of photographing him. She told me that Myerhoff had requested that Furst photograph Ramón. Her statement is tacitly confirmed by Furst's taking credit for the photo (1974: 59). Guadalupe explained that they urged Ramón to walk further down into the canyon, and pretend to fly like a bird. She told me that this event had no cultural significance and that it was done at Myerhoff's request to photograph Ramón. How Furst and Myerhoff decided this photograph of Ramón Medina on top of a boulder illustrated "shamanic balance" is a mystery as tantalizing as determining the real identity of don Juan Matus.

The significance of Ramón's "theatrical performance" (Furst 1974: 60) may never be ascertained. [24] The insinuation that Ramón may have been drunk (Furst 1972a: 153, 1974: 60) must have made this stunt seem even more spectacular to some readers. Commenting on the insinuation that Ramón had been drinking, Weigand concludes that "Furst and Myerhoff were actually endangering his life by encouraging him to leap around" (letter of 20 January, 1991). The effect, though surely not the intent, of celebrating such singular and unverified events has been to dramatically heighten interest in Huichol Indian "shamanism." It was a stunt which amplified the theatrical effect that Delgado's publicity for Castaneda, don Juan, and himself was having. The cumulative effect of the "striking similarities" between Ramón's "Huichol" and don Genaro's "Mazatec" waterfall jumping (not to mention at least 36 other events cataloged by deMille, as well as numerous other pseudo-Huichol incidents still buried inside Castaneda's books) was greater credibility for the mistaken notion that both Ramón Medina Silva and don Juan (or don Genaro) were bona fide shamans. [25]

During the crucial, formative stage of Carlos Castaneda's writing career, much of what he said and wrote about don Genaro (Mazatec) and don Juan (Yaqui) seemed to resemble certain characteristics credited to Huichol shamans by Delgado, Furst, and Myerhoff. Although I do not assert that it is evidence for some colossal conspiracy, each of these UCLA graduates endorsed the fallacy that apprentice shamans are indigenous to Yaqui and Huichol cultures. It is unnecessary, if not impossible, to determine why such erroneous ethnographic similarities appeared. Their existence undoubtedly made Castaneda's work seem more authentic and valid than it was. This must explain why so few anthropologists could identify Castaneda's engaging episodes as "pseudo-ethnography." [26]

Conversely, the correspondence between Huichol literature and events depicted in Castaneda's books greatly increased the public's appetite for and professional anthropology's acceptance of Furst's and Myerhoff's Huichol film and publications. Despite having unmasked Castaneda's literary corpus as fiction, Richard deMille was left with the impression that Ramón's waterfall jumping stunt was genuinely Huichol, truly a manifestation of Mexican Indian shamanism. Like deMille, Hans Duerr, the German anthropologist, credits Ramón with being a true *mara'acame*, accepts Furst's and Myerhoff's error of identifying *quieri* (a powerful sacred plant native to Chapalagana Huichol territory) as jimsonweed, and converts their partially accurate association of it with Huichol sorcery into whole-hearted acceptance of Ramón's waterfall stunts as exemplary of magical flight (Duerr 1985: 77-79, 81). DeMille and Duerr's muddled model of Huichol shamanism is shared by Joseph Campbell and Joan Halifax. Their erroneous view undoubtedly typifies current anthropological consensus.

In light of what Prem Das and Guadalupe Rios have told me, much in Myerhoff's two 1978 interviews with deMille (1990: 336-354, 482-83) can be read as a confession about Carlos Castaneda's involvement with Ramón. Myerhoff's enigmatic statement, which deMille did not probe then, is worth pondering now.

> Even the waterfall episode was not just Carlos reflecting me back to me. There was something besides (Myerhoff in deMille 1990: 346).

What that "something besides" might be must be left for us, the uninitiated, to imagine, unless Castaneda, or Delgado or Furst, repudiates what the journalist Seldes would identify as "the non-conspiracy of silence" (Seldes 1988). The abundant anomalies in their Huichol and "Yaqui" ethnographies, and the silence with which certain questions are met, compel some critics to conclude that some of the "something besides" must be slightly incriminating or embarrassing. Maybe the roar of a jet, or a distant waterfall, drowned out some of Ramón Medina's words. Maybe their Spanish was inadequate to decipher the nuances in Ramón Medina's colloquial phrases. If so, they should have tape-recorded his explanation.

Intending to be more definitive in assessing the extent of collaboration between Myerhoff and Castaneda, I told deMille (in my letter of June 8, 1989) that I was puzzled about why Myerhoff had disguised the identity of Ramón Medina Silva when discussing the waterfall jumping on page 94 of her 1968 doctoral dissertation. I asked him several questions: 1) why Myerhoff waited until 1974, when her *Peyote Hunt* was published, to name Ramón as the waterfall stunt man; 2) why she was so equivocal in interpreting it, insinuating that it was either of two mutually contradictory options, a ritual or a practice session (Myerhoff 1974: 46); 3) why she waited to cite the "strikingly similar" stunt reported by Castaneda; and 4) whether this change in her reporting about the waterfall stunt could be taken as evidence supporting his suggestion (of 25 September 1981) that Furst or Myerhoff would wish to emulate Castaneda only after Castaneda had become a best-selling author. Because Myerhoff left no fieldnotes, but stated there is "something besides" what is known about waterfall jumping, deMille and I remain stranded at the chasm of conjecture.

How deMille got the mistaken notion that Ramón Medina was mentioned on page 94 of Myerhoff's 1968 dissertation may never be revealed. Given deMille's impeccable demonstration of debunking, his silence about this matter is baffling. Some people deduce from deMille's interviews with Myerhoff that she was quietly defecting from the Yaqui and Huichol myth-makers by leaking information about Castaneda's Huichol connection.

The fact that Myerhoff did not name Ramón Medina as the waterfall jumper in 1968 is inconsistent with the lavish publicity he was accorded. Instead of protecting his privacy from invasion by seekers of don Juan style characters, Furst's and Myerhoff's sensational reporting helped Ramón Medina achieve a degree of fame remarkably rare among anthropological informants. Ramón's fame was a direct result of their using his actual name rather than a pseudonym.

It has long been standard anthropological practice to disguise the identity of one's key informants in order to protect their privacy. That Furst and Myerhoff disguised all other peyote pilgrims except Ramón and Guadalupe is perplexing. There is no justification given, just the statement that "All names except those of Ramón and Lupe have been changed" (Myerhoff 1974: 119). The effect, though surely not the intent, of their publicity (which included Furst's film, their books and essays, and Ramón's public appearances in Los Angeles) was to make Ramón a psychedelic celebrity. According to his widow, Guadalupe, a statue of Ramón had been made during his visit to Los Angeles. Dramatizing shamans, or emphasizing the "human interest angle," is acceptable as a marketing tactic, or a journalistic device; after all journalists search for the sensational, exotic, or unusual. But the first priority of anthropologists is to understand the routine and recurrent aspects of other cultures (Werner and Schoepfle 1987: 24). Such extravagant publicity for an informant clearly contradicts scholarly convention. What could have been more important than abiding by the fetters of scholarship and protecting Ramón Medina's privacy? Did Ramón request that they advertise on his behalf?

In 1966, Furst and Myerhoff published an article exaggerating the antagonism between peyote and *quieri* (mistaken for jimsonweed) in Huichol culture. This was simply the first of many Furst publications on psychedelics. The context in which Furst's dramatic depictions of Ramón were embedded suggest the author's intended audience. The waterfall jumping lectures presented by Furst and Castaneda were part of a UCLA lecture series Furst organized on the "ritual use of hallucinogenic plants" (Furst 1990: 77). Because this UCLA lecture series was open to the public, in early 1970, it had the effect of making supposedly shamanic stunts almost as fashionable as psychedelics.

Psychedelics were a subject which held Furst's attention long after Castaneda and Myerhoff had gone on to other pursuits. In 1972, *Flesh of the Gods*, a cross-cultural survey of psychedelics based largely on the 1970 UCLA lecture series, was published (Furst 1990: 78). As this book was being published, Peter Furst participated in an interview titled "Hallucinogenic Rituals and Therapy." After listening to it, I was disappointed by the fact that Furst gave virtually no significant information about the native meaning of the Huichol peyote hunt. Instead, he recited anecdotes about hallucinogens in general, including the chemical called bufotenine found in the species of desert toad Prem Das and company smoked in 1990 (see below). Skillfully skimming over the surface of the Huichol peyote hunt, the effect of Furst's information was to set the stage for the psychiatrist, Stanislav Grof. Dr. Grof, who has observed more than 3,500 LSD sessions (Stafford 1983: 41), eloquently outlined what he regards as a quasi-religious transformation, from death to rebirth, typical among patients receiving LSD in psychotherapy. The 1972 cassette tape interview left me with the distinct impression that members of the psychedelic movement had been encouraged to believe they had much to learn from cultures such as the Huichol. [27]

## On the Trail of Ramón's Peyote Pilgrimages

The Huichol peyote hunt led by Ramón Medina Silva is vastly more famous, but just as aberrant as the waterfall jumping. I have questioned numerous anthropologists without benefit of fieldwork among traditional Chapalagana Huichols. They seem to share the favorable opinion expressed by the acclaimed expert on peyote use, Weston La Barre, in his 1970 review of Furst's film, "To Find our Life." To set the record straight, I shall cite but a few of the many ways in which the Ramón Medina Silva led peyote hunt differs markedly from peyote pilgrimages integral to ritual cycles performed at aboriginal temples (see note 28 and Fikes 1985 for more discrepancies).

Because the peyote hunt reenacts or commemorates the birth or emergence of the Sun-Father, to properly conclude the ritual the temple officers making the pilgrimage must leave a variety of offerings at *Paritecüa* or *Reunar,* the burnt mountain where the Sun-Father first rose (Benítez 1968b; Mata Torres n.d.: 93-97; Fikes 1985: 186-198, 344). Although Furst and Myerhoff knew about the location and significance of the Sun-Father's birthplace (Furst 1968b: 24, 1972a: 171; Myerhoff 1968: 168, 195), the Huichols accompanying them did not deposit offerings there. Thus they failed to reach the final destination of the peyote hunt. Furst and Myerhoff did not clarify the central role played by the immortal wolves (*Camóquite*) in peyote hunting, and the precedent they set for eating peyote raw (Fikes 1985: 186-198, 330-31). That these and other key symbols and prominent sacred places were bypassed suggests that Furst and Myerhoff's peyote hunts set a precedent unique in Huichol history. Both John Lilly and Juan Negrín have participated in Huichol peyote hunts. They (personal communication May 23, 1988) have cited the mixture of pleated and nonpleated costumes worn by peyote seekers accompanying Furst and Myerhoff as proof that it was a pan-tribal excursion which included Huichols from the geographically distinct communities of San Andrés and San Sebastián. Lilly and Negrín have recognized numerous other particulars which indicate that Ramón Medina's peyote pilgrimages have little affinity with traditional Huichol pilgrimages organized by temple officers serving at a specific ceremonial center. The discrepancies cannot all be justified by asserting that Ramón Medina and his companions were unfamiliar with traditional cosmology and ritual.

Ramón Medina knew something about the *Camóquite* (Myerhoff 1974: 181) and *Paritecüa* or *Reunar* (Benítez 1968a, 1968b; Fikes 1985), which he pronounced *Hunaxu or 'Unaxa* (Myerhoff 1974: 81-82, 152). Ramón Medina evidently used *'Unaxa* as a synonym for *Paritecüa* (Furst 1968b: 24, 1972a: 171; Furst and Anguiano 1977: 167-169), and regarded it as the location to which a Huichol "called" by the Sun-Father to be a shaman goes "alone to the sacred mountain and eats peyote" (Furst 1965: 53). If Ramón Medina understood the significance of this sacred site, what caused him and his companions to abbreviate their pilgrimages, and thereby fail to properly conclude their peyote hunts by leaving offerings there? [28] It is possible that the presence of outsiders such as Furst and Myerhoff detracted from the devotions of Huichol pilgrims. Some offense to the ancestors, such as failing to leave offerings at *Paritecüa*, may illuminate why the pilgrims felt compelled to run away from alleged dangers, as Myerhoff reported (1974: 157-58, 243, 1978: 61).

Joseph Campbell (1989) has interpreted this Huichol aberration, running away from danger, as indicative of a profound universal truth. He didn't know that the Huichol fear sickness or other punishments sent by ancestors who are offended when Huichols neglect their ritual obligations. The failure to complete the appropriate ritual at *Pariteçüa* probably explains why in 1966 the pilgrims ran away as if in danger, and why Ramón Medina's uncle, Carlos, did not participate in the 1968 pilgrimage (see notes 28 and 31).

Yaqui specialist Ed Spicer concluded that Castaneda's first book was not truly ethnography, "since don Juan existed in a cultural limbo" (see Beals 1978: 356-57; deMille 1990: 119-120). To what degree might this judgment apply to Furst's and Myerhoff's reports on Chapalagana Huichol culture? Their accounts exaggerated the importance of peyote, and vastly underestimated the premium Huichols place on maize and the rain it needs to grow. Huichol ethnographers such as Lumholtz, Zingg, Weigand, and Fikes have recognized that the Huichol temple ritual cycle is centered around growing maize and soliciting rain from various "Rain-Mothers" (Fikes 1985: 48, 154-158, 238-240). In this respect, it resembles Hopi and other Pueblo Indian ceremonial cycles. Furst's and Myerhoff's "incomplete transition" theory, accepted uncritically by Campbell (1989) and others, indicates a failure to understand how Huichol ritual helps people cope with the uncertainty of maize horticulture in arid and steep terrain (see Weigand 1979b, 1985; Fikes 1985: 47-48). It also betrays an inability to recognize parallels with other cultures adapting to the arid climate of northwestern Mexico or the southwestern part of the United States. Their failure to document rituals inspired by fishing, amaranth cultivation, and Christianity suggest their research was limited to refugee Huichols. Because distinctions between refugee and traditional Huichols were blurred, their informants appear in a cultural limbo which most readers mistake for the real world inhabited by Chapalagana Huichols. They decontextualized their informant, Ramón Medina, so completely that most of their "ethnographic data" are meaningless and misleading.

The anomalies in Furst's and Myerhoff's accounts are only partially attributable to Ramón Medina Silva. Furst originally asserted that Ramón was an "apprentice shaman," in the process of serving an older shaman for five years (Furst 1965: 53). The identity of this older shaman Ramón was supposedly serving was never revealed. In 1977, after almost a decade of broadcasting the news that Ramón Medina had become a *mara'acame*, or "full-fledged singing shaman" in 1968 (Furst and Anguiano 1977: 135), Furst appeared to retreat to a position far closer to that presented here. In 1977 Furst's endnote insinuated that Ramón was caught in a "no-man's land," being neither a traditional Huichol nor a completely enculturated Mexican (Furst and Anguiano 1977: 175). A year later, Furst equivocated again about Ramón's status (Furst 1978: 27, 30). [29] But Furst's 1989 reprint of his 1973 essay, "An Indian Journey to Life's Source," asserted, without any disclaimer, that in 1968 Ramón Medina "became a full-fledged mara'akame" (Furst 1989: 34).

Publishing two inconspicuous disclaimers about Ramón's status was too little too late. Since 1978, neither the general public nor professional anthropologists lacking field experience with traditional Chapalagana Huichols have seriously questioned the authenticity of certain purportedly Huichol events. Those of us who have done fieldwork with non-urban Huichols are still puzzled about why Furst and Myerhoff were unable, or unwilling, to do research with better qualified informants affiliated with specific ceremonial centers. [30] Skeptics will find it incredible that Furst and Myerhoff didn't fathom what the Mexican journalist Fernando Benítez discovered about Ramón: that the annual, temple-chartered peyote hunt tradition had never existed in Guadalajara, Tepíc, or in the region where the extended family compound of Ramón Medina was located (Benítez 1968a: 353-54, 489). It is difficult to believe that Furst and Myerhoff did not consider the implications of the fact that the oldest peyote pilgrim, Francisco, as well as Ramón Medina's wife, Guadalupe, were two of four Huichols making their very first peyote pilgrimage in December 1966 (Myerhoff 1968: 141, 1974: 119). They evidently didn't bother to ask why, in 1965-66, when Ramón Medina was living on the "outskirts of Guadalajara . . . one of the pilgrims came down from the sierra and requested that Ramón lead a group" to hunt peyote (Myerhoff 1974: 118). Scholars who have done research in traditional Huichol *comunidades* understand that traditional Huichols would make the peyote pilgrimages as members of an aboriginal Huichol temple group, or would request that a more experienced Huichol, such as  don José Rios-Matsuwa, or perhaps Ramón's paternal uncle, Carlos, lead the peyote hunt. [31]

Ramón Medina clearly needed supervision or coaching by more knowledgeable Huichol "shamans" such as Carlos and don José Matsuwa. Near the end of Furst's peyote hunt film, don José was seated in the central *ohueni*, the "shaman's chair" typically reserved for the lead singer. Ramón, the alleged shaman, was seated to the right of don José, in a position normally occupied by one of the two assistants (*cuinepohuamete*) of the singing shaman. This is incontrovertible evidence of don José's senior status. But Furst and Myerhoff were unable, or unwilling, to acknowledge this incongruity. Nor were they concerned about the fact that these ceremonial chairs are not taken on temple-chartered peyote hunts. Weigand, Negrín, and Lilly know it is ludicrous for Ramón Medina to be seated in a shaman's chair in the middle of the peyote country (for a photo of this chair see Furst 1969, 1972a: 182, 1974: 42, 1989: 34, 37) Such cumbersome chairs are never carried on temple-chartered peyote hunts. As Weigand observes, "This is 'high' humor" (letter of January 20, 1991).

After Ramón Medina was murdered, in 1971, Anguiano tape-recorded don José (Matsuwa) Rios singing first fruits ritual songs. [32] Yet Anguiano and Furst published ritual texts dictated by Ramón Medina. Given the fact that don José was a better qualified informant, and that his songs correspond to the actual ritual Anguiano observed, there is no justification for omitting don José's 1971 ritual texts.

If Furst and Myerhoff noticed that Ramón Medina relied on better qualified informants, they should have used them instead of, or in addition to, Ramón Medina. Myerhoff claims that it would have been impossible to obtain data from other peyote pilgrims without "giving gross offense to Ramón, who claimed the right (and appropriately so) to provide the correct and official version" (1968: 139). How Myerhoff deduces that it is appropriate to select Ramón Medina, a less-qualified informant, and rely entirely on him for information is more than bewildering. Her defenders may speculate that Ramón Medina somehow convinced her to avoid contact with informants better qualified than he, and overlook any and all evidence which would contradict his version of events. Her critics will point out that she and Furst were well aware that there were

better qualified informants on ritual than Ramón. Furst and
Myerhoff's uncritical reliance on Ramón as their sole key
informant is inexcusable.

My investigation supports Weigand's conclusion,
that Furst and Myerhoff "fabricated a *mara'acame*" (1985:
152). Guadalupe's statements about the cultural irrele-
vance of Ramón's activities at the waterfall, Furst's and
Myerhoff's apparent breach of anthropological etiquette
(i.e., identifying Ramón by name), their failing to acknowledge evidence (e.g., of sexual misconduct) which under-
mined their claim that Ramón was a true *mara'acame*, or
shaman, their misuse of the term apprentice-shaman, and
numerous other profound ethnographic anomalies and errors I have reviewed above and in 1985 (42-51), strengthen
Weigand's conclusion.

DeMille's first two kinds of evidence for debunking
Carlos Castaneda's accounts as fiction (see above "Richard
deMille's Journey and Beyond") may be applicable to
Furst's and Myerhoff's claim that Ramón Medina became
a full-fledged singing "shaman." Their claim is riddled
with several textual inconsistencies (see note 29), and
contradicted by other Huichol scholars such as Benítez,
Weigand, Negrín, and Fikes. Numerous other examples of
Furst's and Myerhoff's data being contradicted by independent knowledge, plus the absence of any fieldnotes to
substantiate Myerhoff's incongruous claims about waterfall jumping, and Furst's refusal to allow examination of his
fieldnotes about this anomaly, should stimulate scholarly
inquiry into the accuracy of their Huichol research. Under
these circumstances, scholars are justified in asking
whether Myerhoff's citing Castaneda's undocumented
allegations about don Genaro's waterfall jumping as "strikingly similar" to Ramón Medina's "practice session" can
best be defined as purely coincidental.

Weston La Barre's favorable review of Furst's peyote hunt film, and deMille's judgement that Myerhoff's *Peyote Hunt* is both authentic and valid (1990: 49, 1990b) seem untenable. Nevertheless, they typify the view still held by most scholars, including Joseph Campbell (1989), and Duerr (1985: 77-81). This erroneous consensus is virtually ubiquitous among those who have not done field work among the Chapalagana Huichol. My research with Huichol shamans compels me to categorize Castaneda's books, and Myerhoff's *Peyote Hunt*, as far less valid than deMille has proposed (1990: 49, 1990b). Ethnographic evidence reviewed above demonstrates that Castaneda's work is largely invalid and unauthentic, having about the same value as von Däniken's *Chariots of the Gods?* and *Gold of the Gods*. Furst's film about the peyote hunt and his publication about the Huichol pre-harvest ritual (see note 32) contain little of value for Huichol scholars. Such sensational products are more valuable when probed for the clues they contain about American popular culture than when taken for orthodox ethnographic research.

## Who Fooled Whom?

Impartial observers will find little evidence to support the notion that Furst, Myerhoff, or Delgado were naive ethnographers constantly duped by a clever Huichol. Some readers will wonder if Ramón Medina may have been fooled, or unwittingly used, by one or more of them. Myerhoff's aversion to being interviewed by deMille until after deMille's book, *Castaneda's Journey*, was published in 1976, suggested to deMille that she was a "Castaneda partisan" (deMille 1990: 338-339). Castaneda's profound impact on Myerhoff is explicitly acknowledged (Myerhoff 1974: 24, 1980: 189), and hinted at in her interviews with deMille. But was she a "Castaneda partisan" because she knowingly collaborated with him, or did her approval of his books indicate she trusted him? What influence did Furst or Delgado have on Myerhoff?

Without benefit of field experience with Huichols, and lacking relevant information supplied by Guadalupe, deMille decided Myerhoff's research need not be scrutinized for evidence of collaboration. Thus deMille did not probe Myerhoff sufficiently in his interviews. She left him with the impression that her research with Ramón Medina was done independently of Castaneda. But deMille did not know what Guadalupe told me, that Myerhoff brought Castaneda to meet Ramón Medina in Mexico. Lacking profound knowledge of Huichol culture, and trusting that Myerhoff's knowledge about it was accurate, deMille concluded that Myerhoff's report of waterfall jumping was authentic, and that it occurred prior to Castaneda's account of don Genaro. Although he cited page 94 of Myerhoff's 1968 doctoral dissertation, "which told how she had been astonished by Ramón's agile leaps at the edge of the chasm" (deMille 1990: 338), deMille must not have been equipped for reading what was printed on that page. There was no Ramón Medina mentioned anywhere on page 94 of Myerhoff's dissertation. In 1968 the leaping was attributed to an anonymous shaman-informant.

> One informant, himself a shaman, was discussing the magical journey... He was speaking figuratively, for the previous day he had put on a virtuoso (and utterly terrifying) performance of his skills in balancing by leaping agilely and fearlessly among towering, slippery rocks that dropped abruptly off into steep

barrancas (Myerhoff 1968: 94).

DeMille's faith in Barbara Myerhoff now hangs on an even more "slender thread," her solitary, unsupported recall of a conversation with Carlos Castaneda (deMille 1990: 482). I shall continue to suspect that Myerhoff was, at least sometimes, Castaneda's collaborator, until Castaneda convinces me this suspicion is untenable. Unless Richard deMille can provide an alternative explanation, I shall assume that Myerhoff told him that Ramón Medina was mentioned as the waterfall jumper on page 94 of her 1968 dissertation. It now appears likely that Myerhoff outsmarted both deMille and Ramón Medina.

According to Pedro Carrasco, Carlos Castaneda hinted that he had not been fooled by Ramón Medina. In one of their conversations, Castaneda laughed profusely while confiding that Ramón Medina Silva was fooling Peter Furst. If Castaneda knew that Ramón was unreliable, or entertaining, it seems likely that he would have alerted Furst or Myerhoff. Given Castaneda's predilection for mystery, it is difficult to interpret his ridiculing of Peter Furst's alleged gullibility. It is possible that Castaneda was covering up his coalition with Ramón Medina, or Myerhoff, by chuckling at Furst in front of Carrasco. Myerhoff might rationalize that Castaneda was merely having fun. She claimed that Castaneda's "imagination was so well developed that all he needed was one accomplice like me or Ramón, and he could get right into that other world of fun he yearned for" (quoted in deMille 1990: 353). Maybe his humor tacitly tested to see whether Carrasco was suspicious. Skeptics will suspect he was setting Ramón Medina up to be the fall guy.

Some readers may suppose that Furst was completely fooled by Castaneda's ethnographic anomalies. Perhaps his Spanish was rudimentary. The enigma remains because Furst refuses to answer any of my questions about his collaboration with Delgado or Castaneda. In 1970, Furst and Castaneda lectured on "shamanic balance" at UCLA. In 1972 Furst tried to legitimize Ramón's waterfall stunt by citing the "striking similarity" to Castaneda's don Genaro (Furst 1972a: 153). Yet at the 1977 meetings of the American Anthropological Association in Houston, Furst gave the Yaqui expert, Professor Jane Kelley, the impression that he had always been cynical about Castaneda's work. He told Kelley then that don Juan's mother was a Yuman Indian, that don Juan was one of those Yaquis deported to Oaxaca (presumably to the Valle Nacionál), and left her thinking that he was the person best able to identify the sources in world religion and ethnography which inspired Castaneda's writing (Jane Kelley, lettters of May 20 and June 16, 1988).

Sometime after September 1975, when deMille's research culminating in publication of *Castaneda's Journey* began, but before March 1976, when Furst completed the preface to his book, *Hallucinogens and Culture*, Furst evidently decided to terminate his public support for Castaneda. Furst did not cite Castaneda even once in *Hallucinogens and Culture*. Such active neglect of Castaneda, and Furst's conversation with Jane Kelley, suggest that publication of *Castaneda's Journey* in 1976 (and/or research connected with it) ended Furst's public support of Castaneda. In 1977, Furst inserted an inconspicuous disclaimer, implying that Ramón Medina "had drifted away from the indigenous culture into the no-man's land between 'being Huichol' and becoming Mexican" (Furst and Anguiano 1977: 175).

In contrast to Furst's predilection for the power of silence, Myerhoff's 1978 interviews with deMille may have been motivated by a desire to clothe certain clues about Castaneda's Huichol connection in a semi-transparent costume. But if Guadalupe's testimony is true, there must be something besides Myerhoff's admission that Castaneda had met with Ramón Medina and Guadalupe in Los Angeles. What Myerhoff did not mention was that in 1965 Delgado and Furst met Ramón Medina, and in 1966-1967, after Myerhoff introduced Castaneda to Ramón – in Mexico – they were all in contact with Ramón (though not necessarily at the same time, or for the same purposes). Myerhoff may have concealed the fact that she introduced Castaneda to Ramón Medina in Mexico in order to reinforce the impression that their reports about shamans (at waterfalls and elsewhere) were obtained independently of each other. Although Myerhoff came close to admitting that "I was completely taken in and a fool," she told deMille she had a "feeling he (Castaneda) is building on an exchange with another person" (deMille 1990: 346-47).

Her feeling that Castaneda was building on an exchange with another person was explained more fully to Professor Ira Abrams, whom she told that don Juan was modeled after her informant. Despite his criticism of Castaneda, Beals was convinced that there was a real person, possibly a "desert rat," from whom Castaneda had learned something (Beals 1978: 359). Perhaps Castaneda had visited María Sabina by mid-1963, as he told Dr. Leary (1983: 168-69). I suspect that most of Carlos Castaneda's model for don Juan was originally built on exchanges with both don José Matsuwa and Ramón Medina Silva.

Information supplied by Ira Abrams and Guadalupe Rios enabled me to read between the lines in deMille's interviews with Myerhoff. Unless Furst is willing to reveal the extent to which Delgado and Castaneda collaborated with him, Myerhoff, and Ramón Medina, the scope and significance of their collaboration will never be known. Their stonewalling efforts illustrate what Castaneda praises as the "power of silence" (Chickering 1988) and what Sykes (1988: 244-256) defines as the "code of silence" academics use to discourage would-be critics. When Richard deMille's books stole the spotlight, Furst's and Myerhoff's public praise for Castaneda's writing ended. Some may infer from this that theirs was merely a temporary convergence of individual interests. It was clearly not a full-blown conspiracy. It is often impossible to establish which of the four UCLA graduates misconstrued elements of Huichol religion. All available evidence indicates that as Delgado and Castaneda began to be exposed, Furst and Myerhoff began diluting and withdrawing their support. Refusing to comment candidly on particular issues or persons is best interpreted as a demonstration of the "non-conspiracy of silence" (Seldes 1988), the "code of silence" (Sykes 1988), or "the power of silence" (Castaneda 1987). Even players in brief coalitions stonewall, or make partial confessions, when threatened by unmasking of their own errors.

Unless Furst, Delgado, or Castaneda decides to elaborate upon clues provided by Myerhoff, Abrams, and Guadalupe Rios, one can only speculate about why they did not do their research with better qualified Huichols in remote areas of the sierra. Some readers will conclude that they didn't care enough about Huichol culture, or professional anthropologists, to do meticulous research at an actively functioning Huichol ceremonial center. Others will wonder if they were afraid of the amoebas, fleas, and scorpions so abundant in the Huichol sierra. DeMille might sarcastically ask if the gigantic winged monster guarding the other world (1990: 412-13) could have prevented them from entering Chapalagana Huichol territory.

Some readers may be tempted to conclude that Ramón Medina was cast in the role of scapegoat or fall guy. However, to contend that classifying Ramón Medina an "apprentice-shaman" was deemed advantageous because his "ignorance" could be cited to deflect responsibility for the singular, sensational, and inaccurate elements discernible in Delgado's lectures, and in much of Furst's and Myerhoff's Huichol publications, would require additional evidence. In fact, Furst and Myerhoff insinuated that Ramón's status, as apprentice-shaman, made him a qualified and reliable informant. As we shall see, most of the anomalies in their work, and that of Castaneda, are best interpreted as a result of an uncanny imperviousness to ethnographic truth.

*Indifference to Ethnographic Accuracy*

Castaneda's books, in which he stars as the sorcerer's apprentice, are essentially allegorical. The problems pervading the eccentric editions of Huichol culture circulated by Delgado, Furst, and Myerhoff suggest their work is far from perfectly factual. Although ethnographic writing is increasingly viewed as less than completely factual (Clifford 1988; Clifford and Marcus 1986; Clifton 1990), there are two other professions which truly reward skilled storytelling. The feature film industry centered at Hollywood thrives on fostering well crafted illusions; making fiction appear plausible. Castaneda's allegories unfold against a Yaqui backdrop, dislocating people and places in ways reminiscent of Western movies. Although he evidently didn't intend it, his sensationalizing of Mexican Indian shamans resembles "disinformation," a type of propaganda familiar to intelligence agencies.

> It involves the deliberate, calculated dissemination of equivocal data, partially true, partially erroneous, in order to conceal something, to divert people from something, to deflect attention in one or another peripheral or tangential direction. But the best lies are always embellishments or variations on the truth, not total fabrications. The most effective disinformation is always structured around a core of validity (Baigent, Leigh, and Lincoln 1986: 268).

It is difficult to determine what motivated the sensational and inaccurate images of super-shamans promoted by the four UCLA graduates. There are some who will be tempted to brand Castaneda's literary hoax as part of a pseudo-religion deliberately devised and widely broadcast in order to defuse 1960s political movements considered subversive of the status quo. Such diverting, hijacking, or coopting of "subversive" political movements has occurred before. [33] Perhaps someday somebody will uncover enough evidence to defend what I believe is a "long-shot" or unverified "hypothesis." The extent to which intelligence agencies influenced psychedelic research is unclear (see above).

This ultimate "political conspiracy theory" seems flawed, not only because evidence to support it is lacking, but principally because there is considerable evidence implicating Castaneda (Bebb 1984; M. Castaneda 1975: 76; Parrott 1975: 81) and Delgado in adventures in unauthorized archaeology. In 1965, Furst and Delgado began collaborating on archaeological, historical, and ethnographic research in Mexico. In August 1965, about the same time Delgado and Furst first met Ramón Medina at Zapopan, Delgado and Furst excavated, evidently without a valid excavation permit, a shaft-tomb at Las Cebollas, Nayarit. Delgado's M.A. thesis included an inventory of artifacts he and Furst excavated from the Las Cebollas' shaft-tomb (Delgado1969: 87), and two diagrams of this shaft-tomb (1969: 123-124). Several of Delgado's drawings appear in Furst's 1966 doctoral dissertation.

The spy thriller scenario is contradicted by the fact that Delgado's visa (allowing him to remain in the United States) was not renewed after Sacramento State administrators and U.S. officials learned from Dr. Betty Bell (letter of April 6, 1970) and José Luis Razo Zaragoza, then secretary of the Instituto de Antropologia e Historia in Guadalajara (letters of 3 August and 10 September 1970) of his adventures in illegal archaeology in Mexico. Despite strident student protests (Burns 1972), news of Delgado's unauthorized archaeology in Mexico helped persuade U.S. officials and Sacramento State university administrators that Delgado would have to leave. After teaching sociology and taking courses in a doctoral degree program at United States International University in San Diego (Hernandez 1972), Delgado returned to Mexico.

It may be only coincidental that the reporter who interviewed Delgado in 1972, Luis Hernandez, has the same name as the man Guadalupe Rios identified as the cameraman of Furst's peyote hunt film. According to Guadalupe Rios, Luis Hernandez was purchasing yarn paintings from Ramón Medina shortly before he was murdered in 1971 (May 3, 1988, interview).

Although spectacular assertions about Mexican Indian shamans may be innocent and infrequent, an erroneous consensus about Huichol culture endures. There is no evidence that a "master-mind" contrived a complicated con-spiracy. Each of the four UCLA graduates may occasion-ally have fooled, or been fooled, by one or more of the others. Whatever the extent of their collaboration may be, it has badly caricatured Huichol culture.

Unlike the systematic strategic lying indispensable to disseminate disinformation, Castaneda's books cheerfully depart from traditional canons of anthropological truth. Their cavalier disregard for ethnographic accuracy is only partially comparable to the best known example of disinfor-mation in anthropology, the Piltdown Man fraud. Although deMille argues that the Piltdown Man fraud resembles Castaneda's pseudo-ethnography (deMille 1990: 112-117), there is a more satisfactory explanation of Castaneda's work, which the culprit himself gave Sandra Burton, the *Time* magazine correspondent, who spent hours interviewing him in preparation for *Time*'s March 5, 1973 cover story. Carlos Castaneda cackled and proclaimed: "Oh, I am a bullshitter . . . Oh, how I love to throw the bull around" (*Time* 1973: 33).

Taking Castaneda's confession at face value leads us to Harry Frankfurt's obscene but apt observations about "bullshit." Frankfurt's remarks may be more profitable than the concept of disinformation for categorizing the core of Castaneda's literary endeavor. The primary problem with Castaneda's ethnography is not that he failed to get things right, but that he didn't try diligently enough to distinguish between what was true and what was false. According to Harry Frankfurt, "the essence of bullshit" is "this lack of connection to a concern with truth – this indifference to how things really are" (Frankfurt 1986: 90). All available evidence indicates that Carlos Castaneda's books were published without taking into account at all the issue of their accuracy. Castaneda skillfully evaded the basic methodological precautions identified as indispensable to gathering accurate ethnographic data (Fettermann 1989; Jorgensen 1989; Spradley 1979; Pelto and Pelto 1978; Werner and Schoepfle 1987; Wasson 1980; Fikes 1985). Such precautions include doing ample fieldwork among traditional Huichols or Yaquis, selecting the best of all possible informants on ritual and shamanism, and cross-checking information obtained from various informants qualified to provide it (Fikes 1985). Castaneda's writing about the "Yaqui way of knowledge," most of Delgado's lectures on Huichol "shamanism," and some of what is contained in Furst's and Myerhoff's publications about the Huichol Indians, were evidently produced without any of the authors having done what responsible scholarship requires, that is, genuinely submitting "to the constraints which the endeavor to provide an accurate representation of reality imposes" (Frankfurt 1986: 90).

Delgado and Castaneda are no longer considered professional anthropologists. "Indifference to how things really are" explains some but not all of the errors in Furst's and Myerhoff's editions of Huichol culture. Although both Furst and Myerhoff have wanted to be taken seriously as Huichol ethnographers, neither of them did fieldwork in the region where traditional Huichol culture was still flourishing. Neither of them verified their more anomalous findings, e.g., that apprenticeship is an orthodox Huichol religious institution, before publishing them. Another unverified and scandalous statement about the Huichol is Furst's assertion, which he attributes to his student, Tim Knab (see note 25), that Huichols employ peyote enemas (Furst and Coe 1977: 91). Unless fieldnotes clearly datable to 1966 can corroborate their reports about Ramón Medina's waterfall jumping, this anomaly should be regarded as unverified and invalid.

Creating bullshit is an improvisational art which includes picking bits and pieces of exotic data from any convenient source, and even inventing ethnographic data when it suits one's purpose. Carlos Castaneda's bullshitting has more in common with bluffing and fakery than with disseminating disinformation. The counterfeit shamans he concocted had both fake and real features. As Frankfurt notes, "What is wrong with a counterfeit is not what it is like, but how it was made ... The bullshitter is faking things. But this does not mean that he necessarily gets them wrong" (Frankfurt 1986: 94-95). As Frankfurt suggests, bullshit artists have more freedom to improvise than liars and are usually less severely reprimanded than liars when their phony baloney is discovered. Although both liars and bullshit artists "represent themselves falsely as endeavoring to communicate the truth," the bullshitter's focus "is panoramic rather than particular. He does not limit himself to inserting a certain falsehood at a specific point, and thus he is not constrained by the truths surrounding that point or intersecting it. He is prepared to fake the context as well, so far as need requires" (Frankfurt 1986: 96).

Weigand concluded (1989b: 148) that Castaneda's use of don Juan as a metaphor to represent aboriginal American ritual was fraudulent. He criticized Furst and Myerhoff for "presenting data derived from artisans residing in cities in Western Mexico as if they were a representation of the life or world-view of the indigenous (Huichol) communities" (1989b: 148). Without access to unpublished notes, scholars may remain baffled about Furst's and Myerhoff's failure to differentiate adequately between Chapalagana Huichols and the more acculturated refugee/ urban Huichols they studied. Does this enigma exemplify "indifference to how things really are?"

"Contextualization," or reporting about the circumstances in which one's informants lived during one's study of them, is indispensable to authentic ethnography (Fettermann 1989: 29-30; Spradley 1979: 124-25). Whatever one decides to call it, camouflaging the ethnographic context in which one's research occurs violates the norms of scholarship. The concealing of ethnographic context was crucial to cultivating academic acceptance of the anomalous ethnographies about the Yaqui and Huichol. Simulating reality, or faking authentic contexts by skillful use of sets, props, and fronts, is clearly a vital element in most Hollywood movies. But, because we are advised that they are fiction, and know they are designed to entertain us, we need not denounce them. The attempt to arrive at scientific truth, via ethnographic authenticity, obliges one to follow rules quite distinct from those which guide production of the Hollywood movies we all enjoy.

Bullshit artists probably flourish most during times of cultural crisis, when "old-fashioned" standards of truth and "establishment" morality have been devalued. Bullshit is most likely to multiply among persons who are expected "to speak extensively about matters of which they are to some degree ignorant" (Frankfurt 1986: 99). The psychedelic movement of the mid-1960s provided a unique opportunity for any academic interested in selling sensational ethnography. By 1964, Dr. Leary's academic credibility was considerably impaired. In 1964, few scholars other than Mircea Eliade were familiar with the "techniques of ecstasy" employed by shamans. Those capable of supplying what the counterculture needed were in short supply. By 1964, if not well before, a huge audience participating in the psychedelic movement was looking for a compass and maps to guide them in the remote realms they inhabited during their altered states of consciousness. The expectations or needs of those in the psychedelic movement far exceeded the supply of accurate scholarly information about how, when, and why plant psychedelics were used. The void about peyote, mushrooms, and other plant psychedelics was neatly filled by Castaneda and other academics willing to exploit the unmet demand for "ecstatic techniques" exuding from America's burgeoning counterculture. In 1968, when Castaneda put don Juan the sorcerer on stage, the audience was so starved for metaphysical meaning they ate up his bullshit as if it were caviar.

Professor William Bright's letter recommending publication of Castaneda's manuscript recognized that the popular market waiting for Castaneda's first book was enormous. Bright's estimate, and the opinions of various others (Baigent, Leigh, and Lincoln 1983: 205; deMille 1990: 109, 124-25), suggest that money-making was an incentive animating the creative writing of the fledgling author who persuaded the University of California Press to publish *The Teachings of Don Juan*. Myerhoff (in deMille 1990: 339, 345, 353) and deMille (1990: 375-76) have speculated that Castaneda's writing about his alleged escapades in Mexico were motivated by the sheer exhilaration of hoaxing.

Future research may help determine which objective: pursuit of profit, and/or prestige, or a penchant for playing intellectual pranks, or some motive yet unknown, best accounts for the sensational and singular ethnographic episodes identified above. Such research must address the issue of unauthorized archaeology in which Castaneda and Delgado were involved. What prompted Furst's and Myerhoff's ethnographic anomalies is unclear (see notes 25, 30, 32). Those who believe more deeply in the "separate reality" than in investigative research may unearth the answer by consulting a trance-channeler, a crystal ball, or one of those CIA operatives who administered LSD to get others to "disclose closely-held secrets."

## *Canonization of Dr. Castaneda's Literary Corpus*

What motivated the four professors who wrote letters recommending publication of Castaneda's first book is a topic beyond the purview of this chapter (see deMille 1990: 131 and note 9). Nor can I assess the degree to which commendation for the first book contributed to its sales. The profuse praise lavished on *The Teachings of Don Juan* by two prominent professors of anthropology, Walter Goldschmidt and Edmund Carpenter, surely stimulated additional scholarly and popular acceptance of the book. Joseph Long declared that had it not been for Goldschmidt's Foreword, "Castaneda's writings might never have been considered more than psychedelic ramblings" (deMille 1990: 131). Because Long ignored the significance of Edmund Carpenter's endorsement, and lacked any knowledge of Castaneda's Huichol connection, he may have overestimated the effect that Goldschmidt's legitimizing Foreword to *The Teachings* had on boosting sales.

The experts' acclaim for Castaneda's first book made unflattering reviews of the second book virtually inconceivable. The *New York Times* book review editor paid for, but refused to print Weston La Barre's 1972 review condemning *A Separate Reality* as "pseudo-profound, deeply vulgar pseudo-ethnography" (in Noel 1976: 39-42). In 1973, Castaneda reaped another reward from his literary success, obtaining his doctorate in anthropology from UCLA with a thinly disguised version of *Journey to Ixtlan*, his third book (deMille 1990: 86-88, 132, 136-138). In 1973, the opinion of American consumers and professional anthropologists was that Castaneda had brought back something new, exciting, and authentic from his Yaqui Indian master. The clothes of the King of Ethnographers, Castaneda, had never appeared more elegant to more readers when deMille's book, *Castaneda's Journey*, announced that the King wasn't wearing any. "So lacking was/is the basis of real knowledge concerning things Indian within academia that it took nearly a decade for Castaneda to be comprehended as the greatest anthropological hoax since Piltdown Man" (Churchill 1988: 23). Churchill's generalization seems less than completely accurate given the evidence about Castaneda's collaboration with Huichol Indians and Huichol "scholars", and the endorsements a few trusted professional anthropologists bestowed upon Castaneda's books.

DeMille's debunking has all but eliminated professional anthropological support for Castaneda's books. Castaneda has become almost as famous as Margaret Mead. His literary legacy is still taken seriously by many scholars (Chickering 1988; Harner 1987; Kramer 1988: 170). He has also helped stimulate an ever-increasing demand for celebrity shamans.

# Notes

6.  Which of these two authors' literary products is most accurate is an issue others may debate. I find little difference between them. Accordingly, I am amazed about what appears to be a double-standard. In books, documentary films, and class lectures professional anthropologists, particularly archaeologists, zealously disputed von Däniken's thesis (1969) that extraterrestrials had influenced cultural development on the Easter Islands, with the huge stone statues, in monuments throughout Central and South America, and in ancient Egypt (with its pyramids and mummies). To explain the contrast between professional anthropologists' vehement condemnation of von Däniken and their initial enthusiasm toward Castaneda's books it is necessary, but not sufficient, to accept Truzzi's distinction between exoheretics (like von Däniken) and endoheretics, or deviant insiders, such as Castaneda (see deMille 1990: 125-26). That Castaneda had awe-inspiring academic endorsements for his first two books, and a doctorate from UCLA for the third one, gave him crucial advantages over those of an uncredentialed writer like von Däniken. Even after deMille demonstrated that Castaneda was essentially an emperor without clothes, many anthropologists spared the UCLA graduate the scathing harangues they heaped on the amateur archaeologist, Erich von Däniken. Even today deMille (1990) and many anthropologists proclaim that Castaneda's books are valid and contain considerable insight into Native American religions. Some anthropologists assert that even though Castaneda's books are fiction, they "have served as one of several stimuli for thinking about alternative textual strategies within the tradition of

ethnography" (Marcus and Fischer 1986: 40). Locating a professional anthropologist who said the same thing about von Däniken's books would be as challenging as finding don Juan or don Genaro.

My investigative research yielded evidence suggesting that some academic anthropologists were reluctant to examine impartially ethnographic anomalies and unverified data published by their colleagues. The formidable obstacles, including perhaps the "code of silence" (Sykes 1988), and the improbability of reaping any rewards, discourage most potential critics. Documenting misconduct is typically delayed. For example, when zoologist Gerrit Miller concluded that Piltdown Man was a fraud, "colleagues persuaded him not to publish his conclusion, saying it was too serious an accusation to make without proof. Exposure had to wait another 23 years" (deMille 1990: 113-114).

7.    In addition to each having 17 separate entries in deMille's Alleglossary (1990: 390-436), Furst and Myerhoff shared two entries, wind-women (1990: 435) and confidence (1990: 402). Myerhoff may have one or two more entries connected with her wandering eye (1990: 352).

8.    Ira Abrams told me this in our telephone conversation of November 29, 1987. Abrams is now a Professor in the Department of Film, Radio, and T.V. at the University of Texas, Austin. One obvious way in which don Juan Matus was modeled upon Ramón Medina Silva and/or don José Rios Matsuwa is that families of both these Huichol men are refugees of the 1910 Mexican revolution. According to Castaneda (1969: 6) don Juan's family was among those Sonoran Indians exiled to central Mexico in 1900. Each of them (assuming don Juan exists) is, therefore, more acculturated than most traditional Huichol or Yaqui Indians.

9.   According to UCLA Professor Walter Goldschmidt (deMille 1990: 131) four professors recommended publication of Castaneda's manuscript. My research indicates they included Pedro Carrasco, William Bright, Edmund Carpenter, and Robert Edgerton. Goldschmidt's endorsement of Castaneda's first book, *The Teachings of don Juan*, is the Foreword. In it he fails to discriminate, calling *The Teachings* "both ethnography and allegory." Bright's letter mentions UCLA Professor Johannes Wilbert's approval of Carlos Castaneda's work. This observation is independently verified by one of Castaneda's fellow anthropology graduate students, Professor Anonymous, who insisted on remaining unnamed. In addition to recommending Castaneda's writing to others at UCLA, Wilbert was the thesis committee chairman of Myerhoff, Furst, and Delgado. Much of Carpenter's recommendation of *The Teachings* is reprinted as the "In Praise of this Book" blurb at the beginning of the Ballantine books edition. Pedro Carrasco explained his reservations about the non-Yaqui content of Castaneda's manuscript, and confided that Professor Hitchcock alerted him to exercise caution if Castaneda asked him to be a member of his thesis committee. Of these four who recommended publication of Castaneda's first book, only Edgerton has flatly refused to supply me with a copy of his letter, and only Edgerton was a member of Castaneda's doctoral committee.

10.   Yet Castaneda compounded the eclectic nature of don Juan's teachings by adding the story that don Juan's mother was a Yuman Indian (Castaneda and Roszak 1968; deMille 1990: 323-324). Even if this assertion were true, how it is relevant to don Juan's teachings escapes me. By 1973, when he wrote the introduction to his doctoral dissertation, Castaneda was begging the question of don Juan's cultural origins altogether. In the introduction to his doc-

toral dissertation (1973), sorcery was depicted as a pan-Indian phenomenon. This strategy, of decontextualizing or "universalizing" sorcery by deliberately obscuring its cultural matrix suggests that some data may have been doctored.

11.    Information about ancestors central to peyote hunting, i.e., *Maxa Tehuiyari*, the deer/child/peyote "deity," and the *Camóquite* or immortal wolves, is in Benítez 1968b: 164-174, 1975: 168; Zingg 1938, n.d.; Fikes 1985. That the dog Castaneda played with was black may indicate his familiarity with Huichol mythology (see note 12). That don Juan carried dried peyote and ate it prior to harvesting fresh peyote in the desert (Castaneda 1969: 91-92) is ridiculously un-Huichol. Although leaving the peyote root in the ground is Huichol, don Juan's sprinkling the wound with sulfur powder (1969: 99) is absolutely ludicrous. Perhaps the sulphur is a sarcastic reference to the Spanish priest, Ortega, who condemned peyote as the "diabolic root" (Furst 1972a: 142), or to Petrullo's book by that name (deMille 1990: 423).

In a similar vein, Castaneda's reports of extraordinary experiences under the influence of jimsonweed and mushrooms have been discredited and pronounced psychopharmacologically invalid by Siegel (1981). But Pollack (1975) and deMille (1978: 181-182) found a South American example of mushroom smoking.

12.    Dedrick has no knowledge of any myths about Yaqui women changing into dogs. Although he says that some Yaqui houses do have trays hanging from the roof, I believe Castaneda combined two elements of Huichol culture to concoct this event. First, in Huichol oral history and ritual *Tatei Yocáhuima* (Fikes 1985: 358) is the female ancestor who could assume the form of a black dog. This "Mother" of the post-deluge Huichols was permanently changed into

human form after *Huatácame*, the founding father, or Noah, of the post deluge Huichols, threw her dog-skin into the fire (Lumholtz 1902: 192-93; Zingg 1938: 539-540; Gutiérrez-López 1968: 18-19; Benítez 1968b: 117-120, 1975: 139-141). Second, inside Huichol houses cheese is often kept on trays hanging from the roof.

Castaneda could have learned the myth about the black dog/human female from Ramón Medina, as did Furst (1968b: 24) and (Myerhoff 1974: 89), or by reading reports of Huichol ethnographers such as Lumholtz, Zingg, Benítez, or Gutiérrez-López. Because small details, such as the fact that cheese is kept on trays hanging from the roof, are usually omitted in Yaqui and Huichol ethnographies, it seems likely that Castaneda observed first-hand where cheese is kept in Huichol houses. Shaking hands by barely touching them (Castaneda 1969: 27) is something else he could have learned by participant-observation among Huichols. Such small grains of truth, and general concepts which are widely distributed among Native Americans (e.g., nahualism), were skillfully, though not always deliberately, combined with meaningless or incorrect data by Castaneda.

13.    Some readers will be tempted to regard Castaneda's "separate reality," one which "transcends" the ordinary reality of consensus, as a parody of the Huichol separation of esoteric-experiential knowledge (grasped only by insiders) and "defensive lies" or ingenious evasions (reserved for uninitiated outsiders). He could have learned of this strategy either first-hand from Huichols, or, from reading Klineberg (1934: 449). When asked what visions they had under the influence of peyote, all Klineberg's San Sebastián informants replied that they saw the Catholic saints. One hesitates in using such harsh words as fraud and conspiracy to describe such intercultural encounters.

Another well known example is Napoleon Chagnon's (1977: 10-11) experience of trying to ascertain the truth about Yanomamo Indian kinship. Such collective hoaxes may be a common obstacle faced by ethnographic fieldworkers. But such intercultural miscommunication differs significantly from concocting caricatures about other cultures. This distinction is explored in detail in Chapter 4.

14. Prem Das clearly emulates Castaneda, claiming to have been an "apprentice" initiated by don José Matsuwa, and writing in much the same style as Castaneda, as Bernard Fontana (1979) recognized in his review of *The Art of the Huichol*. Prem Das says he was introduced to don José Rios (Matsuwa) in Tepíc, at the house of Guadalupe Rios, his adopted daughter (Prem Das 1978: 129). When I called Myerhoff in 1977 to acquire Huichol language tapes, she told me, in no uncertain terms, that her research with the Huichols had ended, and advised me to contact Prem Das.

15. See Fikes (1985: 42-51). Anticipating the charge that I am unfair to Myerhoff (who is deceased), it must be noted that in 1981 she and Furst received, via Richard deMille, several letters from me, signed by Harold, a pseudonym deMille had given me. These letters expressed, among other things, my doubts about Ramón Medina's qualifications as a *mara'acame* and key informant and specifically questioned the basis for Myerhoff's defense of Castaneda's model of Mexican Indian shamanism as valid (see deMille 1990: 353-354). She never responded to any of my letters, nor even to Phil Weigand's (1979b) charge that she and Furst had "fabricated a *mara'acame*." Three questions must be answered by those who are tempted to discredit this research by asserting that Weigand or I am envious. First, who is in a better position to recognize anomalies of Furst and Myerhoff than other Huichol scholars (such as Lilly,

Negrín, Fikes, and Weigand)? Second, if we don't set the record straight who else will? Third, even if Weigand or I were envious, would that automatically invalidate, or inevitably refute, all the specific criticisms being made here? An *ad hominem* attack is always a poor substitute for a rational rebuttal.

16.  Delgado's claim, that the first Huichol shaman is named *"Makiritare,"* is singular and unverified. All available evidence, from my informants, and all others who have published on the Huichol, indicates that the aid of *Caoyomari*, the Creator and tutelary spirit among Huichols, is not now, nor was it originally, gained by seduction, much less by killing four sisters. Seduction and spiritual achievement are diametrically opposed, especially for Huichols aspiring to be healers and singers (Fikes 1985: 40, 54). Among aspiring healers or singers, being seduced is considered a cardinal sin. The deviant who commits such a sin may be recruited to sorcery (see note 18). If this murder motif is not simply Delgado's invention, it could only typify a sorcerer's perspective. It is possible that Delgado's bizarre perspective influenced Myerhoff's defamation of *Caoyomari*, as "one who makes others crazy" (Myerhoff 1974: 85). The linguist, Joseph Grimes (1981: 24), defines *Caoyomari* as the god who acts as a messenger between the deities and the Huichol singer. This positive image of *Caoyomari* is also evident in Benítez (1968a, 1968b), Negrín (1975, 1977, 1985), Mata Torres (1974: 12, 17, 58), Preuss (1909: 206, 212) and Fikes (1985).

17.  This dichotomy between right (good) and left (evil or sinister) was either lent to, or borrowed from, Castaneda or Furst (1965: 45, 60-64, 71). Huichols do typically face east when reckoning the directions in ritual (Fikes 1985: 105-06).

18.  Myerhoff mentioned that five years of sexual fidelity

were required of aspiring Huichol shamans, and that those who fail to abide by their vows "are in danger of becoming sorcerers" (1968: 98, 1974: 100). As Phil and Celia Weigand note, "acts of sorcery are dramatically punished," and accusations of sorcery are pursued with such vigor that feuds often result (Weigand and Weigand 1991: 58, 59). Aspiring shamans whose sexual misconduct breaches their vow to the ancestor associated with *quieri* are likely to practice sorcery. "Soon they will cause so much harm that someone will eventually kill them for revenge" (Valadez 1986: 38). Valadez goes on to describe the Huichol (good) shaman's constant struggle to reverse the damage done by sorcerers.

My research suggests that among Huichols the struggle between good and evil is intense. Eliade (1964: 509) concluded that the shaman's struggle against demonnic forces and disease was nearly ubiquitous. Furst cites Eliade, and suggests that Ramón Medina typified this commitment to "the shaman's supernatural war against demonic forces" (Furst 1965: 70-71, 75). However, Furst's interpretation of warrior figurines from archaeologically known (and now extinct) cultures adjacent to the Huichol region as shamans engaged in supernatural conflict (Furst 1965) has met with little acceptance among archaeologists. Taylor (1970) is among those who have questioned Furst's use of Huichol data to interpret art from West Mexican shaft-tombs. But Castaneda's books are full of confrontations between rivals (deMille 1990: 429, 434-35) and having a "worthy opponent" (Castaneda 1972: 214-230) is evidently essential to becoming a "man of knowledge."

19.    Although there are indeed far fewer women healers, and virtually no female singers, there is no mythological taboo or justification for this. In fact, it is because Great-grandmother-Germination was a great healer and singer,

that women can aspire to master such skills (Fikes 1985: 86, 347-48).  It seems hard to believe that Delgado didn't observe what Benítez reported, that the mother and sister of Ramón Medina Silva were regarded as shamans among the refugee Huichol (Benítez 1968a: 355-57).

20.  Perhaps Harner's Jivaro model of apprenticeship has unduly influenced recent trends in Huichol and "Yaqui" ethnography.  Apprenticeship is an appropriate way to describe how Jivaros acquire "power to bewitch or cure exclusively through purchase" from an established practitioner (Harner 1972: 118).  Castaneda has known Harner since at least 1962 (deMille 1978: 99) and Harner steadfastly insists that Carlos Castaneda is a bona fide shaman (deMille 1990: 22, 249; Harner in Nicholson 1987: 4). However, there is no hard evidence to prove that Harner is in any way responsible for the liberties other academics may have taken with his work.

To her credit, Myerhoff eventually recognized that there is "no apprenticeship as such" among the Huichol (1974: 99).  Like Castaneda, Delgado, and Furst, New Age entrepreneurs such as Prem Das and Brant Secunda used the term "apprentice" well outside its authentic context, Jivaro culture.  In doing so, they compounded the misrepresentation of Huichol culture.  We must recall that Delgado, Prem Das, and Secunda became self-selected guides to altered states of consciousness at a time when such personalities were scarce and highly sought. I suspect they have, presumably unwittingly, glamorized their own work by glorifying their Huichol teacher, and by distinguishing themselves from anthropologists burdened by an "outmoded" relationship with Huichol informants. They have transformed themselves, so they say, into the apprentices of shamans and sorcerers. They proclaim that they are extraordinary individuals who have mastered the secrets of shamans. This claim facilitates marketing their shamanic skills to American consumers.

Americans lack the group learning process, or shared function orientation (Fikes 1978) characteristic of Yaqui and Huichol ritual cycles. New Age seminars occur within a stratified social system resembling those of India and Europe much more than those in most of aboriginal America. In his October 15, 1963 letter to Dr. Osmond, Huxley wrote about the emotional contexts in which the learning of new ways of the mind should be placed. "The Indians tried to solve the problem by means of the guru system. But this lends itself to all kinds of psychological and social abuses (you should hear Krishnamurti on the subject of gurus!), and something less dangerous will have to be worked out" (Bedford 1974: 732). Some of these abuses have been suggested by Faber (1977: 378).

21.    In addition to being contradicted repeatedly by the data of Huichol experts (see notes 16-20 above), Delgado's credibility is further strained by his attempt to conceal his connection with Furst. At about the same time they first met Ramón Medina at Zapopan, Delgado and Furst excavated, evidently without a valid excavation permit, a shaft-tomb at Las Cebollas, Nayarit in August, 1965. Delgado's M.A. thesis included an inventory of artifacts he and Furst took from the Las Cebollas' shaft-tomb (Delgado 1969: 87), and two diagrams of this shaft-tomb (1969: 123-124). Several of Delgado's drawings appeared in Furst's 1966 doctoral dissertation. But, in his  public lectures he asserted that Rene Millón had introducted him to the Huichols (Morotti 1970). Professor Millón denies having any knowledge of Delgado or his Huichol study (Millón's letter of January 28, 1988).

In his interview with Luis Hernandez (1972: 5), Delgado stated that his M.A. from UCLA was awarded in

Anthropology. His master's thesis and an official UCLA document prove that his M.A. degree was granted in Latin American Studies on June 14, 1969. In 1966 Delgado entered UCLA as a graduate student in Anthropology, but transferred to Latin American Studies shortly before completing his master's thesis. Such discrepancies make it rather hard to accept at face value any of the thrilling tales Delgado told about don Juan, Castaneda, and his own shamanic powers.

22. Perhaps Furst has in mind Harner's essay, "Jivaro Souls," first published on pages 258-272 in the April, 1962 issue of *American Anthropologist*. In this 1962 publication (available long before Furst, Castaneda, and Myerhoff began interpreting spectacular events at waterfalls), Harner describes how the *arutam* soul can be acquired by vision-seekers at sacred waterfalls (1962: 260-61) and through the kind of extraordinary witchcraft, theft, and murder (1962: 262-63) one associates with characters in Castaneda's books. Harner, who qualifies as Castaneda's third most cited source, with 16 entries (deMille 1990: 413-415), again describes how Jivaro boys make pilgrimages to sacred waterfalls to acquire an *arutam* soul residing there (Harner 1972: 91, 105, 134, 136).

23. See deMille (1990: 343). But, Myerhoff never characterized Ramón's waterfall stunts as tricks. What are we to make of the fact that her characterization of Ramón as a trickster was not made public until after deMille's debunking of Castaneda? At any rate, Myerhoff's is clearly not a conventional anthropological usage of the word trickster. I used the word here to convey the meaning Myerhoff must have intended in asserting that Castaneda's teachings are impressive but half humorous (deMille 1990: 339).

Similarly, Ray Clare (1988) argues that Castaneda's books are really trying to enlighten readers about sacred clowns, specifically the Yaqui Pascola clowns. But, among Native Americans, coyote stories are recited and sacred clowns perform their antics in front of audiences who know full well that rules of conduct are being breached and truth mocked. Sacred clowns who ridicule norms (often those of Anglo or Hispanic culture) in such a community of shared values are indeed seen as humorous. Similarly, Dr. Duerr has implied that Castaneda's tutelary animal, the Coyote, is "usually lying or at most tells only half the truth" (Duerr 1985:113). But Castaneda has never confessed that his adventures with don Juan are only another coyote story. If he had, we would all be laughing, and Castaneda's books would be classified as fiction.

Professional anthropologists and youthful Americans who read Castaneda's books did not know enough about Yaqui or Huichol culture to appreciate what Myerhoff and Clare would like us to believe was merely Castaneda's clowning. Readers of Castaneda are fooled. They do not see Castaneda or his characters as foolish. Nor did Castaneda intend for them to see don Juan as foolish. The serious and sincere tone Castaneda conveyed in his 1968 interview with Roszak makes it absurd to assume that Castaneda was constructing a parody of some esoteric American Indian tradition he had allegedly learned. Of course the books do contain humor, and may best be interpreted in light of Castaneda's life. For example, the fact that don Juan shares his name with the Spanish seducer in the Trickster of Seville may not be coincidental (deMille 1978: 190, 194). As deMille hints (1990: 370-72), Castaneda may have combined sex and sorcery. Sexual imagery is also indicated by the two "tutelary animals" of Castaneda. If memory serves me, certain body parts of crows and coyotes are used in love potions or charms by rural Mexicans.

24. The fact that this waterfall is located well outside Chapalagana Huichol territory, in a public park near Guadalajara (which Weigand has identified as Parque Dr. Atl), immediately implies Ramón Medina's pose does not represent any authentic Huichol practice. Guadalupe Rios' statement, that the photo of Ramón encapsulated an activity which had no religious significance for the Huichol, suggests that Ramón's behavior was significantly misinterpreted. It is possible that Guadalupe was ignorant about some esoteric knowledge Ramón could have acquired. But such conjecture would be more credible if Myerhoff had deposited fieldnotes describing the details of this milestone in Huichol ethnography and if Furst had not refused to allow me to examine his fieldnotes.

25. Lacking any proof that don Juan exists makes it pointless to speculate about his qualifications. Neither Roszak (in his 1968 interview of Castaneda) nor Wasson (see deMille 1990: 328), nor even the IRS (de Mille 1990: 521), much less any of the millions of his book buyers yet know what don Juan does for a living. With regard to Ramón Medina, I noted that a traditional Chapalagana Huichol singer, one who is qualified to recite myths and songs in public rituals, must have made at least ten peyote hunts while serving the community as a temple officer at a particular ceremonial center during two different five-year terms. Huichol healers must have served at least five years as a temple officer (Fikes 1985: 72-77). Ramón Medina was not serving as a Huichol temple officer when Furst and Delgado met him at Zapopan. According to Furst, at that time Ramón had only made two peyote hunts (letter of July 25, 1981). Ramón Medina evidently knew about the orthodox Huichol singer's ten year learning process (Myerhoff 1974: 101), and although it was garbled, or perhaps misunderstood by Myerhoff, about the importance of the

aboriginal Huichol temple ritual cycle absent among the refugee Huichol (Myerhoff 1974: 179).

Negrín has some data which suggest that a superdevout Huichol may become a shaman or *mara'acame* without serving as a temple officer at a particular ceremonial center (personal communication April 1, 1991). This is presumably a comparatively rare and rather recent development. Both Weigand (personal communication April 9, 1991) and I know that pilgrimages to the *quieri* plant may be made outside the temple ritual cycle, but believe that such knowledge must supplement that gained by serving as a temple officer. The widespread Huichol fear that *quieri* may be used in sorcery may make active participation in the temple cargo system especially crucial for those involved with *quieri*.

Ramón Medina was not simply unqualified for healer or singer status. The sexual infractions Myerhoff reports he committed during his quest to become a *"mara'akame"* (Myerhoff 1968: 153, 1974: 134) would have disqualified him from becoming a healer, much less a singer (Fikes 1985: 54). As Weigand deduces (1985: 151), it is primarily because Ramón Medina was not a traditional *mara'acame* that his data "are laden with misrepresentations, fabrications, and half-truths that traditional Huichols deride and are upset about. . . . He [Medina] was cynically exploited, even after his tragic murder, and turned into something he was not."

Like Weigand, I am convinced that Ramón Medina is not exclusively responsible for all ethnographic errors and anomalies appearing in the literature of Furst and Myerhoff. It appears that Furst and Myerhoff (1966, 1972; and Furst 1978: 24-26), overlooked some of what Ramón Medina knew about the Huichol sacred plant, *quieri*, in order to validate their overly simplistic model of good (peyote) versus evil (*quieri*). Negrín (personal communication April 1, 1991) believes that Zingg's equally simplistic description of *quieri*, and his misidentification of it as jimson weed (1938: 211-217), provided the prototype for Furst and Myerhoff's model. Several Huichol informants told Benítez (1968a: 280-284, 1968b: 101) that *quieri* could aid one in deer hunting and violin playing. Ramón Medina told Benítez (1968a: 285-86) that the ancestor associated with *quieri* provides aid in violin playing. Ramón Medina may also have known what his widow, Guadalupe, told me (March 22-23, 1991, interview), that *quieri* is useful in deer hunting and diagnosis of disease. She proclaimed that Ramón had made pilgrimages to a particularly well-known *quieri* to obtain aid in violin-playing.

It is not possible to determine who is responsible for the defamation of the Huichol culture hero, *Caoyomari*. Myerhoff does not provide a source for her translation of *Caoyomari* as "one who does not know himself" or "one who makes others crazy" (1974: 85). Guadalupe knows nothing, and asserted that Ramón Medina had never mentioned anything to her about the "bird of a thousand colors" (March 22-23, 1991, interview) which Myerhoff saw after having ingested peyote (Myerhoff 1974: 42-44). Furst's report, citing his student, Tim Knab, that Huichols use peyote enemas is preposterous (Furst and Coe 1977: 91). Weigand suspects that the peyote enema story is fabricated (letter of January 20, 1991). Knab's report (1977: 85) that the Huichol ingest *quieri* through the anus is unverified and outrageous. Could Knab's outlook have been unduly influenced by non-Indians who take enemas to ingest LSD? 26. See La Barre in Noel (1976: 39-42) for more of this "stinging criticism." Prior to October, 1976 at least 18 anthropologists had publicly accepted the don Juan books as fact (deMille 1990: 120). Castaneda's intellectual ability, or commercial success, was impressive enough that his UCLA doctoral committee awarded him a Ph.D. in anthropology for a thinly disguised version of *Journey to Ixtlan*, his third book. DeMille (1990: 86-87, 130-132), Beals (1978) and I are troubled by the fact that Castaneda could obtain a doctorate for what was essentially his third book. We also question why his books are still advertised as nonfiction. According to Jason Green, "an overwhelming majority of Americanists thought Castaneda's first book was authentic ethnography" (telephone conversation of January 19, 1988). Professor Green (a pseudonym) talked at length about Castaneda's career at UCLA but subsequently refused to be quoted.

The inability of academics to recognize things Indian (Churchill 1988: 23) is only part of the reason why Castaneda's books became popular. The veneer of validity about Mexican Indian shamans that fooled Green, deMille (1978b), and others is a result of publishing misinformation about Huichol, Yaqui, and Mazatec religions.

27.    Furst's fascination with psychotropic plants is evident in several other publications (see Furst 1972a: 283). He published a paper, "Morning glory and mother goddess at Tepantitla, Teotihuacan" in 1972, an essay, "Drugs, chants and magic mushrooms" in 1975, a book, *Hallucinogens and Culture* in 1976, an article, co-authored with Michael Coe, "Ritual Enemas" in 1977, and a book *Mushrooms: Psychedelic Fungi* in 1986. In his 1990 essay, published in *The Sacred Mushroom Seeker*, Furst attacked the "powers that be" with the rhetoric of a psychedelic partisan, lamenting the fact that although alcohol and tobacco are legal, they are much more harmful than psychedelics (Furst 1990: 73).

28.    Although Ramón Medina told Myerhoff that the ancestors at *Hunaxu* (the place where the Sun-Father was

born) should be greeted, they bypassed this sacred mountain in 1966 without leaving offerings (Myerhoff 1968: 168, 195, 1974: 82, 152). Judging from Furst's film, John and Colette Lilly estimate that the peyote hunters were about 20 kilometers away from *Paritecüa* (i.e., *Hunaxu*) when the hunt, or film version of it, was concluded. Ramón Medina and his companions were also unable to collect the yellow root used for face painting (Myerhoff 1968: 200, 1974: 147). There are simply too many other peyote ritual details missing for scholars to ascribe much ethnographic value to this film. Missing details include: departure from and return to a ceremonial center or *toquipa*, (Dreben 1986; Fabila 1959:100-101), and wearing turkey feathers and squirrel tails in their hats (Lumholtz 1900: 188; Preuss 1909: 211-212), gathering and using the root used for yellow face paint, leaving a cross with money attached, depositing deer antlers and other offerings at various shrines, (Benítez 1968b, 1975; Dreben 1986). The fact that Ramón Medina clearly knew about peyote hunt obligations that Furst and Myerhoff either prevented him from fulfilling, or didn't care about enough, suggests their peyote hunts were abbreviated. The questions of why so much was omitted, and with what impact on Huichols, remain unanswered. Scholars such as Joseph Campbell (1989) celebrate peyote hunt anomalies, such as running away from alleged danger, as indicative of a great universal truth. I have speculated that fear of punishment from ancestors offended by violation of some taboo, e.g., pilgrims failing to leave offerings at the birthplace of the Sun-Father, may explain why they ran away.

29.   Myerhoff (1974: 60) mentions displaced Huichols who lived scattered among Mexicans in communities outside the sierra, but without including Ramón Medina. Benítez makes it clear that there is no way to exclude

Ramón from membership in that refugee Huichol group (1968a: 353-382, 489). The inconsistencies in Furst and Myerhoff's reports about Ramón Medina's status are bewildering. Furst proclaimed that Ramón had become a full-fledged shaman or *mara'acame* in 1968 (Furst 1968b: 16, 22, 25, 1969, 1972a: 144, 154, 169, 175, 184, 1974: 42, 45, 58-60). In 1977, in the text of his article, Furst (and Anguiano 1977: 135) proclaimed that Ramón had become a full-fledged singing shaman in 1968, but in an inconspicuous endnote Furst (Furst and Anguiano 1977: 175), hinted, without providing the details supplied by Benítez, that Ramón Medina was only a gifted artisan who interpreted traditional Huichol culture while living in an alien environment. That this disclaimer appeared one year after deMille's book, *Castaneda's Journey*, was published is fascinating. This less flattering image of Ramón Medina, and a similar revelation published a year later (Furst 1978: 27) still did not yield a completely candid characterization of Ramón Medina. The details of his tragic murder were never reported. If a more contextualized and accurate representation of Ramón Medina had been disseminated several years earlier, New Age interest in Huichol "shamans" might never have been so intense. If the particulars of Ramón's life had been as fully explained as they were by Benítez (1968a: 353-382), the Furst-Myerhoff portrait of Huichol culture would have been infinitely less sensational.

Myerhoff didn't wait for deMille's debunking to undermine her claim that Ramón Medina had become a true *mara'acame*. In a footnote Myerhoff claimed (1974: 101) that in 1971 Ramón told her there was another "level" of the *mara'acame*'s training, an additional five years of study. This begins to approximate reality. Two terms, each involving five consecutive years of service as a temple officer, are a necessary but not sufficient requirement for becoming a Huichol singer. The question of why, over the years, such textual inconsistencies and belated corrections appear in Furst's and Myerhoff's writing is puzzling. Defenders of Furst and Myerhoff will argue that Ramón Medina must have misled them. Others will ask if disclaimers and belated corrections indicate that Furst and Myerhoff are answering objections of critics. Textual inconsistencies about Ramón Medina's status, and field investigation of Medina's social situation, led Weigand to conclude that Furst and Myerhoff "fabricated a *mara'acame*." Discrepancies in their reports about Ramón Medina resemble contradictions Dedrick recognized in Castaneda's incongruous portrait of don Juan. Dedrick reasoned that such contradictions invalidated the claim that don Juan was a Yaqui. Although Ramón Medina was a refugee Huichol, it would be ludicrous to credit him with being a bona fide Huichol singer.

30.     The high-caliber scholarship evident in Myerhoff's *Number Our Days* is completely free of the problems evident in her Huichol work. There are good reasons for the dramatic contrast between Myerhoff's Huichol ethnography and her sensitive portrait of a community of elderly Jews in Venice, California. Her Huichol ethnography is of marginal value partly because, as Myerhoff admitted, she was "not able to live among the Huichols in the sierra" (1974: 17). Nor did she cross-check texts dictated by Ramón Medina with other Huichol informants (Myerhoff 1974: 18).

     After reviewing her Huichol publications, her interviews with deMille, and talking with Guadalupe, I find it difficult to believe she was forever duped by a crafty Castaneda. Is it possible that she was a hoaxer in league with Castaneda? Or, could Furst have unduly influenced the course of her Huichol research? Furst, her senior, was "director of the Regional Center of the Latin American Center" at UCLA when Myerhoff first came to Guadalajara as a graduate student in 1965 (Myerhoff 1974: 37). Although I want to believe it is unlikely, it is possible that Myerhoff manipulated Furst and others.

Ramón was also the primary, if not the sole informant of Furst. Furst has never, to my knowledge, candidly explained why he was unable, or perhaps unwilling, to do research with well-qualified informants on ritual residing within the traditional Chapalagana Huichol homeland. Until he does, his motives and research "methods" will remain almost as enigmatic as those of Castaneda.

31.    Carlos, Ramón's paternal uncle (Benítez 1968a: 360), was making his ninth pilgrimage in December 1966 (Myerhoff 1974: 120). In the 1968 peyote hunt filmed by Furst, Carlos was evidently replaced in his role as Sun-Father by don José Rios Matsuwa (Myerhoff 1974: 127-28; Furst 1972a: 155, 159). I say "evidently" because elsewhere Myerhoff implies (1974: 128) and Furst asserts (July 25, 1981 letter) that in 1968 don José functioned as *Tatutsi*, Our Great Grandfather. Attempting to justify this confusion, Myerhoff compounds the distortion of traditional Huichol culture by erroneously stating that the names of peyote pilgrims are changeable from year to year (1974: 129, 1968: 222). Genuine Huichol temple officers making peyote pilgrimages assume the names of particular ancestors they represent for five consecutive years (Fikes 1985). Huichols fear that omitting key elements in rituals may anger the ancestors, and bring sickness as a result. It is, therefore, likely that Carlos, Ramón's paternal uncle, decided not to participate in the 1968 peyote hunt because certain key components of the ritual were omitted in the 1966 peyote hunt (see note 28).

32. On August 10, 1990, Celia Garcia-Weigand interviewed Marie Areti Hers. In 1971, when Hers acompanied Marina Anguiano (Furst's coauthor of the 1977 article on the first fruits ritual) and her husband to observe the Huichol festivities at El Colorín, Hers was directing archaeological research in the region subsuming the Coras, Huichols and Tepecanos. She has nearly 20 years of field experience, including ethnography, in this region. She is at the Instituto de Investigaciónes Estéticas at the UNAM. The highlights of her inteview with Celia Garcia-Weigand, which I translated from Spanish, are summarized below.

Marina Anguiano was accompanied by her husband and Dr. Hers. They met Guadalupe Rios in Tepíc, Nayarit in December 1971. Ramón, Lupe's husband, was dead. Guadalupe purchased several items needed for the ritual, including cigarettes, alcohol, candles, and fruit. Marina's costs were paid for by Furst. They all went to the village of El Colorín to observe the first fruits ritual. The old Huichol shaman at El Colorín (identified as don José Rios by Furst and Anguiano) told them it was very late to celebrate the first fruits festival. It was well past harvest time. This was the first Huichol ritual Hers had seen. She was amazed at the fact that all the younger Huichols at El Colorín were so talkative. They spoke in Spanish and anticipated questions their visitors might ask about the meaning of the ritual. They were evidently accustomed to dealing with anthropologists. This was quite unlike what Hers observed later at a first fruits ritual at Las Guayabas, a Huichol ceremonial center near San Andrés Cohamiata. The elders at Las Guayabas were not at all interested in talking with her. Hers stated unequivocally that she felt the El Colorín ritual was largely a farce, that the Indians gave the outsiders what they wanted or expected. Songs sung in the Huichol language by the older singer, don José, were tape-recorded. He and another singer sang for two days and a night. He tried to heal Marina's twisted ankle. He was not used as an informant. Marina took notes, as per Furst's instructions. It was her first ethnographic research. She did it innocently. In this type of fieldwork the Huichols didn't matter. Instead of doing long-term fieldwork with Huichols they arrived at El Colorín with money and finished their business there in three days.

The first fruits ritual, called *Tatei Neixa*, or Dance of our Mother, has been described by Lumholtz (1900: 155-157), Preuss (1909: 207-210, 1907:189), Zingg (1938: 482-500) and Fikes (1985: 170-186). Zingg (n.d.: 139-167), Benítez (1975: 141-151), Myerhoff (1974: 210-214), and Fikes (1985: 288-297) have published the myth explaining how maize was first acquired. The real significance of this ritual was never understood because the ritual Anguiano observed at El Colorín was abbreviated, and perhaps because Ramón Medina was not a well qualified informant. Furst and Anguiano (1977: 98) concluded that the ritual was performed primarily to indoctrinate children with the peyote hunt tradition rather than to foster appreciation for the life-sustaining first fruits of corn and squash. An unadulterated Dance of our Mother, i.e., first fruits ritual, includes intermittent dancing all night around a fire. In the abbreviated version Hers and Anguiano witnessed in December 1971, such dancing lasted only an hour because "everyone was anxious for us to hear the interpretations of a musical group, made up of the Rios Medrano brothers, of Mexican folksongs . . . sung in the mestizo villages (Furst and Anguiano 1977: 147). Replacing Huichol ritual with Mexican folksongs is indicative of the acculturation Benítez documented in this refugee Huichol region.

According to Anguiano and Furst (1977: 135) the singer was don José Rios, Guadalupe's uncle. According to

Hers, don José's singing was tape-recorded. Yet Furst translated and reprinted a harvest ritual text Ramón had dictated for him and Myerhoff in 1966 (Furst and Anguiano 1977: 110, 122,125). They also reprinted a chanted version of this 1966 narrative, one sung by Ramón Medina shortly before he was murdered in 1971 (Furst and Anguiano 1977: 150-170). Ramón Medina's song is so riddled with anomalies and unexplained places and events, that it has little, if any, ethnographic value. Why they didn't use don José's song, which accompanied the ritual Anguiano observed, is an enigma. Anthropologists typically prefer to work with the best qualified informants available and analyze ritual songs corresponding to the actual rituals from which they are derived.

There is another anomaly. Furst attempted to justify the fact that this particular harvest ritual was delayed until December 22. Such a long delay, of two to three months, is highly irregular. It suggests, when added to the two problems discussed above, that this ritual was performed in greatly abbreviated form, primarily to satisfy anthropologists. Furst's assertion, that the absence of peyote delayed the ritual, is not corroborated by harvest rituals I have observed being performed without peyote in early October. The other excuse Furst offers is more plausible, that Huichols can appease ancestors if rituals must be delayed beyond their normal date (Furst and Anguiano 1977: 135-36). Does Anguiano have fieldnotes to confirm Furst's explanation of this anomaly?

33.    I did not try to prove, nor do I now believe, that an all-encompassing conspiracy existed between Furst, Myerhoff, Delgado, and Castaneda. However, I prefer to risk being falsely branded a "conspiracy theorist" than to ignore considerable evidence suggesting that certain anomalies, most notably waterfall jumping, are a concomitant of

collaboration between two or more UCLA graduates. Additional research about the scope and significance of Castaneda's Huichol connection is needed. In the meantime, I hope my debunking of numerous ethnographic anomalies about Huichol religion will make New Age seekers wary about equating improvised shamans with aboriginal Huichol healers and singers.

Many of the New Age myth-makers appear to be proselytizers of a new religion. This religion seems to be drifting away from its anchor in the historical and cultural world. How will the revised standard version of Huichol culture, an edition severed from the aboriginal temple ritual cycle and marketed as another New Age commodity, appear two hundred or two thousand years from now? Despite obvious differences, studying the politics and marketing of Christianity may be instructive.

The possibility that the political-religious movement led by Jesus Christ was hijacked or coopted has recently been discussed by Baigent, Leigh, and Lincoln in *Holy Blood, Holy Grail* and *The Messianic Legacy*. They argue that the version of Christianity disseminated by Paul and his followers gradually detatched itself from Judaic history, law, and political struggle against Roman domination. They claim that the historical details of Roman domination of Jewish politics at the time of Christ were all but eliminated, and that bits and pieces of non-Hebrew mythology were superimposed on a badly tattered portrait of Jesus.

Photo: Juan Negrín

**Huichol singer and children**

# CHAPTER THREE

## *THE MARKETING OF HUICHOL "SHAMANS"*

After Ramón Medina Silva was murdered, don José Rios-Matsuwa became the most renowned of all "shamans," with Eduardo Calderón running close behind (Joralemon 1990). In addition to being the most likely prototype for Castaneda's don Juan, don José Rios-Matsuwa is Guadalupe de la Cruz Rios' uncle (Anguiano and Furst 1977: 135, Furst's letter of July 25, 1981) and foster father (Prem Das 1978: 129). As was true of Ramón Medina, Myerhoff and Furst failed to protect don José's privacy by giving him a pseudonym. Whether intentional or not, their breach of anthropological etiquette was the first step in marketing don José. [34]

Following the trail to glory blazed by Delgado, Furst, Myerhoff, and Castaneda, Prem Das and Brant Secunda have transformed their Huichol master, don José Matsuwa, into a famous New Age personality. In the process, don José's Spanish surname, Rios, was replaced by Matsuwa, a Huichol word meaning pulse, wristguard, or bracelet. With Myerhoff's apparent blessing, Prem Das proclaimed that he was don José's apprentice. During the past 20 years don José's self-proclaimed apprentices, Prem Das and Brant Secunda, widely popularized his teachings and sold him as a shaman. Although there is evidence suggesting that don José may have been a Huichol shaman, there are also anomalous statements that hint that he fooled his handlers, or that investigating his social status didn't matter much to them. Whatever his status is, Castaneda's don Juan was

129

surely partially inspired by him.    Since I have not yet had the opportunity to review complete texts of the songs and myths he allegedly recites, nor the pleasure of meeting him, I can not deliver an informed judgment about his status in the Huichol refugee community, El Colorín, in which he lived until his death in 1990.

In the meantime, I can be quite judgmental about the latest Huichol star to climb aboard the shaman's bandwagon.    Ramón Medina's widow, Guadalupe de la Cruz Rios, was featured in a September 22, 1989, feature story in the *Santa Fe New Mexican* (Baker 1989).    The story complementing the huge color photograph of Guadalupe implied that she is not simply a shaman, but a singing shaman (curiously the Spanish word "cantadora" is used rather than the standard Huichol phrases which designate "singer").    Until I can hear and translate Guadalupe's songs I shall steadfastly play the part of a skeptic about her promoters' claim that she is a Huichol singer (see note 36).

My misgivings about marketing Huichol shamans may do little to deter those eager to accept the "shaman" trademark attached to Guadalupe, and formerly to her uncle (and foster father) don José Rios Matsuwa.    As the Judeo-Christian heritage is abandoned by certain segments of our society, New Age capitalists compete to meet unmet psychological or religious needs by marketing Huichol shamans (as well as a variety of other Native American celebrities, trance-channelers, Asian gurus, etc.).    Given what is evidently an enormous market gap in metaphysical meaning, many of their customers may be satisfied.    However, whether or not non-Indians think they derive benefits from attending ceremonies and seminars with such luminaries as Michael Harner, don José Matsuwa, Lynn Andrews, or various Asian gurus is not at issue here.

With respect to the marketing of Huichol shamans

three issues deserve discussion. First, orthodox Huichol teachings and teachers have not been marketed. Nor has their edition of Huichol culture been widely dispersed. They are simply too busy healing their relatives, growing corn, and performing rituals to be marketed. The public's knowledge about Huichol culture will increase gradually as Weigand, Negrín, Lilly, Liffman, Hers, Shadow, Bauml (among others) and I publish more of our data. This should, in turn, promote truth-in-advertising. Once consumers know the details about traditional Chapalagana Huichol culture, they are free to make informed decisions. Setting the ethnographic record straight (as I have attempted here) is a prerequisite to informed consent. If consumers still want a placebo after it is advertised for just that, then the choice is theirs.

Second, while consumers remain enamored with "shamans," real life problems impinging on Chapalagana Huichols are worsening. The profound economic and political problems facing Chapalagana Huichols have hardly been mentioned in the popular publications and films about the Huichol. Such neglect of the less glamorous aspect of their lives is obviously more a matter of taking responsibility for those one studies than of championing consumer rights. Such benign neglect, or default in discussing political and economic problems, is an anthropological blind spot that Professor Vine Deloria has eloquently criticized (1969: 83-104).

Besides neglecting to discuss the political, social, and economic problems endemic among Huichol refugees, Delgado, Furst, and Myerhoff have left a legacy of confusion and misinformation about traditional Huichol ritual and shamans. Fernando Benítez, the Mexican journalist, was correct in stating that the most traditional of Huichol shamans in San Andrés Cohamiata were vitally involved in defending their communal lands against Mexicans attempting to seize them (Benítez 1968a: 276-277). Huichol temple rituals and symbolism attune them to their environment (Fikes 1985), not to some fantasy land. It is precisely because the Huichol singers who taught me and Negrín recognized the value of their customs that they were annoyed by Mexican encroachments into their forests and pastures, upset by restrictions on their deer and peyote hunting, and threatened by attempts to steal their lands.

At certain times Myerhoff left the impression that Ramón Medina was a defender of his people (1974: 73, 100). Elsewhere she and Furst implied that Huichol symbolism "eliminates the need for dealing with the question of why . . . Spaniards steal Huichol land" (Myerhoff 1974: 261; Furst and Anguiano 1977: 172). (For a critique see Fikes 1985: 48-49.) As noted above, this contradiction exemplifies, or approximates, what deMille defined as "textual inconsistency." If Myerhoff's portrait of Ramón Medina as a defender of his people were true, it seems inconceivable that the symbolism he informed her and Furst about had eliminated the need for defending Huichol land. [35]

Third, an estimate of damage or harassment to traditional Huichols has never been attempted. A confession about my own limitations is appropriate here. I have not tried to prove how Castaneda's writing may have inspired some possible benefits to non-Huichols. Harvey Cox, a theologian who took peyote with Mexicans in a group therapy session (1977: 32-51) implies it was a therapeutic event. He also admits that Huichols did not want uninvited outsiders to participate in their peyote rituals. My research did not systematically survey benefits some American youth inspired by reading Castaneda's books might avow. It is my impression that the warning of Mel Faber, a former

Castaneda colleague (deMille 1990: 298-305, 386-87), now a professor of English specializing in psychological studies, is warranted:

> Don Juan's erratic, injurious acting-out lead one to believe that certain features of the program are inimical . . . to the individual's welfare, and I am thinking particularly about the massive, persistent use of powerful hallucinogenic drugs, the struggle to control one's dreams, the radical, permanent withdrawal from other human beings, the reliance upon shock and terror and betrayal to "shake up" the organism, and the attempt to cut oneself off entirely from the past (Faber 1977: 378).

The exact number of fatalities and "bad trips" prompted by reading Carlos Castaneda's romantic story about flying under the influence of jimsonweed (*Datura*) is undocumented. This represents what may be the most clearly damaging effect of Castaneda's books (see above,"Flying High with Don Juan as Co-pilot"). If I were more of a crusader, I would have explored such problems, and perhaps interviewed Castaneda's ex-wife, Margaret, about why she said that don Juan broke up her marriage with Castaneda (M. Castaneda 1975: 77).

Since 1976, I have received several reports describing incidents in which traditional Huichols have been harassed, jailed, shot at, and almost murdered by guru-seekers and Mexicans acting on the misinformation and propaganda now in circulation. Reciting details of such anecdotal evidence in the absence of systematic research is inappropriate here. I will mention only the report which had the greatest impact on me. In 1977 the Huichol healer-singer with whom I lived told me that while he and his family were making a pilgrimage to collect peyote a foreigner ("gringo") asked to accompany them. While the Huichol family was lodging at a friend's house in Zacatecas, the foreigner pulled out a knife and tried to stab my Huichol father (Bonales). The attack came shortly after the stranger had inhaled some powder through his nostrils. The Zacatecas police had to be summoned to restrain the attacker. Weigand, Negrín, and Valadez (1986: 4-6) are also concerned about the threat such outsiders pose to traditional Huichols. According to Valadez (1986: 5) a Huichol "tribal leader feels the Mexican government is cracking down on Huichols who go the the desert to gather peyote. He cites as the reason for this the involvement some Huichols have with outside tour groups." In 1989 peyote pilgrims from the community of San Andrés were jailed and robbed by Mexican police and soldiers because they were transporting peyote (Ruz Buenfil 1990: 69). Sounding the alarm about the negative impact sensationalizing celebrity shamans is having on the Huichol may help minimize further damage.

Professor Kelley reported that as of 1980, Castaneda fans no longer looked for don Juan among the Yaquis, as they once did (see deMille 1990: 33). She and John Dedrick are sure that Castaneda's books have done no real damage to Yaquis. I have no evidence to dispute their judgment that harm to Yaqui Indians has been minimal. The Yaquis offer relatively little to guru-seekers in search of don Juan. They are somewhat more acculturated than Chapalagana Huichols.

Castaneda's books have contributed greatly to the mystique surrounding Huichol Indians and their peyote rituals. His pop anthropological legacy has been supplemented by Furst's film, and by lectures and publications of Furst, Myerhoff, Delgado, Prem Das, and Brant Secunda.

As a result, Huichols became a focal point of New Age interest. Searchers for don Juan types have flooded the more accessible areas inhabited by refugee Huichols. It is precisely because don Genaro and don Juan exist only in imagination that searchers for magic have "discovered" flesh and blood Huichol "shamans" such as Ramón Medina, his widow, Guadalupe, and her relative, don José Rios (Matsuwa).

The volume of intruders in Huichol territory has increased not simply because the Yaquis seem less colorful than Huichols, but because many episodes in Castaneda's early writing were stimulated by collaboration with Ramón Medina Silva (and possibly other Huichols), and UCLA colleagues involved with Ramón Medina; i.e., Furst, Myerhoff, and Delgado. To many readers, the don Juan books must have been credible because much of their content looked like what was supposedly Huichol. The combination of Castaneda and Huichol evident in the essays of Prem Das is paradigmatic here (Prem Das 1978, 1979; and note 14).

By 1975, the anomalous version of Huichol culture popularized by Furst, Myerhoff, and Delgado (and indirectly by Castaneda), had fired the imagination of scores of New Age seekers. According to Furst (1975:18):

> There has been a veritable pilgrimage to Huichol-land of alienated middle-class romantics, who, though ignorant of the meaning of "being Huichol," come in search of gurus comparable to Carlos Castaneda's don Juan and of instant religious revelation via the peyote trip.

The degree to which Furst and other academics helped launch "the minor plague of would-be mystics' (1975: 19) on Huichols is unclear. But evidence indicating that there was communication between Carlos Castaneda and three other researchers of Huichol culture, all of whom were endorsed by UCLA's Department of Anthropology, or Latin American Studies, makes it perfectly clear that this plague of guru-seekers unleashed upon Huichols is in no way accidental. Highly sensational lectures, publications, and Furst's film about Huichols, have, in concert with Castaneda's books, set off an avalanche of public interest in topics which were, before 1964, of importance primarily to sedate scholars such as Mircea Eliade.

American youth, suffering from a crisis of meaning which became especially acute as the credibility of the "establishment" diminished in the mid-1960s, abandoned tangible political objectives to pursue "tales of power," of a "supernatural" sort, disseminated by a disorganized group of collaborators interested in profiting from meeting the unmet demand for gurus and mysticism. The Delgado-Furst-Myerhoff version of Huichol culture was inherited, and is being passed on with little if any modification, by Prem Das, Brant Secunda, and others. Their version of Huichol culture and "shamanism" is *the* version known to today's New Age consumers.

Like Gordon Wasson, I am outraged by marketers who bastardize ancient rituals and cheapen the tremendous personal sacrifices, unbending dedication, and humility required of bona fide Huichol and Native American healers and ritual specialists (those defined as "shamans"). My admiration for authentic aboriginal American ritual practitioners is what animates my criticism of those who prostitute and trivialize their teachings.

The curandero (healer) who today, for a big fee, will perform the mushroom rite for any stranger is a prostitute and a faker, and his insincere performance has the validity of a rite put on by an unfrocked priest (Wasson 1972: 193).

If New Age entrepreneurs such as Prem Das, Brant Secunda, and Larain Boyll [36] were not still actively selling Huichol shamans and passing on the distorted version of Huichol culture they acquired from the four academic allies graduated from UCLA, the debunking presented here might have only academic interest. In 1990 popular magazines such as *Shaman's Drum* and *High Times* published provocative pieces on the Huichol peyote hunt. Brant Secunda and Lorain Boyll are still holding seminars. Prem Das, formerly Paul Adams, may only be temporarily inactive, after well over a decade of leading New Age seekers on peyote hunts in the Mexican desert.

In 1990 five American citizens, whom Prem Das led on an expedition to eat peyote and smoke the secretion of a psychedelic toad, became the first foreigners to be arrested in the state of Nayarit (Mexico) for possession of peyote. These five were apprehended immediately after they and Prem Das arrived back in Tepíc, the capital of Nayarit, and the city where Prem Das and his Huichol wife reside. Three members of the group, including Leo Mercado, a member of the "Peyote Way Church of God" (see Appendix A), were imprisoned in Nayarit from early May until early July 1990 (Trebay 1990).

This non-Indian group was not satisfied with attempting to follow the straight and narrow path of the Huichol peyote hunters. In addition to eating peyote, they "smoked the dried secretions of a desert toad whose toxin produces an effect 'somewhere between nitrous oxide and Ecstasy'." The secretions on the skin of this toad contain bufotenine, a chemical listed on Schedule 1 (Anderson

1980: 207; Grinspoon and Bakalar 1979: 312). One of the seekers, Carlo McCormick, "thought that was the greatest thing on Earth" (Trebay 1990). At the time they were arrested in Tepíc, the quintet possessed forty kilos of peyote. Leo Mercado had made a bouquet of twelve peyote buttons "to give to the 110-year-old shaman, don José Matsuwa" (Trebay 1990). Leo Mercado and his girlfriend Raven Winston had first met don José Matsuwa in 1988, after returning from their first peyote-eating expedition with Prem Das.

Huichols, even those totally independent of the "shamans" marketed by New Age entrepreneurs, have for twenty years been plagued by more than their share of such New Age seekers. If Huichol elders understood how much the unprecedented influx of shaman seekers was stimulated by publications of academics who had misrepresented their culture, their response would surely approximate the conclusions on page 6 of a 1989 report of the American Indian Science and Engineering Society:

> Research and publishing on American Indian topics is valuable to non-Indian scholars .... Indian culture as an economic commodity has been exploited by the dominant society with considerable damage to Indian people ... Community-based research in Indian communities needs to be conducted in conjunction with the endorsement by tribal authorities for the purpose of ensuring that the finished product has value to Indian people and is educationally beneficial.

Several ways to guard Huichol and Native American communities against sensational research and publishing incursions can be imagined. One safeguard against misrepresentation of their cultures would be to require non-Indian researchers to obtain the informed consent of Indian authorities in the community where they intend to do research. Another deterrant would be to restore and reward the Boasian commitment to collecting accurate ethnographic data, before engaging in theory-building.

One of my primary objectives is educating non-Indians about the difference between bona fide Native American shamans, or medicine people, and Indian celebrities advertised by entrepreneurs and academic opportunists. Native Americans north of the Mexican border are becoming increasingly critical of teachers in academia and those in the New Age movement who profit from marketing Indian spiritual traditions as a commodity (Churchill 1988). In 1986, the Traditional Circle of Elders, an elite group of native healers and ritual practitioners, told the American public that

> people of our respective nations are complaining that their ceremonies, pipes, and sweatlodges are being violated by non-Native individuals and Native American individuals who purport to be "medicine people." This is a violation of our human rights, group rights, and a violation of our religious freedoms. The exploitation of the sacred symbols of our ceremonies causes pain and distress among our people, and denigrates the fundamental instructions of our cultures and teachings. We cannot prevent people from throwing their money away on so-called "Indian ceremonies" but we can challenge those who misuse our sacred pipes, sweatlodges and ceremonies. So now once again we demand that these violations cease.

Native American leaders such as Oren Lyons and Vine Deloria are annoyed by the fact that persons Indians recognize as traditional Indian spiritual leaders are often rejected because the publicity for plastic medicine people has brought them unmerited but immense credibility (Churchill 1988: 23, 1990: 94). Indian activists are outraged by such unauthorized selling of their spirituality. Some condemn it as a form of "cultural genocide" (Churchill 1988: 24, 1990: 94). Accordingly, since 1984, members of the American Indian Movement (AIM) have diligently attempted to end the activities of those regarded as plastic medicine people. The seminars of Sun Bear and others have been physically disrupted and AIM members are "demanding that local book stores stop carrying titles, not only by Sun Bear, and his non-Indian sidekick 'Wabun,' but charlatans like Castaneda, Lynn Andrews and Hyemeyohsts Storm" (Churchill 1990: 98). Scholars who lament such tactics (and rightly so) should provide more accurate information about Native American religions to students and consumers, and vigorously correct misconceptions about Native American religious practitioners and religions as they did when Erich von Däniken's books became best-sellers.

The parody of orthodox Huichol religion is being peddled by a few non-Indian marketers and their paid Indian performers. How many of the thousands of guru seekers turned-on by tales of power circulated by New Age entrepreneurs have disturbed or victimized traditional Huichol healers and singers is unknown. If this book reduces the volume of disenchanted youth searching for don Juan type characters, and prevents damage from being done to conservative Chapalagana Huichols, it will have served one of its primary purposes.

*From Cognitive Dissonance to Clarity*

The most enchanting subjects in my research on the aboriginal Huichol temple ritual cycle emerged naturally as I did old-fashioned Boasian-style ethnographic research. [37] I learned first-hand how the Huichol Indians had masked their most esoteric lore, and the hidden core of their rituals from unbelievers, including certain anthropologists and missionaries (Fikes 1985: 277-80). I was amazed that Huichol esoteric teachings about wolf-nahualism and *quieri* had remained essentially hidden from outsiders, including several Huichol ethnographers. After I uncovered such data, I consulted with Lilly and Negrín about whether to refrain from publishing some of it, especially that which seemed too sensitive, or possibly sensational. Because the tide of New Age fascination with pseudo-shamans is so high, it seems advisable to debunk misconceptions about Huichol culture before presenting accurate information to the public.

My analysis of ethnographic anomalies popularized by Castaneda and other academics was aroused largely by the conflict between their dramatic depiction of shamans and my research among the most conservative of Chapalagana Huichols. The contrasts between the Huichol culture I knew, and the distorted version of it popular today were so enormous, and the clues about Castaneda's involvement with Ramón Medina so tantalizing, that I had to discover why.

Respect for the wisdom, sacrifices, and service to their people provided by several Huichol singers I have known compels me to set the record straight. [38] They helped me learn how to be true to myself by learning from my dreams and visions. They taught me that the presence of mind in nature (Bateson 1972) is far more pervasive and subtle than our scientific paradigm can measure. Their conviction that all sources of subsistence are sacred increased my reverence for life and stimulated what I am convinced is a primordial or universal vision of human destiny: to nurture the child (that they worship as *Maxa Tehuiyari*) and confront ignorance and evil in the here and now. I learned much of value from Huichol singers who were never, and will never, be marketed. I want to share some of what I learned from them with those who will never have the opportunity I did.

Aspects of their pre-Columbian culture, though rapidly vanishing now, still offer much of value to the "civilized world." But to learn more from them, we must now protect them from schemes born of folly and greed. They, like ourselves, are increasingly imperiled. If their wisdom has moved us, one way to honor it, and them, is to engage in action which contributes to the survival of their culture, and in the process bring reform to our own.

Anomalous accounts of Yaqui and Huichol shamans published after 1965 have, for the past twenty years, helped inspire New Age entrepreneurs whose activities have fed consumers starved for metaphysical meaning. Perhaps what Prem Das told me is true, that participants in the peyote hunts he organizes gain something of value. But while peyote remains illegal his customers will have to risk taking a trip to jail. Their escapades may also prompt Mexican officials to restrict bona fide Huichol peyote hunts (see Valadez 1986: 4-6).

Knowing that traditional Huichol culture still remains a reality quite separate from the version New Age consumers have been buying should make a difference to some of them. The theory of cognitive dissonance suggests that having knowledge of the schism between traditional and commercial Huichol activities should trigger anger or incredulity in some consumers. Because I assume that academic endorsements of unverified but spectacular ethnograpic episodes originally misled today's promoters of Huichol shamans, I hope that my debunking efforts will encourage them to insist on increased accountability for academic anthropologists.

During the past 25 years the marketing of Ramón Medina and don José Matsuwa (and now Guadalupe Rios), as Huichol shamans has been effective for two reasons. First, despite Weigand's pioneering efforts (1979b, 1985) there has been inadequate scholarly criticism of the eccentric edition of Huichol culture first popularized by Furst, Delgado, Myerhoff, and, indirectly by Castaneda. Second, there is widespread consumer acceptance of the distortions circulated by academic experts, and subsequently exploited, presumably naively, by Huichol popularizers such as Prem Das, Brant Secunda, and others. Future Huichol scholars, and today's consumers of New Age seminars, may benefit from being exposed to this criticism derived from those who have done bona fide ethnographic research among Chapalagana Huichols. Without accurate knowledge about Huichol ritual specialists, how can consumers give their "informed consent," reject, or contest claims first made popular by UCLA-endorsed "experts" doctored in anthropology, and subsequently broadcast by entrepreneurs marketing a popular but erroneous edition of Huichol culture?

My primary objective in setting the Huichol ethnographic record straight is to increase respect for traditional Huichol culture, and rekindle interest in the type of anthropology illustrated by Franz Boas. I have yet to participate in New Age seminars of any kind. They may be tremendously useful for some participants. I have not looked for evidence to indicate that entrepreneurs are doing anything except naively passing on misinformation previously legitimized by the good University of California, Los Angeles seal of approval. For now, the blame for caricaturing Huichol and Yaqui culture must be born by Castaneda, Delgado, Furst and Myerhoff, all graduates of UCLA's Anthropology and Latin American Studies Departments. [39] This exposé may produce little change among consumers in the Huichol tributary of the New Age movement. For some, emotional needs for self-transcendence (some will say escapism) and larger-than-life personalities may overpower the capacity for critical thinking. They may well be involved in constructing a quasi-religion, one originally inspired by the charismatic Castaneda. The formation of this quasi-religion, one now being promoted by Castaneda partisans such as Michael Harner, Prem Das, and Brant Secunda, is "at least as interesting as Moses, Wovoka, Joseph Smith . . . and the movements they inspired" (Beals 1978: 361). The cultural crisis of the 1960s, which precipitated the demand for gurus and shamans, and the complex relationship between contemporary New Age celebrities and consumers of their seminars on shamanism, are part of a social movement worthy of further investigation.

# Notes

34.  Perhaps Furst recognized don José Matsuwa as a "shaman" ripe for celebrity status. Of course don José may have tricked Furst, especially if Furst was less than fluent in Spanish. After all, Prem Das (1979) portrays don José as a shaman whose sense of humor rivaled that of don Juan. It seems ironic that Furst failed to recognize that don José functioned as if he were a singing shaman. He played the part of lead singer in Furst's film and Furst's letter (July 25, 1981) suggests that in 1970 don José diagnosed Guadalupe's illness and performed a ceremony to heal her of arthritis. Yet if Furst recognized don José was a *mara'acame*, why would he conceal that fact?

Some might speculate that Furst honored Castaneda's request to conceal the identity of his Huichol master (given the alias don Juan). Or, perhaps Furst learned too late to appreciate don José's senior status and thus to acknowledge that Ramón Medina was a poorer informant. But the fact that Furst and Anguiano did not publish, or perhaps bother to translate, don José's harvest ritual song suggests that Furst may have wanted to avoid the embarrassment that disclosure of his utter dependence upon an underqualified informant, Ramón Medina, might bring. Other scenarios can be imagined.

35.  According to Myerhoff, Ramón Medina felt that Huichols who knew how to read and write should defend their people and lands, honor their history, and practice faithfully their own customs (1974: 73). Indeed today's *mara'acame* should be bilingual and literate "to protect his people from 'those land-grabbing Spaniards with their maps and titles'" (1974: 100). Overlooking the image she

evoked about Ramón Medina's political commitment, and erroneously referring to Spaniards rather than Mexicans as the outsiders now stealing Huichol land, Myerhoff concludes that Huichol religion denies "the gratuitous and cruel losses by refusing to relinquish the past" (1974: 262). This is a textual inconsistency and a preposterous assertion (Benítez 1968a: 274-77; Negrín 1977, 1985). Furst endorsed Myerhoff's fanciful notion about Huichol symbolism facilitating escapism (Furst and Anguiano 1977: 171-72). Neither Mexican encroachment nor erosion of aboriginal Huichol subsistence and religion was denied by any of the finest exponents of Huichol symbolism I could find in Santa Catarina. Fernando Benítez came to the same conclusion about shamans he knew in San Andrés (1968a: 276, 1975: 175-76).

36.    Tours to visit Guadalupe de la Cruz Rios in Mexico have been led by Larain and Bob Boyll, the Directors of the "Four Winds Circle", a non-profit organization based in Mill Valley, California. Guadalupe, whom they advertise as a "traditional medicine woman of the Huichol Indians," has also performed "Huichol ceremonies" at various locations around the San Francisco Bay. Four Winds Circle has also organized tours to the Huichol peyote country. Guadalupe's visit to Santa Fe, New Mexico was arranged by Raymond Carr, a Santa Fe gem dealer (Baker 1989).

There is an anomaly in the Spanish language version of Furst and Myerhoff's 1966 essay which suggests that even Guadalupe's relationship with Ramón Medina was confused. Phil and Celia Weigand (letter of January 20, 1991) reported that Guadalupe Rios was identified twice as the sister ("hermana") of Ramón Medina (Furst and Myerhoff 1972: second plate following page 96, and page 193). As Weigand notes, "This is a rather crucial difference for an ethnography" (letter of 20 January, 1991).

37.   By Boasian-style research I mean doing a comprehensive ethnographic survey of a specific culture, including its ethnohistory, social organization, and mode of
ecological adaptation.  Such research involves investigating geographically contiguous cultures.  The hallmark of
Boasian style fieldwork is meticulous recording of ethnographic data.  My Huichol research is based on a whole-
hearted devotion to the Boasian approach in anthropology,
including political activism on behalf of Native Americans.
Boas was, when necessary, a political advocate for Northwest Coast Indians (Rohner in Helm 1966: 200-203).
Leslie White, an outspoken critic of Boas, led a movement
to make theoretical concerns, namely "cultural evolution,"
paramount in anthropology.  By the mid-1960s the Boasian
tradition was fading fast.  Abandoning Boasian style research in the quest for grand theory or "validity" (deMille
1990) surely made it more difficult to detect the ethnographic anomalies dicussed here.

38.   Since 1976 I have lived a total of over fifteen months
with Huichols residing in the temple district of Santa
Catarina. In the course of my field research I have observed
numerous temple rituals, tape-recorded ritual songs of four
bona fide Huichol singers, and made pilgrimages to several
sacred sites.  I have spent at least nine months translating
ritual texts from Huichol to Spanish, and Spanish to English.  My library and film archival research on Huichol
culture has taken well over two years.  This investigative
research and writing has taken over three years.

39.   I agree with Susan Eger-Valadez (1986: 4-6) that
New Age guided tours to Huichol villages, sacred sites, and
even to gather peyote are a threat to Huichol culture.  But,
unless Susan Eger-Valadez (herself a UCLA graduate in
anthropology) has incontrovertible proof that those she ac-
cuses are cynically exploiting what they know to be disin-

formation, her attack seems to illustrate a classic case of "scapegoating" or "blaming the victim." Whether the New Age seminars represent a case of the blind leading the blind, or of opportunistic entrepreneurs profiting by supplying placebos to the proverbial believers born every minute, or of academics misleading the entreprenuers, who in turn unwittingly mislead consumers, are conclusions which should be reached following extensive research with New Age entrepreneurs and their clients.

# CHAPTER FOUR

## EXAMINING FAITH AND POWER
## IN THE IVORY TOWER

### Consensus and the Credibility Gap

Castaneda's association with Huichols and collaboration with Huichol experts yielded an apparent congruence between Huichol and Yaqui (and maybe even Mazatec) "shamanism." Widespread dissemination of unverified and singular accounts of Mexican Indian "shamans" has produced an erroneous anthropological consensus. This process differs drastically from the way in which Huichol Indians camouflage their religious beliefs from non-Huichols using the strategy of defensive lying.

To interpret the difference between defensive lying and sensationalizing other cultures we must distinguish the distrust Huichols display toward outsiders from the trust the American public places in professional scholars. Because Huichols have suffered violent conquest and disruption of their culture by Hispanic intruders, they have learned to conceal esoteric truth from uninitiated outsiders who might use such knowledge against them.

Carl Lumholtz, the first Huichol ethnographer, reported that "They don't tell the truth, except when it suits them" (1900: 7), and that "They are quicker to invent a lie than any Indians I have met" (1902: 24). Lumholtz's observation, that many Huichols "are clever enough to put on an external show of Christianity toward people from whom they expect some favour" (1902: 22) was unwittingly validated by the psychologist Otto Klineberg.

When Dr. Klineberg asked what visions they had under the influence of peyote, *all* Klineberg's San Sebastián informants replied that they saw the Catholic saints (1934: 449). My Huichol informants' reports about their peyote experiences make it obvious that the Huichols who lied to Klineberg were deliberately disguising authentic peyote visions from an outsider they had no reason to trust. He was there less than two months in 1934, during a period of violent regional political turmoil in which Christian militants (called Cristeros) combated government forces. Although the Cristero revolution was officially concluded in 1929, violence in rural areas such as San Sebastián continued for almost a decade (Weigand 1979a).

Reports from the colonial era in Mexico establish the antiquity of this Huichol cultural defense. A Franciscan priest reported that Huichol men justified giving peyote to their sons on the grounds it would make them wise, skillful matadors, and agile tamers of horses (quoted in Furst 1972: 143). In 1722, when Spaniards launched the attack which subjugated the Cora Indians inhabiting the Mesa de Nayarit, a region west of the Huichol, they were accompanied by Huichol Indian allies from the communities of San Andrés Cohamiata and Santa Catarina (Negrín 1985: 14-16, 1977: 12-13). Misleading untrustworthy outsiders continues.

According to Furst and Anguiano (1977: 174) Ramón was initially "given to subtle distortion of Huichol traditions so long as he was not wholly certain of his questioners' intentions toward the native culture". Myerhoff mentions that Ramón told the Franciscan priest, Ernesto Loera, that the flower of the *quieri* was a sacred flower which protected the shaman, but peyote was used by sorcerers. After noting that Ramón's statement is the opposite of the actual situation, Myerhoff asserted (1968:

19-20; see also Furst and Myerhoff 1966: 7) that Ramón justified misleading Father Loera because Loera only wanted to study Huichol religion in order to change it. But Furst and Myerhoff suggested they had overcome Ramón Medina's reluctance to divulge accurate information (Furst 1968b: 25). Furst asserted that "Ramón eventually became not only a valued friend but sufficiently convinced of the value of accurate recording of the traditional culture.... to insist on, more than invite, actual participation in the peyote pilgrimage, without which, he said, it would be impossible to understand anything of Huichol culture" (Furst and Anguiano 1977: 174).

Professional anthropologists regularly assume the reports provided by their colleagues are reliable. They are members of the same culture and practitioners of a profession dedicated (at least originally) to the pursuit of accurate information. While theories are often contested, authenticity of data derived from research is normally taken for granted. Skepticism about the findings of purported research is still the exception (Nova 1988). When unauthentic ethnography is condoned, or covered up by colleagues, debunking is delayed and made more difficult. DeMille discovered that some anthropologists acted as if stonewalling and misleading researchers was justified (deMille 1990: 136-38). Condoning such academic dishonesty ultimately imperils the fund of credibility the profession enjoys with the public it serves.

For what reason would Castaneda deflect attention away from his involvement with Huichols by claiming don Juan was Yaqui? Certain Castaneda partisans will credit him with protecting his informants' right to privacy. If Guadalupe and I are correct in concluding Castaneda learned nothing profound about Huichol esoterica, it defies logic to suppose he was hiding anything from the uninitiated, or shielding Huichols from them. Perhaps only his relationships with Ramón Medina, Peter Furst, Barbara Myerhoff, and Diego Delgado were disguised by implying that don Juan's teaching constituted "a Yaqui way of knowledge". His misuse of data, and his presumably sporadic collaboration with Ramón Medina, Myerhoff, Furst, and Delgado, resulted in caricaturing Yaqui religion. Creating this caricature contrasts conspicuously with Huichol evasions and defensive lies designed to impede untrusted outsiders from gaining access to esoteric truth.

Numerous affinities in their reports, e.g., about apprenticeships and shamanic balance at waterfalls, made detecting the defects in Castaneda's work more challenging. The consensus that Castaneda's books constituted authentic ethnography was also facilitated by alleging that his apprenticeship opened the doors of perception to a separate reality. These factors, and the presumption that academics should trust their colleagues, may clarify why almost all anthropologists initially endorsed Castaneda's work as authentic. Academic endorsement of the first book, and awarding a doctorate for the third book, increased Castaneda's fund of anthropological credibility. This in turn enhanced enormously public acclaim for Castaneda's writing in its formative stage.

Consensus (even among experts) does not necessarily guarantee truth. Despite the popularity of bloodletting as a form of medical treatment it proved to be hazardous to a patient's health. There was also a time when Castaneda was a hero among anthropologists. Waterfall stunts continue to be construed as exemplary of shamanic balance. Until somebody examines critically "data" others have supposed was accurate, the Huichol edition of the allegory about the Emperor's New Clothes will continue enchanting uninformed academics and disciples of New Age entrepreneurs.

My research made me skeptical about the model of Mexican Indian shamanism accepted by deMille. It has vividly reminded me that unverified and extraordinary claims about other cultures may produce scholarly consensus and New Age community. But the separate reality they sustain is both illegitimate and short-lived. Those who create such illusions, whether for themselves or for others, are constantly challenged by those seeking truth.

Castaneda is dealing with the central issues of our times, asserted Lawrence Chickering (1988) in reviewing Castaneda's latest book, *The Power of Silence,* for the *Los Angeles Times.* Investigating the foundation beneath Castaneda's literary edifice has revealed what is surely the central issue to the human condition. The capacity for trust is, as Eric Erickson suggests (see Rappaport 1979: 212), integrally connected with the human species' unusually long period of dependency.

We may briefly consider how trust is developed in our society. Infants are utterly dependent on mother to provide milk and nurturing. Trust in mother may, as Erickson insists, be the foundation upon which one's character is built. Families begin to socialize children who are subsequently dependent on schools, churches, and various social institutions to provide knowledge. Inasmuch as public schools routinely foster obedience to authority among students (Bateson 1972: 162; Fikes 1978; Henry 1965; Illich 1972: 76-79; Philips 1972: 89), they help nurture adults predisposed to trust that authorities of reputable institutions always provide accurate information.

America's public universities are, among other things, essentially repositories of public trust. The power of the academic depends upon the trust readers place in their institutions (Baigent, Leigh, and Lincoln 1986: 169-170).

Academic experts are empowered by the trust readers place in official endorsements indicating that ethnographies about Yaqui, Huichol, or other cultures are non-fiction. Castaneda's inability to document don Juan's existence, and Furst's refusal to answer questions or provide fieldnotes about activities observed at a waterfall near Guadalajara, violate the trust academics writing non-fiction share with other scholars. Lacking first-hand knowledge of Yaqui or Huichol culture makes readers especially dependent upon reports offered by experts. When experts attribute unverified data to their "teachers" or informants, but fail to provide documentation for such data, can their claims be taken seriously? Readers are unable to contest the experts' claims unless they have independent access to the experts' fieldnotes, and, in certain cases, even to members of the cultures the experts studied. Without access to fieldnotes, how can other scholars verify anomalous events reported by their colleagues? If fear of academic disapproval intimidates colleagues and makes them reluctant to probe anomalous ethnography, what will enable non-specialist readers to recognize anomalous ethnography endorsed by experts they have been taught to trust? How shall illiterate "informants" have the opportunity to defend themselves and their cultures?

Castaneda's claims that he was a sorcerer's apprentice and that don Juan's teachings constituted a "Yaqui way of knowledge" are unsupported by photographs, fieldnotes, or tape recordings. Castaneda's assertion, that his master, don Juan Matus, prevented him from obtaining such ordinary ethnographic evidence, may exemplify a special form of subterfuge: "Diabolical lies are not simply false transmissions they are lies that tamper with the very canons of truth" (Rappaport 1979: 242). [40] In 1992 the American Anthropological Association passed a resolution recognizing that "unpublished anthropological materials" are "irreplaceable and essential for future research and education". This resolution, approved by over 97% of those who voted on it, directed anthropologists to preserve unpublished materials in their possession. How anthropologists respond to cases that test ethnographic etiquette, e.g., Furst's refusal to supply fieldnotes about shamanic balance and Myerhoff's failure to preserve them, remains to be seen. Unless academic associations set clear limits and display greater commitment to enforcing professional standards by chastising unacceptable conduct the time-honored presumption that colleagues are always truthful may be seen as less than credible.

When Native American coyote stories and sacred clowns break taboos, that all members of society recognize as taboos, they are right to laugh at them. When Hollywood movies take events or people out of their authentic contexts we are entertained because we are warned that it is fiction. What shall we do when academic experts test the canons of truth?

The spectacular but unverified events popularized by Castaneda, Furst, Myerhoff, and Delgado resemble a political problem originally identified as the credibility gap. The covert operations conducted by our secret government (Moyers 1988) have a virtual counterpart, insufficient accountability of university professors (Sykes 1988). Professors are, as everybody knows, neither elected by the students they supposedly serve, nor, in the case of anthropologists, accountable to the cultures they claim to study. The checks and balances academia has today seem incapable of averting a professor's abuse of confidence or misuse of power.

Americans are increasingly skeptical about the willingness of political candidates to keep campaign promises.

The media's constant exposure of abuses in our political system reassures us, at least sometimes, that the media is playing its role as watchdog. But who should keep anthropologists accountable? To improve their credibility with Native Americans and the public, professional anthropologists must vigorously enforce adherence to exacting ethnographic standards.

## Distinguishing Anomalies from Esoterica

Drawing the line between ethnographic anomalies, or mutations, and data which are patently spurious is difficult. Anomalies are presumably more numerous than phony data. Walter Stewart and Ned Feder, the only federally funded investigators of scientific fraud, have reason to believe that "as much as one-fourth of all scientific data published each year may be fraudulent or otherwise tainted" (Henderson 1990: 58). According to Stewart, "It is awfully easy to get phony data into the scientific literature" (Henderson 1990: 59). An obvious reason for this proliferation of phony data is that publishing original research is indispensable, both to achieve tenure, and to obtain the almighty research grant.

There are numerous well-documented examples attesting to how difficult it is get widely acclaimed but tainted research out of circulation (Sykes 1988: 241-256; Nova 1988). Years may pass before anybody is able, or willing, to expose a scientific fraud. The Piltdown Man forgery circulated as standard science for 41 years (deMille 1978: ix). [41] Most of the problem can be traced to the justifiable fear that most scholars have about jeopardizing their own careers by "blowing the whistle" on a reckless colleague. Therefore, as one might suspect, any estimate of the extent of fraud in science is imprecise. Some scholars believe that debunkers like Stewart and Feder have some irrational reason for exaggerating the extent of the problem. Others, citing the formidable risks and obstacles to "whistle-blowers", as well as the absence of career rewards associated with exposés of spurious science, wonder if Stewart and Feder's estimate understates the extent of the problem in the social sciences.

As deMille concluded, Castaneda's report about don Genaro's daring deeds at the waterfall, and his claim to have mastered estoteric wisdom contained in the "Yaqui way of knowledge" taught by the Yaqui sorcerer, don Juan Matus, are evidently fraudulent. It may be that such spurious data are less likely to be detected when they intersect topics which are little-known, illicit, or taboo. Under these circumstances, evaluating the accuracy of previously published ethnographic research may be complicated. Scientific verification depends on, among other things, the possibility of replicating controlled experiments conducted by previous investigators. In archaeology, once the data are obtained, by excavating the site, replication is impossible. This is one reason why archaeologists insist on meticulous recording of all details of their excavations. Ethnographers have yet to agree upon comprehensive standards for obtaining accurate data, despite the obvious need for such standards.

Even when we conduct our research in what we assume is the same culture, the reports we publish differ somewhat. Unless the culture core has disintegrated, ethnographic reports are never unique. Cultures do change, and different regions of the same culture may have been exposed to different influences, in varying proportions, over time. Fieldwork is, in effect, conducted at different times in a culture's history. Even though truly scientific replication is not possible, there are methods for insuring that ethnographic data are accurate (Pelto and Pelto 1978: 26-7, 34-35, 38, 286-87). When differences of interpretation arise among ethnographers doing research with members of the same culture, they are usually defined as a result of researchers having done fieldwork at different times, or in different places. Sometimes, as in the case of Derek Freeman's criticism of Margaret Mead, conflicting theoretical perspectives or "paradigms" are invoked to explain disagreements (Clifford and Marcus 1986: 102-03). Differences between informants also account for legitimate disagreements. Historical, regional, and individual differences comprise a reality so complex that it would be hard to overstate the need for scrupulous reporting about the qualifications of our key informants, and about the ethnographic context in which we do our fieldwork.

Fraud, or extreme imperviousness to ethnographic truth, should only be suspected after the variables mentioned above have proven inadequate to explain ethnographic anomalies. In addition to the three rules of evidence deMille and I have used as debunking tools, he has asserted that the refusal to submit fieldnotes "for examination violates the norms of scientific conduct and amounts to prima facie evidence of fraud" (deMille 1990: 61). Castaneda has never produced any of the tape recordings, photos, or fieldnotes anthropologists require to certify the existence of an alleged informant. Accordingly, deMille has argued that "the don Juan books are a transparent fraud" (1990: 354). Furst has refused to submit the fieldnotes required to document Ramón's purported demonstration of shamanic balance at a waterfall near Guadalajara. If he has notes, I can imagine no compelling reason for denying access to them. Myerhoff's fieldnotes contained nothing at all about the waterfall incident. Perhaps a hungry packrat devoured her notes.

Castaneda's only defense is his claim that routine ethnographic verification was impossible because his master, don Juan, would not permit it. Some may have confidence in Castaneda because he claimed to be a sorcerer's apprentice, not a mere ethnographer. But Castaneda's inability to produce tangible evidence of his informant's existence is inexcusable for those of us who have documented esoteric teachings. It was an appealing excuse because a legacy of European conquest has obscured so much Native American esoterica.

It is not accidental that the mushroom rituals Gordon Wasson announced in 1957 had remained outside the purview of non-Indians. Next to the ability to transform one's self into a wolf, jaguar, puma, or other animal (Castaneda supposedly became a crow), the willingness to revere and ingest potent mind-altering plants was construed as the most tangible proof of diabolic influence at work among Mexican Indians. When Castaneda proclaimed he had learned the long-lost "secrets" of nahualism and psychedelic plants from his Yaqui teacher, few anthropologists were willing to question it. Many of them must have hoped that the pre-Columbian "secrets" to which Castaneda had gained access had really been preserved, despite the Catholic "veneer" Yaquis had assimilated.

Anthropologists ready to believe that Castaneda had entered the occult realm of sorcery or shamanism were well aware that Spanish priests had felt it was their sacred obligation to combat Satan, and that their religious mission justified punishing and executing natives who used peyote, mushrooms, and other plants in healing, foretelling the future, and other fantastic feats. They knew the story of how the persecution of Aztecs engaged in psychedelic or sacramental plant use had quickly defamed the sacred plants (which were revered as the incarnations of deities) and driven practitioners underground (Schultes 1940, 1941, 1970, 1972; Dobkin de Rios 1984: 142-145). They knew the sacred mushroom eaters of Mexico had been cautious for good reason (Wasson 1980: 199-214). Like those who were seduced by the Piltdown Man hoax, they were predisposed to believe.

The virtual taboo on revealing esoteric information to non-Indians meant that few missionaries or anthropologists had recorded much of the core of aboriginal American religious belief and practice by 1953, when Aldous Huxley first took mescaline; in 1955, when the Wassons rediscovered Mazatec Indians' sacramental mushroom use; or even by 1960, when Carlos Castaneda's alleged apprenticeship with the Yaqui man of knowledge named don Juan began. This enormous scholarly void about shamanism and esoterica was exacerbated by the premium placed on anthropological theory. This trend had, since at least the time of Leslie White, begun to devalue the Boasian school's emphasis on meticulous data collection. By the mid-1960s more and more anthropologists were inattentive to authenticity because of their involvement in the quest for validity, cultural universals, and grand theory. Accurate information about such esoteric and sensational subjects as shamanism and psychedelic plants was scarce at a time when popular demand for such information was escalating rapidly. In 1968, most anthropologists were inclined to regard Castaneda's don Juan as an Indian survivor of Catholic witch hunts. Wasson, Castaneda, Furst, Myerhoff, and others who allegedly brought back pre-Columbian lore were welcomed as heroes.

In 1968, when the psychedelic movement's yearning for metaphysical meaning was peaking, Carlos Castaneda's account of his apprenticeship was bound to become an instant best-seller. Academics eager to popularize the secrets of Mexican Indian shamans were presented with a superb opportunity. The ways in which their sensational publications, films, and lectures would impact Mazatec mushroom eaters and Huichol peyote hunters were of little concern to those intent on exalting their version of shamanism. Few if any people could have predicted in 1968 that academic endorsement of misleading ethnographies about Mexican Indian shamans (Yaqui, Huichol, and Mazatec) would become the source of an important tributary of the New Age movement.

## Exiting the Magical Mystery Tour

I have described Carlos Castaneda's place in the psychedelic or New Age movement. I have interpreted how Castaneda, whether by covert means or by collaboration with one or more of his academic allies, perpetrated one of the most elaborate anthropological hoaxes in this century, thereby stimulating several entrepreneurs to market shamanic techniques to a new generation. I have contrasted authentic Huichol and Native American ritual practitioners with those advertised as "shamans".

The obstacles to completing the research for this book have been frequent and formidable. If I mention the obstacles placed in my path, it is to help clarify why my style may sometimes seem too strident to please readers who lack, as I did until now, the experience of doing this type of investigative reporting. I would also remind readers who complain that some passages in this book are too harsh, that it should not be too surprising if it resembles the pugnacious criticism many archaeologists unleashed on their equivalent of Carlos Castaneda, Erich von Däniken. [42] Both these best-selling authors produced books which are most accurately characterized as largely invalid and unauthentic. The impetus behind most of their ethnographic anomalies is a pronounced tendency toward the melodramatic or sensational. Sensational ethnography annoys scholars because it highlights only the most exotic and fashionable aspects of another culture. Although it often becomes quite popular, such ethnography is too narrowly focused, selective, or biased to be of use to scholars. Like Castaneda's account of his apprenticeship with don Juan, Furst's and Myerhoff's publications and film about the peyote pilgrimage epitomize the sensational. Huichol peyote hunting was torn from its cultural context, the annual Huichol ritual cycle (Benítez 1968a, 1968b, 1975; Fabila 1959; Fikes 1985; Lumholtz 1902; Zingg 1938; Negrín 1975, 1977, 1985; Weigand 1985). Its connection with *Hicüri Neixa*, the peyote dance believed to help bring the first rains, was never explained, probably because this ritual had disappeared among refugee Huichol. Despite its many problems, their abbreviated and anomalous version of peyote hunting is still greedily devoured by New Age seekers (Furst 1989), and accepted by anthropologists as a totally authentic portrait of traditional Chapalagana Huichol ritual. Furst's and Myerhoff's preoccupation with peyote led them to underestimate the centrality of maize, and rain, in Huichol religion and adaptation. Huichol culture is misrepresented primarily because of their bias toward the sensational.

     Like Castaneda's don Juan, Ramón Medina was left in an ethnographic never-never land. Common to Castaneda, Furst, Delgado and to a lesser extent, Myerhoff, is the failure to candidly and completely illuminate the ethnographic context from which their data were derived. They simply do not furnish enough accurate background information about their key informants for scholars to evaluate the authenticity of their data. Understanding Ramón Medina the way Fernando Benítez described him, as a somewhat acculturated Huichol, is vital for scholars concerned with clarifying errors, omissions, and anomalies evident in Castaneda, Furst, Myerhoff, and Delgado. Most of the misconceptions about traditional Huichol rituals and ritual practitioners can be identified. However, precise identification of the source of every anomaly in the Huichol record is complicated because of the collaboration between Castaneda, Furst, Myerhoff, Delgado, and their chief informant, Ramón Medina.

When I first began this research I was inclined to blame Ramón Medina first, and give the UCLA graduates the benefit of the doubt. Today, I tend to hold them responsible for most ethnographic errors, omissions, and anomalies. Unless these researchers have fieldnotes and tape recordings to verify their most anomalous findings, it seems unfair to hold Ramón responsible for their assessments. Interpreting misconceptions, errors, and anomalies in Huichol ethnography forced me to consider how scholars should remedy, or better yet prevent, sensational ethnography from disturbing members of other cultures. It also convinced me that anthropologists must become more accountable to the cultures they study and the public they inform.

My investigative research and writing were sustained by the faith that most people will choose truth over illusion, once they know the difference. I will be pleasantly surprised if my conclusions are controversial enough to rekindle the kind of radical probing of higher education associated with critics such as Sykes in *Profscam*. I will be particularly pleased if some of the New Age seekers who reflect on this book, and their experiences, will recognize they have been taken on a detour and decide it is time to chart a new course. If this book helps them recognize how much of the information circulating about shamans is overly simplistic, trivial, and misleading, it will have served one of its primary purposes.

My ultimate objective is to inspire anthropologists and New Age seekers to greater appreciation and respect for the achievements of Huichol healers and singers. My experiences and research have convinced me that they and other Native American spiritual leaders have much of value to teach us (see Fikes and Nix 1989). However, to properly value what Native American shamans have to offer, we must remain skeptical about our civilization's uncanny ability to turn everything into a commodity.

In today's consumer society, with its instant coffee, frozen dinners, and fast foods, even psychological and religious transformations are simplified and shortened to render them suitable for mass marketing. As Vine Deloria laments, learning shamanistic techniques in a few short seminars typifies many quasi-religious activities which have acquired legitimacy. New Age seekers are vulnerable "to every kind of mercenary hustler imaginable. It's all very pathetic, really" (Deloria quoted in Churchill 1990: 94).

> Consumerism has rendered the short cut respectable . . . any short cut is a marketable commodity . . . The 1960s labeled such commodities "plastic", and spurned them. "Plastic" became synonymous with shoddiness (Baigent, Leigh, Lincoln 1986: 203).

Many who participated in the development of the 1960s counter-culture now support New Age events sold over-the-counter by entrepreneurs. What New Age seekers must learn from Timothy Leary, Carlos Castaneda and other gurus from the psychedelic sixties is that it is not enough to be a non-conformist, to be out of formation, to belong to a counter-culture. We must get our culture back on course again. To do so, requires, among other things, retaining what is viable and valued in our culture, such as critical thinking and high ethnographic standards. Scholars who have studied authentic shamans should join Indian activists taking action to prevent trivialization, if not desecration, of native spirituality. We must also work diligently to protect the inalienable right of Huichols and other Native Americans to freely exercise their religions. The best way to show our appreciation for those Native Americans who are still able to perform rituals which stimulate heartfelt reverence for the earth and its web of life is to help defend their traditional way of life.

# Notes

40.    Since lying is predicated upon the human capacity for speech (which entails the capacity for displacement) the possibility of fabricating a separate reality has always been with us. But there is little comfort in knowing that the "generation of the lie" which vexed Hebrew prophets and mystics of the age which produced the 12th Psalm (Buber in Rappaport 1979: 242) has endured. In fact, this generation is plagued by diabolical lies and other forms of deceit "even more than the times of the psalmist" (Rappaport 1979: 243). Despite the risks and the lack of rewards, there are still crusaders willing to uncover the shoddy foundations of any separate reality created by tall tale tellers in business, evangelism, academia, and government. But to effectively deter deceit obstacles impeding truth-tellers ("whistle-blowers") must be eliminated and rewards for successful debunking increased.

41.    In 1942 a report about Amala and Kamala, two "wolf-children" allegedly raised in India, was published. Many scientists, including Robert Zingg, accepted it as true without attempting to verify its content. In 1959 two doctors published the results of their investigation of the fabled wolf-children. They could not find the village, Godamuri, the supposed site of the wolves' den, anywhere in India. Nevertheless, at the end of 1973, "a textbook on sociology reproduced the story as if no one had ever questioned it" (Montagu 1974: 19).

42.    Erich von Däniken's sensational writing elicited nearly universal condemnation among professional anthropologists. It was as if they really believed that neglecting to criticize bogus data and slipshod theory made one an

accomplice in its propagation. Similarly, Franz Boas complained to President Theodore Roosevelt that the popular film Edward Curtis made about the Kwakiutl Indians was sensational and staged. Incidentally, Faris (1990: 54, 71-72) has concluded that Curtis staged a Navajo ceremony called Nightway.

# CHAPTER FIVE

## *CHAPALAGANA HUICHOL HARVEST AND PEYOTE RITUALS*

### *Profile of Chapalagana Huichol Culture and History*

More than 8,000 Huichol Indians inhabit the rugged Chapalagana river basin in northwestern Mexico (see page viii). Their nearly inaccessible mountain and canyon country contains little arable land. Chapalagana Huichol [43] have preserved a rudimentary form of slash and burn horticulture. The rains which come between early June and October are indispensable to Huichol survival. Without adequate rainfall, their primary crops (corn, beans, and squash) will not prosper. In addition to maize horticulture, a variety of wild plants (e.g., prickly pear cactus, maguey, and mesquite) and animals (e.g., rabbits, deer, and fish) are available at different elevations and different times of the year. Extended family compounds, called *ranchos* in Spanish, are concentrated in a habitation zone about 1,500 meters above sea level (Fikes 1985). Within this micro ecological zone, which is one of five distinct habitats defined by Weigand (1972), *ranchos* are widely dispersed. They are generally located on level ground near water and farm land.

Huichol marriages typically involve members of different *ranchos*. They sanctify a procreative unit and a division of labor based on gender. Huichols have essentially egalitarian gender relations, and a system of bilateral kinship and inheritance. [44] They prefer to select first-born sons (of the first wife) as *rancho* leaders. Huichol land is held communally and several Spanish-imposed political offices are unpaid but crucial in transactions with non-Huichols. Among the most traditional Huichol, an individual's prestige is determined largely by community service. Healer, singer, and *cahuitero* are distinct religious practitioners whose social status is predicated primarily upon the extent of their community service as aboriginal temple officers. [45] Although their prestige may be considerable, Huichol healers and singers are merely part-time ritual practitioners. Healing, performing funeral rituals, making pilgrimages to the *quieri*, and learning the secrets of wolf-nahualism are activities done outside the purview of the temple ritual cycle.

Carl Lumholtz, the first ethnographer to study the Huichol, discovered through first-hand experience the existence of 19 or 20 aboriginal temples (Lumholtz 1900: 9-10, 1902: 27). Additional data obtained by Weigand and I suggest that temple officers in Huichol ceremonial centers were participants in a vast network of regional trade and ceremony long before Spanish conquest. All available evidence indicates that since 200 A.D. the aboriginal Huichol temple ritual cycle has governed vital subsistence activities (i.e., deer and rabbit hunting, fishing, and maize horticulture) and regulated trade of sacred items (e.g., peyote, conch shells, and feathers) with members of neighboring cultures. The annual cycle of rituals is performed to honor various ancestor-deities who personify natural phenomena. Rain-Mothers are particularly important. Temple rituals replicate the world-organizing precedents the ancestor-deities set, and dispose them to protect human health and provide abundant subsistence.

The Huichol language most closely resembles that spoken by their western neighbors, the Cora Indians of

Nayarit (see Figure 1). Cora is the nearest living language to Nahuatl (Aztec). Similarities in social organization and religion between Huichol and Cora are profound and pervasive. Both of these Uto-Aztecan cultures were integrated into a system of regional trade and common ceremony prior to Spanish conquest. The ceremonial centers which still exist today among Chapalagana Huichol were central in the life of this pre-Hispanic system.

Despite sporadic efforts of Franciscan missionaries, Huichols have preserved an aboriginal ritual cycle more elaborate than that of most other Indians of North and Middle America. Christian elements in aboriginal ritual are obvious, but syncretism has remained relatively insignificant, at least in Santa Catarina. It has been more than 100 years since Franciscans resided in Santa Catarina. Some of my Santa Catarina informants fear that allowing missionaries to reside continously in their community would inevitably entail losing some of their land. This well-justified fear may explain why Huichol ritual practitioners, led by *cahuiteros*, perform Easter week ceremonies themselves.

The 4,107 square kilometer homeland reserved by Chapalagana Huichol is half the size it was before Spanish conquest. In 1722 Spaniards conquered the Cora capital at the *Mesa del Nayarit* (see Figure 1). It was then that the Spanish crown established three *comunidades indígenas* (indigenous Huichol communities): Santa Catarina Cuexcomatitlán, San Andrés Cohamiata, and San Sebastián Teponahuaxtlán. Spanish colonization of what remained Huichol-controlled territory was retarded because mineral wealth and fertile land were relatively scarce. Nevertheless, San Andrés and San Sebastián were politically subdivided. From them two new units, Guadalupe Ocotán and Tuxpan de Bolaños, were created. Only Santa Catarina, the Huichol community where my ethnographic research was conducted, has resisted subdivision. The Mexican revolution and the Cristero rebellion dislocated thousands of Chapalagana Huichol. Many of these refugee Huichol live in Mexican-controlled territory south of the Chapalagana Huichol, e.g., in Tepíc and El Colórin. In recent years virgin pine and oak forests, and excellent pasturage for cattle, have enticed Mexicans to invade, or lease at incredibly low prices, Huichol communal lands. Huichol resistance to Mexican exploitation of their resources continues.

**Aboriginal Huichol temple and ceremonial center**

*Dance of Our Mother*

Huichols prepare to celebrate the first fruits ritual of *Tatei Neixa* (Dance of Our Mother) when the constellation called *Tzimanixi*, identified as the Pleiades by Lumholtz (1900: 57), appears in October. The appearance of the Pleiades and the ripe maize are harbingers of the new year. Among Huichols the new year is synonymous with revival of life. New corn and children are key participants in this ritual. Both promise revival of Huichol life. This harvest ritual symbolically rehearses Huichol cosmogony and recapitulates the tribe's mythical history. This is done, as Eliade might recognize,

> to introduce the newborn child ritually into the sacramental reality of the World and culture and thus to validate the new existence by announcing that it conforms with the mythical paradigms.... And one cannot "begin" anything unless one know its "origin," how it first came into being (Eliade 1968: 33).

The myth and songs recited during this ritual remind Huichols how the world was organized, how maize was acquired, and how they differ from other animal species. The maize myth presented in Appendix B reveals that the marriage between the father of the Huichols, *Huatácame*, and the maize maidens is of paramount importance. Equating wives with maize, this myth sanctifies the biological fact of mutualism existing between maize and Huichols. The marriage between Huichols and maize suggests that horticulture is seen as an enduring and overriding commitment in Huichol subsistence and ritual.

In translating two versions of this myth and talking to

Huichols about it, I concluded that for them mutualism with maize implies more a tragic breach of unity than a progressive emancipation from foraging. Adopting slash-and-burn horticulture (seen as establishing, suspending, and reinstating a relationship with the maize maidens) is definitely recognized as an event which irrevocably altered their mode of adaptation to the environment. Because *Huatácame's* mother offended the maize maidens, they must forever be offered the blood of sacrificial animals in order that maize grow. As Fernando Serratos [46] stoically proclaims, "Because of the sacrifices made by *Huatácame*, the rituals must be made." Although the need to respect and nurture maize is expressed throughout the annual ritual cycle, it is never so poignantly dramatized as in this harvest ritual.

In 1979 and 1980 I observed the *Tatei Neixa* ritual performed by the singing shaman, Julio García, at two different *ranchos* near Santa Catarina. The events I observed corresponded closely to the four published accounts of this ritual. [47] Because the sequence of events in this ritual has been adequately described elsewhere, only its major themes require clarification here. In addition to recapitulating the origin of maize and thereby acknowledging its abiding partnership with Huichols there are three main reasons for performing this ritual: (1) to honor *Tatei Yoahuima* (Blue-Maize-Mother) and *Nihuetzica Nonotzi* (the Corn-Child); (2) to protect human health, especially that of children; and (3) to express gratitude to *Tatei Huerica Huimari* and the Rain-Mothers for their help in growing the maize.

In this harvest ritual, as in the planting ritual of *Namahuita Neixa* described by Zingg, *Tatei Otoanaca* (Maize-Mother) is represented by a chair dressed in Huichol women's clothes and stuffed with ears of corn

(Zingg 1938: 488). That this effigy of the corn goddess occupies the central place on the temple altar and is "literally covered with female finery" attests to the Huichol's abiding dependence on maize, the central theme in all versions of the maize myth (Benítez 1975: 141-151; Myerhoff 1974: 210-214; Preuss 1907: 189; Zingg n.d.: 139-167). As Zingg noted, reciting how maize was acquired on the first night of this ritual is

> of prime importance in their religious life, since it explains the foundation of the world in times of the ancients, the establishment of the races of mankind, and the functions of the various gods. The myth continues to explain the mythical *raison d'etre* of corn to the Huichols (Zingg 1938: 483).

Both my versions explain how maize was acquired, why it became so difficult to raise, and why blood sacrifices are an enduring and indispensable component of the annual ritual cycle.

According to Serratos (see Appendix B), when *Huatácame* first obtained maize at *Quitotometa* it was essentially a human female. After the maize maidens he married were mistreated by his mother, he was obliged to anoint the corn husks with deer blood in order that the maize return again. Emphasizing the hardship resulting from *Huatácame's* mother's primordial offense justifies their belief that maize must be scrupulously treated and offered blood sacrifices. The biological fact of interdependence between humans and maize is transformed into a moral imperative by equating maize with wives. The *cahuitero's* version of this myth reveals its didactic function. He emphasizes that this myth promotes marriage, and states that since ancient times it has been recited as part of the

Huichol marriage proposal.

There are some people who base their lives in accordance with this precept. Others have not understood it. Our men abandon their wives and our women abandon their husbands. These people lack wisdom.

Like Serratos, his description of maize as young women dressed in various colors suggests that a fundamental unity between maize and Huichols once existed. Only after the maize wife was mistreated by *Huatácame's* mother did estrangement between maize and Huichols occur. His version makes it obvious that by equating maize with wives Huichols affirm their enduring dependence upon both. Because maize was originally, and is ultimately, human it must be treated well. Reinforcing their reverence toward maize is the belief that failure to honor it may bring hunger or illness as a punishment.

It bears repeating that this "humanistic" view of maize is more than mere poetry or folklore. On the one hand, maize is utterly dependent upon humans for its propagation. As a consequence of centuries of genetic manipulation by humans, corn cannot survive or reproduce without human care. It now requires human nurture (i.e., planting kernels at appropriate distance from each other, weeding, and protection from predators) in order to survive (Iltis 1983; Jolly and Plog 1976: 223; Mangelsdorf 1974). On the other hand, Huichols are utterly dependent upon it for their survival. It feeds them. To assert as they do that they are married to maize is scarcely an exaggeration of what ecologists define as mutualism (Clapham 1973).

The interdependence between maize and Huichols is a fact of human ecology. To interpret this as a partnership between husband and wife lends a certain dignity to

Huichol horticulture and reminds them that each is largely responsible for the other's survival. Although maize is not regarded as a product of genetic manipulation, Huichols can be credited with having a realistic understanding of its crucial role in their adaptation because, as Rappaport suggests, "The criterion of adequacy for a cognized model is not its accuracy, but its adaptive effectiveness" (1979: 98).

Of course Huichol action is predicated upon the belief that maize is a gift originally bestowed and perpetually nurtured by diverse ancestor-deities. That is why Huichols feel safe about consuming maize only after it has been offered to the ancestor-deities in this first fruits ritual. By consuming foods originally given by the gods, Huichol children are rendered susceptible to sickness. Eating such "sacred" foods as maize, squash, fish, and deer makes children unwitting participants in the world established by the ancestor-deities. To insure children's health, they are transported, along with their offerings, to *Pariteciia*, the birthplace of the ancestor-deities.

The Sun-Father, the deer, and their guardian (or *master*) all dwell at *Pariteciia*. In this ritual, new corn is presented and Huichol children formally introduced to these and other ancestor-deities residing at *Pariteciia*. In the song which narrates the journey to *Pariteciia* the Rain-Mothers and Sun-Father are explicitly acknowledged as owners of corn and children and ritually offered the new ears of corn. *Tatei Yoahuima* (Blue-Maize-Mother) is also acknowledged and honored as the owner of the Corn-Child. All this ritual activity must occur before the new ears of corn can be safely consumed by people. Offering the "divine" parents (or owners) of children and corn the first fruits is assumed to guarantee their goodwill and thereby insure that all produce harvested may be eaten safely.

Protecting one's health is certainly the most obvious

reason for performing this ritual. [48] Whereas badgers, ants, other animals, and Mexicans consume corn irreverently (i.e., without performing the *Tatei Neixa* ritual), for Huichols to do so would constitute an offense punishable by sickness or death.

Even tiny babies thus participate in honoring the gods which have given this good harvest of green squash (and corn, while even beans were represented by a few bunches on the altar). ... Without this ceremony, the food is so ritually unclean that eating it would kill the Huichols (Zingg 1938: 489).

My informants all made it abundantly clear that before maize may be safely eaten it must be offered in this ritual to the Sun-Father residing at *Pariteciia*. To do otherwise is to risk illness or death. According to Serratos:

The singing shaman takes the children [*tiihuainorixi*] the new ears of corn, and all the offerings to present to the Sun-Father at *Pariteciia*. The Sun-Father wants us to respect *Nihuetzica* [the Corn-Child]. If we don't, we may have stomach aches, or corn may grow inside us and make us sick. That is why one must hunt deer and perform the ritual of *Tatei Neixa* before the ears of corn can be eaten.

Similarly, the *cahuitero* explained that after the maize is planted in June, it is strictly forbidden to eat ears of corn.

Ears of corn can only be eaten after *Nihuetzica* [the Corn-Child] is offered to the Sun-Father in the ritual of *Tatei Neixa*. The Corn-Child originally appeared at the birthplace of the Sun-Father. After receiving his offering of ears of corn, the Sun-Father eats the Corn-Child. If people neglect to offer the Corn-Child to the Sun-Father before eating the first fruits, they may become sick or even die. To prevent this, the singing shaman asks the Sun-Father five times for permission to eat the ears of corn. And the singing shaman offers the Corn-Child chocolate, cornmeal, votive arrows, gourd bowl offerings, and candles.

Jerónimo Bonales remarked that maize is in a dangerous condition until after this ritual is performed and that eating corn prior to performing this ritual might cause the Sun-Father to send a scorpion to sting the offender. Whereas my informants' concern with making ritual offerings to the Corn-Child and feeding him to the Sun-Father to avoid illness is evident enough, the rationale behind it requires further explanation.

Especially significant is the *cahuitero's* statement that offerings of chocolate, cornmeal, votive arrows, gourd bowls, and candles are made to the Corn-Child. It is precisely these offerings which are made before hunting and after killing deer. As I have noted (Fikes 1985), deer cannot be summoned, or killed safely, unless such offerings are made. These offerings are essential not only to solicit deer and protect one's health, but also to insure the eventual return (or reincarnation) of the deer. Maize must be similarly treated to insure its return and to protect human health.

In his song the *cahuitero* tells the Corn-Child that he must be presented at *Maxa Tecüa*.

For you *Nihuetzica* we have made all these offerings since ancient times. At *Pariteciia* we baptise the

Corn-Child and present those who conduct the baptism [i.e., *taocaritame*]. ... Here I am offering you your Corn-Child. Now I shall cook *Nihuetzica.*

Because cooking the corn entails killing *Nihuetzica*, he must first be offered to the Sun-Father. In the Cora counterpart to this Huichol harvest ritual it is explicitly stated that although the Corn-Child is killed by the fire, he is reincarnated as the evening star, returning to his house above us (Preuss 1909: 207-208). Numerous passages in Huichol songs indicate that this ritual facilitates the return of the Corn-Child to his celestial home.

It may be recalled that the birthplace of both the Corn-Child and the Sun-Father, *Pariteciia*, is simultaneously the exit from the underworld and the entrance to the celestial realm. *Pariteciia* is presumably an "*axis mundi*" (Eliade 1964) or an "earth navel" (Ortiz 1969). In the *cahuitero's* song both the Corn-Child and Huichol children are introduced to the ancestor-deities residing at *Pariteciia*. After the squash and corn are ripe, the ancestor-deities, taking the form of blue hummingbirds, butterflies, etc., carry the Corn-Child, Deer-Person, and Huichol children to *Cuanameyapa*, *Maxa Teciia*, and *Pariteciia*. Arriving at Pariteciia, the singer presents the children, the Corn-Child, and the other offerings to the Sun-Father and to *Tatei Huerica Huimari*. As my *compadre* explained, the children and the Corn-Child are baptized or blessed there by these two celestial parents.

In Bonales' version of this song the children and their assemblage of offerings are presented by the singer to ancestor-deities residing at numerous shrines including *Yozyapa*, *Yoz Tecua*, or *Cuanameyapa*. *Cuanameyapa*, considered the place where life began, is a lookout point where the earth boiled and thickened before the great deluge. As Bonales sings:

> My ancestor-deities we are going to *Cuanameyapa*.
> Permit the children to pass. Do not harm them
> because they bring you all your offering. The chil-
> dren will eat the corn, but Blue-Maize-Mother do not
> harm us. . . . This ritual is performed according to
> precedents established by the ancestor-deities. . . . In
> response to this song they have accepted the children.
> . . . The children are flying well and the young chil-
> dren without wings are being helped by the ancestor-
> deities. At the earth's intersection [*hixüapa*] the
> children are ascending toward *Yoz Tecua* with the aid
> of the ancestor-deities.

It must be clearly understood that only at the earth's
intersection is ascent from the underworld to the terrestrial
or celestial realm possible. A Tewa informant has captured
the meaning of the Huichol word, *hixüapa* (earth's intersection):

> An earth navel is like an airport. You notice how
> airplanes, no matter where they go, always have to
> return to the airport. In the same way all things –
> game, people and spirits – always return to the earth
> navel (Ortiz 1969: 24).

Both children and new corn return in this ritual to the
earth's intersection (*hixüapa*). Maize is eaten and children
blessed by the ancestor-deities residing there. Huichol
children are said to visit their celestial mother, the lunar
deity, and, as Preuss suggests, the Corn-Child returns to his
celestial matrix. As the *cahuitero* sings, the Blue-Maize-
Mother, the *haicü* and the maize of various colors are all

present at this intersection. Like the "souls" of deceased Huichols, which return via the underworld to join their celestial parents, i.e., Sun-Father and *Tatei Huerica Huimari*, the Corn-Child is apparently reborn after being consumed by the Sun-Father and other ancestor-deities.

After arriving at *Cuanameyapa*, the final destination of children on this ritual pilgrimage, the entire itinerary of the trip is recited in reverse and then Bonales informs the male ancestor-deities (*cacaomama*) that having been duly entertained, they may rest:

At last all of you have tasted the ears of corn. I shall give you no more. *Tei Yoahuima* [Blue-Maize-Mother] you have heard this song we sing for you each year. Blue-Maize-Mother you accompanied me but now we have returned. If *Na'arihuame* is willing we shall make this journey again with the children. We are grateful to you *Huerica* for the help you gave to the younger children as they were flying. You did not let them fall.

Inasmuch as it is the key to the "hidden" meaning of this ritual, the connection between the *Huerica* and the celestial mother merits further comment.

My *compadre* identified this particular *Huerica* as a large black bird resembling a buzzard, and Bonales informed me that *Tatei Huerica Huimari* can assume the form of a buzzard. Similarly, Palafox Vargas noted (1978: 74) that in this ritual the children are carried on the wings of the *Huerica*, a bird which incarnates *Tatei Huerica Huimari*. That this bird is a messenger, or incarnation, of the celestial mother is especially appropriate given her identity as the mother of Huichol children and of *Nihuetzica* (the Corn-Child). Closely associated with the moon and dwelling in the center of the sky, she and her surrogates, the eagles, are credited with protecting the Corn-Child (see Fikes 1985). According to the *cahuitero*, the guardians of the Corn-Child include the yellow eagle, the red eagle, the blue eagle, and the great *Huerica*. Because these eagles protect the growing corn from predators such as rats, ground squirrels, and badgers, they are given offerings of corn beer, tamales, and meat at the peak called *Paritecüa*. The fact that Serratos credits *Tatei Huerica Huimari* with facilitating abundant harvests (see Appendix B) suggests that she is indeed the prototypical Mother to whom this dance (and harvest ritual) is dedicated.

We need not digress to consider the striking similarities between this prototypical Huichol mother and her Cora, Aztec, and Pipil counterparts (Thompson 1939: 142-144). All that remains to be clarified here is the symbolism surrounding the departure of the Rain-Mothers (i.e., the culmination of the rainy season). Numerous excerpts from songs and symbolism of various offerings proper to this ritual indicate that *Tacützi Yürameca* (Great-grandmother-Germination) and the Rain-Mothers are preparing to leave the Huichol sierra just as this ritual is performed.

Both Great-grandmother-Germination and the Rain-Mothers are especially active during the Huichol rainy season. In his song the *cahuitero* states that the Rain-Mothers are the owners of maize and of Huichol children and that "this song is dedicated to *Tacützi Yürameca*." According to Bonales, each year after the *Tatei Neixa* ritual is performed, a replica of *Tacützi's* cane (illustrated in Berrin 1978: 144-146) is deposited at her shrine. This act acknowledges that the power of germination symbolized by, or as Huichols would say, embodied in her cane, is on the wane as the rainy season ends.

During this ritual each child carries a "god's eye"

(*tzicori*) as the song transports them toward *Cuanameyapa*. Among other things, the *tzicori* represents the corn and squash flowers which have just blossomed. According to Serratos, the *tzicori* is also a marker for the first five years of a child's life. After the ritual is over, the *tzicori* is taken as an offering to the *Aitzárica* and to *Tatei Matinyeri*. Offering the *tzicori* to Rain-Mothers residing at these springs (shrines) helps insure the children's health inasmuch as the *tzicori* is considered a *nierica* (mirror) through which Rain-Mothers may see, and thereby guard, the children throughout the year which is about to begin. Thus the replica of *Tacützi's* cane and the *tzicori* offered to the Rain-Mothers are veritable indexes of their departure and the impending change of seasons.

Explicit in the *cahuitero's* song is the recognition that this ritual marks the end of the rainy season (*tocárita* or *tocáripa*) and the beginning of the dry season (*taxáricü*). Addressing the Rain-Mothers assembled at *Paritecüa*, the *cahuitero* (representing *Iromari*) asks them for their permission to take the children there. As the end of this pilgrimage song he (as *Iromari*) bids the Rain-Mothers farewell:

Here I shall end this rainy season ritual. Here I shall stop my Rain-Mothers. We shall meet again my ancestor-deities . On exactly this day we will see each other again. If you permit me to live until then I shall sing this very song. ... Here I am reciting the events of your life my ancestor-deities. Do not be offended. I am offering you your Corn-Child. ... At this time of the rainy season [*tocáripa*] you request that we perform this ritual. The seasons are changing. Hold on, and walk in the intersection [*hixüapa*] my children [*tühuainorixi*].

Amen.

In his version of this song Bonales promises to make this journey to *Cuanameyapa* again with the children, "if *Na'arihuame* is willing." What his promise means is that provided the rains return again next year there will be another harvest (and therefore a first fruits ritual). *Tatei Na'arihuame* is said to be the first Rain-Mother to appear each year. Coming from the east (from *Tatei Matinyeri*), she brings the rain back again to the Huichol sierra each June. That explains why two plumed serpent sticks carried by the two dance leaders in the *Hicüri Neixa* ritual (see page 189) are offerings to, or replicas of her: she must be induced to return so that the maize can be planted in a wet cornfield.

That *Tatei Neixa* marks the end of the rainy season is clearly indicated by the fact that Bonales and the *cahuitero* bid farewell to the departing Rain-Mothers and promise to meet them again next year. Yet this ritual also heralds the beginning of the dry season. Returning from *Cuanameyapa,* Bonales sings, "I brought back the children and the *cacaomama.* My *cacaomama*, find no fault with this song. My *cacaomama* I brought you back to stay inside the god-house." Identified as male ancestor-deities, the *cacaomama* presumably replace the departing Rain-Mothers. The succession of the seasons is symbolized by a relocation of ancestor-deities. Wet and dry seasons are distinct but complementary aspects of Huichol life. Performance of their annual ritual cycle is intended to perpetuate this fundamental unity in duality.

Of all the Huichol rituals (which Zingg classified as *either* a wet *or* a dry season ceremony) only *Tatei Neixa* was defined as a combination wet and dry season ceremony (Zingg 1938: 482). Preuss also recognized that this harvest ritual heralds, if not facilitates, the changing of the seasons

(Preuss 1909: 208-212). However, admitting that it facilitates or commemorates the transition from wet to dry season must not cause us to ignore its dominant characteristic. Above all else, this ritual celebrates the revival of life. Celebrated at the climax of the rainy season, this ritual acknowledges that Huichols have been granted new life. The rain controlled by various Rain-Mothers has bestowed life upon maize, beans, and squash. These crops in turn feed the Huichols and their children. The rainy season, is, after all, the only time of year when these life-sustaining crops can be grown in the Huichol sierra. This coincidence of rainy season, life, and darkness (caused by cloud-covered skies) is nicely illustrated by the word *tocari*, which simultaneously connotes night, rainy season, and life (Palafox Vargas 1978: 73; Preuss 1907: 185). Health and life for Huichol children is largely based on harvesting plenty of corn, beans, and squash. To obtain abundant harvests requires the presence of the Rain-Mothers. Accordingly, children bring ritual offerings to the departing Rain-Mothers (of all world directions) present at *Cuanameyapa*. Their abiding dependence on the Rain-Mothers is epitomized by Bonales' statement that if *Na'arihuame* is willing, we shall make this journey again next year.

Photo: Smithsonian Institution

**Huichol peyote dance leader carrying plumed serpent stick**

*The Peyote Hunt*

A comprehensive ethnographic account of the Huichol peyote hunt will not be provided here because the itinerary and the observable details of the annual peyote pilgrimage are described in Benítez (1968b, 1975), and Mata Torres (n.d.). Although each of these investigators notes that peyote gathering is symbolically equated with deer hunting, the supreme importance and chief attributes of the ancestor-deity being hunted remain obscure. Consequently, the primary purpose of the peyote hunt, as conceived by Huichols, still requires clarification.

*Eating Deer-Person's Heart*

The peyote hunt is, for my informants, primarily a commemoration, repetition, and re-enactment of a primordial hunt for Deer-Person (*Maxa Tehuiyari*). To appreciate their perspective two caveats must be kept in mind. First, Deer-Person is not a "dying god" but rather a master of physical metamorphosis, an omniscient and omnipresent Creator and tutelary spirit. Second, the immortal wolves (*Camóquite*) which originally ate him are not villains, but heroes who set a precedent still valid for Huichol peyote hunters. On the one hand, the peyote hunters are seeking the Creator and tutelary spirit, Deer-Person. On the other hand, they are following in the footsteps of those immortal wolves who originally ate him and thereby acquired his wisdom.

Although various ancestor-deities are honored during the peyote pilgrimage, the final destination of the hunters is *Pariteciia*, the home of Deer-Person. Peyote is understood to be the *iyari* (heart-soul-memory) of their tutelary spirit, Deer-Person. Eating peyote enables Huichols to partake of Deer-Person's wisdom. The extreme reverence Huichols feel toward Deer-Person (and for peyote, his heart or incarnation) is vividly illustrated in the song Bonales learned on his first pilgrimage as a temple officer (See Appendix C). As Bonales' song and the testimony of all my informants indicate, there is no doubt that peyote is regarded as what Wasson (1980) has called an "entheogen." Under its influence Bonales actually sees the ancestor-deities, including the peyote deity. He calls Peyote a great teacher, especially of songs, and notes it has the power to erase the minds of careless people. Consistent with the widespread Mesoamerican understanding of the sacred mushrooms (Wasson 1980), the peyote deity speaks through him, the shaman. Also familiar to Mesoamericanists will be the Huichol's identification of peyote as the "flower of God." But neither its parallels with other Mesoamerican entheogens nor its mind-expanding, visionary, or "hallucinogenic" effect on humans is at issue. Our concern here is the meaning that eating the heart of Deer-Person has for Huichols.

The statement attributed to peyote itself, "If you come to know me intimately, you shall be like me and feel like I do," suggests that Deer-Person, incarnate in peyote, is considered a most compelling ego ideal. This suggestion is well confirmed by the *cahuitero*'s characterization of Deer-Person as the supreme teacher of Huichol singers and healers, and as having been the first to learn the amaranth song, which is associated with healing.

It is because of the wisdom of Deer-Person [*Maxa Tehuiyari*] that shamans [*mara'acate*] exist. That is how we Huichols are able to diagnose diseases with our *nierica* [mirror] and *iyari* [memory-heart-soul], which are the eyes of Deer-Person. That is our method of curing. Thus we follow the study of Deer-Person.

But why do Huichols believe eating peyote facilitates access to the wisdom of Deer-Person?

Hultkrantz has noted (1953: 400-401) that the heart is the organ typically preferred in cannibalistic ceremonies of North Americans. Among Huichols, and perhaps Native Americans generally, the heart is regarded as the locus of intelligence and of the soul which survives death. The *iyari* (heart/soul) contains the mind or memory of the "deceased" and presumably persists even after the physical body disintegrates. Accordingly, the hearts of ordinary deer are only consumed by Huichol elders after first being offered to the ancestor-deities. Being the *iyari* of *Caoyomari*, their Creator and tutelary spirit (Negrín 1975: 17), peyote merits even more scrupulous treatment; i.e., the prohibitions and offerings associated with the peyote hunt. To eat peyote, the heart/soul of their Creator and tutelary spirit is, in effect, to assimilate his memory, knowledge, or being. This understanding of peyote, as *Caoyomari's iyari*, illuminates the deeper meaning of peyote's statement, "If you come to know me intimately, you shall be like me and feel like I do." To become one with *Caoyomari* is to share his concern for promoting cosmic order. The state of trance or ecstasy which Huichol singers value is the prerequisite for maintaining that order established by *Caoyomari*.

As may be surmised, before consuming the heart of this omniscient tutelary, Huichols are obligated to honor and re-enact a precedent which established the existing ecological order. In deer hunting, as in its symbolic equivalent, peyote hunting, wolves are acknowledged as having set the precedent Huichols must follow. In a text dictated by Serratos, *Maxa Tehuiyari* (Deer-Person) is credited with being an outstanding hunter and a master of metamorphosis; i.e., a child deity capable of assuming human, deer, and peyote form. After being apprehended near the Pacific Ocean by his sisters, Deer-Person manages to escape from them and various ancestor-deities, including the sun and fire, who hold him captive. Traveling toward the east, Deer-Person is hunted by various divine hunter-ancestors; including the *Camóquite* (immortal wolves). Also called *ahuatámete*, these wolf deities (or constellations) finally caught Deer-Person and ate him raw.

> But he was no longer a boy. He had taken the form of the Blue-Deer [*Maxa Yoahui*]. He took that form in *Huíricüta*. That is the reason that one eats the peyote raw. Because of the precedent set by the *Camóquite* it is not cooked.... The child [i.e., *Maxa Tehuiyari*] remained there in *Huíricüta*. That is why peyote is so far away. Nowadays when one goes to *Huíricüta* and eats the peyote it is eaten raw because the *Camóquite* ate the child raw. To commemorate the wolves eating the deer raw the peyote hunters must do likewise when they eat his heart [peyote].

My informants clearly indicate that the wolf is a source of inspiration and a powerful tutelary spirit. Their deference toward wolves is expressed in the act of eating peyote raw. My informants insist that wolves are like children and servants of the Sun-Father. Preuss suggests that the "deer" (peyote) shot by peyote hunters symbolizes the stars which are eclipsed by the Sun-Father during the dry season. As he explained, the Huichol peyote hunters represent deities in the service of the Sun-Father (Preuss 1909: 211-212). Also, in the service of various ancestor-deities, including the Sun-Father, are the *Camóquite*. By eating Deer-Person they set the precedent which helped create the existing order that Huichol temple officers are obliged to recreate.

Huichol esteem for wolves transcends the fact that they are credited with setting precedents still valid for peyote and deer hunting ritual. Inasmuch as they caught and ate Deer-Person, the Huichol Creator and tutelary spirit, wolves may be respected as rightful heirs to his wisdom. Might Huichols have concluded that wolves are, like themselves, partially responsible for maintaining ecological order?

For individual Huichols, the peyote hunt facilitates acquiring the wisdom of Deer-Person (and, by implication, becoming a healer and/or singer). Because of their understanding of the power inherent in the *iyari* (heart/soul), Huichols do not feel uncomfortable about eating the child deity's heart. In fact, this is the surest way to gain his wisdom. From their hunter perspective Deer-Person was destined to become peyote and thereby provide a source of inspiration for them. As Serratos' text indicates:

> The boy was destined for this purpose: to take the form of deer and of peyote. As the deer escaped from the ancestor-deities, he took the form of peyote there in *Huíricüta*. Peyote grows in clusters which resemble the shape of a deer. That is why we shoot it with our arrows.

Hunting this tutelary spirit incarnate in peyote is, on the one hand, a vision quest, and, on the other hand, an initiation rite organized by Huichol temple groups. Supplementing the individual hunter's vision quest is the overriding goal of the temple group: to perpetuate the existing ecological order and thereby prevent chaos (i.e., deviation from Huichol tradition).

## Recreating the World

In addition to hunting for Deer-Person, temple officers commemorate the birth of the Sun-Father and invoke the aid of the Rain-Mothers. At *Tatei Matinyeri*, the official entrance to the peyote country, various Rain-Mothers and fertility deities are visited and presented with offerings. At *Paritecüa*, the final destination of the peyote pilgrims, Deer-Person, Sun-Father, and (if Mata Torres is correct) Great-grandmother-Germination are visited. The pilgrimage to *Paritecüa*, rehearsed in the first fruits ritual, allows the temple officers to greet the ancestors convened there and insures that the new year is properly inaugurated.

According to Benítez-Sánchez, at the end of each year the ancestor-deities are debilitated. Although they have abandoned their bodies, their womb remains in the peyote country, where they reassemble at the end of the year. On the rock altar of *Parietzie,* where light first appeared on the earth's surface, their umbilical cord remains rooted. The heart or memory of the ancestor-deities arrives there and their spirits reunite within a magical enclosure. In this manner, the spirits of the ancestors visit each other "at the end of the year in order to be reborn with a new spirit, just as we do after dying" (my translation of Negrín 1977: 123). It is apparently this annual reunion or rendezvous which compels Huichol pilgrimage. As Eliade might recognize, the temple officers' annual pilgrimage to *Parietzie* complements, if it does not actually re-enact, the eternal return of their ancestor-deities.

Huichols are convinced that the world established by the ancestor-deities is effectively recreated by proper performance of ritual (Fikes 1985). Of all the events commemorated in Huichol ritual, the most significant is probably the birth of the Sun-Father. His birth is re-enacted each year by the temple officers in order to commemorate his perpetual return. As Preuss noted (1909: 211-212), Huichol temple officers commemorate or recreate the birth of the Sun-Father by traveling to his birthplace and adorning their hats with turkey feathers and squirrel tails. But, their pilgrimage to *Paritecüa*, the "burnt hill" where the sun first rose, has additional significance.

In his funeral ritual song, the *cahuitero* sings that both people and ancestor-deities are born there and that *Paritecüa* is the final terrestrial stop made by the souls of deceased Huichols before joining their celestial parents, Sun-Father and *Tatei Huerica Huimari*. It is also the resting place of all the ancestor-deities, including Deer-Person. According to my *compadre*, this peak is the birthplace of all the ancestor-deities and is still inhabited by them, as well as by yet unborn children. It may be recalled that new corn and Huichol children are transported there in the first fruits ritual. *Paritecüa* clearly has all the attributes of a world navel, a sacred intersection through which life perpetually passes. It is viewed as both the exit from the underworld and the entrance to the celestial realm. As demonstrated by the Sun-Father, *Paritecüa* is the passageway where ascent from underworld to sky is possible.

Representing the point of rendezvous for people and ancestor-deities alike, it is fitting that peyote hunters leave offerings there. According to Serratos, the peyote hunters leave yarn painting prayers (*huehuiya*), gourd bowls with coins, maize, deer antlers and blood, votive arrows, and

"god's eyes" (*tzicori*). [49] With these offerings they help
sustain the Sun-Father and ask for rain. At a nearby spring,
as at *Tatei Matinyeri*, temple officers again petition ancestor-deities for rain prior to obtaining water required for
rainmaking rituals to be performed in the sierra.
Perhaps more than any other Huichol ritual, the
peyote pilgrimage helps secure climatic continuity, maintaining the alignment between earth and sun and insuring
adequate rainfall. By making offerings to the diverse
ancestor-deities reunited at *Pariteciia*, Huichol temple
officers do their part in perpetuating the cosmos. Only then
do they merit the health, rain, and abundant subsistence
they solicit from the ancestor-deities who inhabit and control their world. Yet making the prescribed offerings does
more than merely promoting harmonious relations between
Huichols and the diverse ancestor-deities personifying and
controlling their universe.

Huichols apparently assume their offerings revive
and sustain the beings who originally established the ecological order they both inhabit. The temple officers' annual
pilgrimage to *Pariteciia* is required not simply to help
recreate the existing order initially organized by the ancestor-deities, but also to nourish the deities at a time when
they are debilitated. Feeding them is indispensable to
perpetuating the world they personify and control. Performance of ritual *plus* presentation of prescribed offerings
is what insures the succession of wet and dry seasons and,
by implication, guarantees health and abundant subsistence
for Huichols.

Hardly less important than *Pariteciia* is *Tatei Matinyeri*, another "earth navel" which Huichols honor as the
goddess (birthplace) of children. Zingg reports that
Huichols see this group of perennial springs in the desert as
a womb or pregnant woman and believe that unborn chil-

dren come down from above through this womb in a manner Preuss recognized as identical to Aztec and Cora conceptions (Zingg 1938: 623). According to Benítez (1975: 127) and Mata Torres (n.d.: 61-65), the peyote country (known as *Huíricüta* or *Parietzie*) is entered through this womb (or these perennial springs).

Home to all the Rain-Mothers except the Pacific Ocean (Benítez 1968b: 246, 270), visiting *Tatei Matinyeri* is mandatory for peyote hunters. This Huichol shrine is identified as the birthplace of all the female ancestor-deities and as "Our Mother who watches over us" (Negrín 1977: 95). My *compadre* explained that in order to solicit rain, *Tatei Matinyeri* is offered deer antlers, candles, chocolate, cornmeal, etc. Her water is then carried back to the sierra for use in temple rituals such as the Peyote Dance (*Hicüri Neixa*).

Entering the sacred peyote country through *Tatei Matinyeri*'s womb, the peyote hunters travel to *Paritecüa*, their final destination, birthplace of the Sun-Father and home of *Caoyomari*. In the Huichol universe *Paritecüa* represents the gateway linking terrestrial and celestial realms. It is where the sun's ascent to heaven occurred and where the soul's return to its celestial parents is possible. Complementing *Paritecüa* is *Tatei Matinyeri*, the womb through which descent to earth from heaven is possible. Both are regarded as supreme sources of life, as intersections between planes of existence, as sacred centers where existence is radically transformed. Both must be visited and honored by temple officers seeking to recreate the world they inherited from the ancestor-deities.

All available data suggest that the peyote pilgrimage is intended to reinstate ritually the existing ecological order. In retracing the route of the ancestor-deities, in commemorating their world-organizing exploits, and by making offerings which sustain them, Huichol temple officers help preserve the order they created. Also indicative of their commitment to recreate the cosmos is the hunt for that great tutelary spirit, *Maxa Tehuiyari* (Deer-Person). Eating peyote, the heart/soul of *Caoyomari*, who is the architect and chief custodian of existing order, is the royal road to complete identification with him (as Bonales' song, in Appendix C, plainly tells us). Significantly, the way in which peyote is harvested epitomizes the Huichols' recognition of nature's regenerative power. As Furst (1972: 176) and Mata Torres (n.d.: 79) observed, the roots of the peyote cactus are left in the earth in order that this "flower of God" may blossom again.

Inasmuch as the peyote pilgrimage occurs in the interval after the maize is ripe but before it is planted again, it may be characterized as the first of the dry season rituals. Upon returning from the peyote hunt (which is now held virtually anytime between October and April), the temple officers journey to the Pacific Ocean and then to the shrines of other Rain-Mothers (see page 208). These dry season pilgrimages are clearly designed to solicit rain, an element indispensable to Huichol survival.

**Huichol peyote dancer with yellow face paint**

Photo: Smithsonian Institution

**Huichol singer seated on chair watches women grinding peyote**

# Notes

43.  My principal informants call themselves *Toaporitari*, thereby emphasizing their affiliation with *Toapori*, the particular Huichol ceremonial center where the Catholic church of Santa Catarina stands. Santa Catarina is the name they use to refer to their particular *communidad indígena*. When defining themselves as a distinct ethnic and linguistic group they call themselves *Huixáritari*, the plural form of *Huixárica*. The word "Huich" means dog in the Tarascan Indian language. This Tarascan word is probably the basis for "Huichol", the name Spaniards have given the *Huixáritari*. I use the word Huichol merely for the sake of convenience. Chapalagana Huichol is sometimes used to distinguish inhabitants of this homeland from those refugee Huichol residing south of it.

My use of the word Huichol should not lead readers to conclude that regional variation in language and culture is unimportant. The linguist, Grimes (1964:    13), has distinguished three major dialect divisions which correspond to natural barriers in the Chapalagana river region. Weigand (1981) and Negrín (1985: 13) have independently identified four major aboriginal zones.

44.    There is considerable evidence to support Weigand's prediction (1978:  110-11), that the desire to accumulate cattle (and thereby become wealthy) will expedite subordination of Huichol women and its concomitant, the agnatic principle of inheritance (i.e., passing property from fathers to sons). Since Lumholtz noted (1902: 253-54) that cattle wealth could contribute to the creation of a class-stratified society, vaccines have helped increase Huichol cattle production and stabilize herd size. The Mexican government

has selected Huichol men with the largest herds to receive loans for the purchase of more cattle. Weigand has concluded (personal communication 1983) that this intensification of cattle production has already facilitated modifications in the system of bilateral kinship and inheritance characteristic of traditional Huichol society.

45.    In this context it should be noted that the Huichol word *mara'acame* is used to designate an animal, plant, or person credited with having "supernatural" power. It is clearly a vague term which does not distinguish between healers, singers, and *cahuiteros*. In the Huichol hierarchy of religious practitioners, healers are accorded less prestige than singers, who are, in turn, less influential than *cahuiteros*. The authority of the *cahuitero* extends into the political realm (Fikes 1985: 75).

46.    To help maintain my informants' right to privacy, the names of Huichol singers used here are purely fictitious. The four singers whose songs and myths were tape recorded were all residents of the aboriginal temple district of Santa Catarina (Fikes 1985: 7-15). The qualifications of my *compadre*, the father of a boy I baptised, and my relationship with him, are summarized elsewhere (Fikes 1985: 12-13).

47.    Zingg's report (1938: 482-500) on the 1934 ritual at Ratontita is the most accurate and complete account available. Lumholtz (1900: 155-157) and Preuss (1909: 207-208) provide accurate but abbreviated descriptions. Anguiano's account of the *Tatei Neixa* performed at El Colorín, Nayarit is of questionable value inasmuch as Mexican folksongs had replaced much of the aboriginal meaning of the ritual (Furst and Anguiano 1977: 147), and for other reasons discussed above, in note 32.

48.    Both Cora and Huichol informants make it clear that the notion held by Anguiano and Furst (1977: 98), that the

primary purpose of this first fruits ritual is to impregnate
young minds with the peyote tradition, instead of fostering
reverence for the first fruits of horticulture, is untenable.
Neither version of the song I have translated mentions
peyote or the peyote hunt. Although this first fruits ritual
song recapitulates the itinerary of the peyote hunters, it is
obviously integral to a ritual performed to insure that new
ears of corn can be safely consumed. Similarly, in the Cora
counterpart to *Tatei Neixa*, Padre Ortega (1754: 24) was
told that if any person ate of the first fruits before he was
blessed, his god would punish him with a terrible attack of
herpes.

49.   Of the four scholars who published accounts of the
peyote hunt, only Fernando Benítez actually climbed to the
summit of *Pariteciia*, which he called "Reunar." His photographs (Benítez 1968b) and the description of the ritual
he witnessed there are, therefore, unprecedented and invaluable. He observed offerings of votive arrows, corn
flowers, candles, and a stuffed deer's head being deposited
in the "opening from which the new-born sun had sprung"
(Benítez 1975: 72). Subsequently, while a prayer was
being chanted, he saw deer blood and corn beer sprinkled on
the ground. Furst, Myerhoff, and Mata Torres did not
witness the ceremony performed on top of Reunar. Mata
Torres reported (n.d.: 96) that offerings deposited there included votive arrows, candles, gourd bowls with peyote,
and a representation of the goddess *Tacützi Nacahúe* with
the canoe in which she and *Huatácame* survived the great
deluge (Mata Torres n.d.: 96).

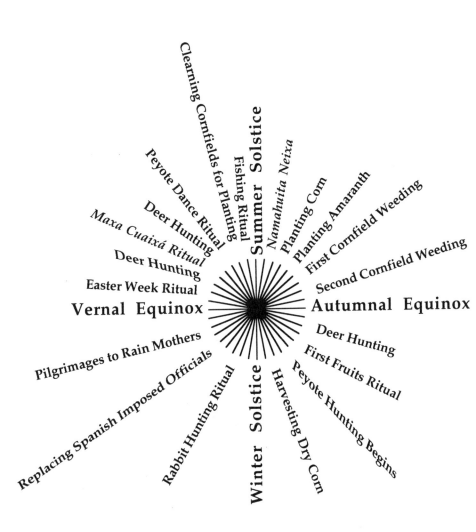

Clearing Cornfields for Planting
Fishing Ritual
Peyote Dance Ritual
Deer Hunting
Maxa Cuaixá Ritual
Deer Hunting
Easter Week Ritual
Summer Solstice
Namahuita Neixa
Planting Corn
Planting Amaranth
First Cornfield Weeding
Second Cornfield Weeding
Vernal Equinox
Autumnal Equinox
Pilgrimages to Rain Mothers
Deer Hunting
First Fruits Ritual
Replacing Spanish Imposed Officials
Rabbit Hunting Ritual
Peyote Hunting Begins
Harvesting Dry Corn
Winter Solstice

Figure 2: *Huichol subsistence & ritual cycle*

**Quanah Parker, Comanche, peyote meeting evangelist**

# APPENDIX A

## *PEYOTE: DIVINE CACTUS OR DANGEROUS DRUG?*

Peyote or *Lophophora williamsii* is a small spineless cactus which grows in a 100,000-square-mile area south of the Rio Grande – in the Chihuahuan desert of northcentral Mexico. It is one of the slowest growing plants in existence. Because thousands of collectors fail to leave its roots in the ground, peyote is threatened with extinction.

Native American veneration of peyote may be 10,000 years old (Stewart 1987). Radiocarbon dates on a peyote button necklace found in a burial in a desert cave in northern Mexico indicate that peyote was used at least a thousand years ago (Adovasio and Fry 1976; W. Taylor 1966: 84, 1972: 175). Furst has asserted that peyote was used by at least 200 A.D. (1972a: x, 1972b). My correlation of events in Huichol oral history with Weigand's archaeological survey of the region surrounding the Huichol homeland indicates that Huichol peyote pilgrimages may have originated around 200 A.D. However ancient peyote use may be, by the time Spaniards arrived it was widely used by the natives of Mexico (LaBarre 1969).

From the time Europeans "discovered" aboriginal Americans using peyote, their ability to use it has been hampered. In 1620 the Spanish Inquisition denounced peyote as diabolic and made use illegal (Anderson 1980: 2-7). Persecution of Mexican Indian peyotists included torture and death (Stafford 1983: 104). Today most non-Indians still regard peyote as a dangerous drug, a psychedelic similar to LSD. It should be clear that my identification of peyote as a "plant psychedelic" is intended only as a convenience for non-Indian readers. Huichol Indians revere peyote as the heart/soul of their Creator (Fikes 1985: 188-189). The Creator of peyote can bless them with healing ability and teach songs. Members of the Native American Church (NAC) believe peyote is a "divine medicine" and credit it with healing them and teaching songs. Such reverence or deification of peyote indicates that Wasson's term, "entheogen" (1980), more accurately conveys the Native American perspective on peyote.

## Huichols as Magnets for Psychedelic Seekers

Castaneda claims (1969: 27-34) that the first time he ate peyote was on August 7, 1961. My interview with Guadalupe de la Cruz Rios suggests that Carlos Castaneda ate peyote with Huichols sometime in 1966. In 1966, Furst and Myerhoff became the first professional anthropologists to go on a Huichol peyote hunt (Myerhoff 1978: 56). Their accomplishment came as the psychedelic movement was reaching its zenith. Castaneda's books, in concert with Furst's and Myerhoff's publications, Furst's movie, and Delgado's lectures, greatly stimulated interest in peyote among members of the psychedelic movement. In the 1970s, Prem Das and Brant Secunda began marketing don José Rios (Matsuwa) as a Huichol shaman. By 1976, the Huichol had become a magnet for psychedelic seekers (Anderson 1980: 175). Since then, Huichol "shamans" and peyote hunts have become a fashionable commodity for more and more New Age seekers.

The Huichol have become increasingly popular because there is, as yet, no Yaqui Indian who fits the description of Castaneda's don Juan, and because the Yaquis are far more acculturated than the Huichol. Huichol Indians have preserved a more elaborate and essentially non-Christian ritual cycle in which peyote is consumed sacramentally, i.e., revered as the heart-soul of the creator, *Caoyomari* (Fikes 1985). Since the mid-1960s, many psychedelic advocates have been especially fascinated by Huichol peyote rituals (Stafford 1983: 104-106, 120-123, 129, 133-34, 140-41, 143, 146, 149). Some of them have devised peyote rituals which combine elements borrowed from Huichol and NAC rituals, in a "somewhat hokey" manner (Stafford 1983: 120).

## Native American Church

Anthropologists believe that religious use of peyote among Native North Americans began spreading rapidly after 1880. Today there are well over 100 NAC chapters dispersed within the United States. Members of various Native American societies learned to venerate peyote from enthusiasts such as John Wilson (LaBarre 1989: 151-161; Stewart 1987: 86-93) and Quanah Parker (see photo, page 209). Members of the NAC are usually enrolled in a federally recognized tribe and most have at least 25 percent Indian blood.

Participants in the all-night rituals of the NAC sing, drum, pray, meditate, and consume peyote. A fire burns in the center of a circle of twenty-five or so worshippers. Both Christian and Native American symbols are employed during the meeting (Aberle 1966; La Barre 1969; Slotkin 1956; Steinmetz 1990; Stewart 1987). All worshippers have the opportunity to sing and to play the drum while others sing. Singing accounts for at least sixty percent of ritual devotions in NAC meetings. Worshippers are led by a ritual specialist called the Roadman. Worshippers are not allowed to leave the ritual, except with the Roadman's permission, or, during a brief intermission (after the eagle bone whistle is blown four times). The Roadman shows the way to the "peyote road", a way of life characterized by high moral purpose and family values. Church members are expected to abstain from alcohol, care for their families, and demonstrate love toward one another. Members of the NAC proclaim that peyote is a divine medicine, which when used sacramentally, has healed them of alcoholism, tuberculosis, and various other ailments.

Peyote is regarded as a gift from God. It eliminates the craving for alcohol, the most widely abused drug in Indian country. It is not eaten to induce visions. It heals and teaches righteousness. Peyote is eaten, or consumed as a tea, according to a very formal ritual. It is reverently passed clockwise around the circle of church members several times during the course of all-night prayer services.

## Non-Indian Peyote Use is Illegal

Legal penalties for eating peyote in America or Mexico are still fully applicable. Many of those seeking the kind of adventure associated with Castaneda's don Juan must have seen legal barriers as a separate, and irrelevant, reality. As Furst points out (1975: 18), by 1975 seekers of don Juan-type characters had inundated the Huichol. The search for magic and mystery south of the border continues unabated. Valadez (1986: 4-6) has attacked those who lead New Age versions of Huichol peyote hunts, noting, among other things, that they jeopardize bona fide Huichol peyote pilgrimages. In 1990, Americans returning from a trip to the place where Huichols hunt peyote were arrested with forty kilos - 88 pounds - of peyote. Much of the decline in peyote use among non-Indians within the United States may be a result of their collecting peyote south of the U.S. border, and participating in Huichol-like peyote hunts. In the 1960s and early 1970s peyote use was at an all time "high" among non-Indians in the United States. Although peyote use among non-Indians has never been a significant problem, one of the biggest busts occurred in the late spring of 1971, when U.S. Drug Enforcement Administration (DEA) officer Joe Keefe seized 80 pounds of peyote from a Yale University student in New Haven, Connecticut. Keefe recalled that he had been prepared to purchase LSD in liquid form when the student suddenly offered him this huge quantity of peyote. But by the early 1980s, DEA drug seizure statistics show that peyote possession or sales violations had declined dramatically. DEA agents confiscated a grand total of 5.6 kilograms (about 12 pounds) of peyote in 1981. No peyote was seized in 1980, 1982, or 1983. In 1987, only two kilos were confiscated. Inexplicably, peyote seizures were much higher in 1988, 30.5 kilos, and 1989, 51 kilos (Frank Shults, personal communication, 1990). What accounts for this increase, and whether it represents a trend are unknown. Nevertheless, the volume of non-Indian peyote use still ranks far behind use of marijuana and psilocybin mushrooms, the two most popular plants among the counterculture.

Perhaps the NAC will remain relatively unattractive (and undisturbed by non-Indians) as long as the Huichol serve as a magnet or "lightning rod" to absorb non-Indian interest in plant psychedelics. At any rate, the amount of peyote used by non-Indians will never rival the use of chemical psychedelics, which are more convenient, or even psilocybin mushrooms, which are less nauseating. Non-

Indian experimentation with peyote is limited, not only because peyote is illegal, but because it tastes exceedingly bitter. Eating peyote is likely to produce nausea and vomiting. After eating just one peyote, William James, the famous psychologist, became violently sick for 24 hours (Stafford 1983: 112, 133). Barbara Myerhoff is unique, and incorrect, in asserting that for Huichols, and others, peyote tastes "shockingly sour" (Myerhoff 1978: 68).

In the late 1880s the German psychopharmacologist, Dr. Louis Lewin, initiated scientific study of the various alkaloids present in peyote. Peyote's chief psychoactive component, mescaline, was first isolated in 1897 by Arthur Heffter, Lewin's rival (Stafford 1983: 110). Mescaline is clearly preferred by non-Indians, who began experimenting with it after it was first synthesized in 1919 (Stafford 1983: 110). The number of mescaline experimenters increased dramatically after Aldous Huxley's *Doors of Perception* popularized it.

In the late 1950s some non-Indians tried peyote. One of the most famous of them, beatnik poet Allen Ginsberg, revealed that the second part of his most famous poem, "Howl," was written as he wandered up and down the streets of San Francisco after eating peyote (Stafford 1983: 115). In the late 1950s non-Indians inhabiting Greenwich Village began using peyote recreationally. They could obtain it legally by mail from Texas suppliers, or over the counter at the Dollar Sign Coffee House in New York's lower East Side (La Barre 1969: 230).

The first arrests for non-Indian peyote distribution came in May 1960, when 311 pounds of peyote was seized from the proprietor of the Dollar Sign. The peyote confiscated from this raid was never returned to the proprietor, despite the fact that no law prohibiting peyote use existed at that time (La Barre 1969: 230).

Recreational peyote use among non-Indians continued throughout the 1960s. Miniscule as it may be, non-Indian use of peyote has had, and continues to have, a negative impact on non-Indian perception of the NAC. In 1964, California's Fourth District Court of Appeals ruled that "the use of peyote in Indian religious ceremonies constitutes enough of a threat to public safety to make the act illegal without violating constitutional rights of religious freedom" (La Barre 1969: 236). La Barre questioned why Indians who use peyote sacramentally "should be directly penalized in the alleged indirect interest of other potential users *ultra vires*", and warned that carrying this line of reasoning to its logical conclusion would mean that "any departure from conformity to any orthodoxy is illegal" (1969: 236-37). How prophetic he was. As we shall see, when the Supreme Court ruled in 1990 that the NAC use of peyote in religious rituals is not protected under the First Amendment of our Constitution, it cleared the way for state legislatures to outlaw sacramental peyote use simply by passing allegedly neutral, generally applicable laws against peyote.

The U.S. Supreme Court's ruling in *Smith* seems especially aberrant given the 1964 California Supreme Court ruling in *People vs. Woody*, the decision which overturned the Fourth District Court of Appeals ruling cited above. Using the compelling state interest test, the California Supreme Court ruled in *Woody* that Navajo railroad workers using peyote in "honest religious rites" were protected by the First Amendment of the United States Constitution (Anderson 1980: 168).

*Native American Peyote Use is Imperiled*

Even before non-Indians became fascinated with psychedelics Indian use of peyote was deemed dangerous. In 1918, the Bureau of Indian Affairs was lobbying Congress to pass a law prohibiting peyote use. Responding to this threat, James Mooney, an anthropologist affiliated with the Smithsonian Institution, called for a congress of "Roadmen". Mooney was instrumental in helping the Oklahoma delegation of peyotists become the first Native American Church congregation to obtain a legal charter (La Barre 1969: 217).

Since then, the NAC has periodically been forced to defend its First and Fourteenth Amendment rights to use peyote as a sacrament and medicine. (A legal history of NAC struggles can be found in La Barre 1989 or 1969: 223-24 or Stewart 1987). "After taking peyote, Indian men become ax murderers and their women tear off their clothes in a sexual frenzy." Such defamatory statements were circulated in anti-peyote pamphlets in the mid-1930s (Weil, personal communication 1990; Anderson 1980: 164). Such propaganda must have incited legislators to favor a federal law to ban Indian use of peyote in 1937. Like several earlier bills, the 1937 U.S. Senate bill (S. 1399) was defeated, in part because anthropologist Franz Boas and his associates defended the Native American Church in their statement to Congress (La Barre 1969: xii, 223).

The threat to religious freedom for the NAC became more tangible in 1965, when a federal law outlawed peyote (albeit with an exemption granted by the Commissioner of Food and Drugs for the "non-drug use in bona fide religious ceremonies of the Native American Church"), and in 1970, when peyote was classified as a Schedule 1 controlled substance. The Comprehensive Drug Abuse and Control

Act of 1970 provides for a punishment of up to 15 years in prison, a fine of not more than $25,000, or both for individuals convicted of trafficking in peyote. This federal anti-drug law outlawing peyote was passed without the consent, or proof of harm, to the majority of those who use it, i.e., the 250,000 or more members of the Native American Church. However, the DEA has adhered to a regulation which exempts the listing of peyote as a controlled substance in Schedule 1, to protect the "non-drug use of peyote in bona fide religious ceremonies of the Native American Church" (Anderson 1980: 208).

Until the Supreme Court's decision in *Employment Division of Oregon v. Smith* in 1990, NAC members felt secure knowing there was an exemption protecting them from prosecution for their sacramental peyote use. Similarly, during prohibition, wine used in the context of communion was permissible. But the U.S. Supreme Court ruled in *Smith* that the NAC use of peyote in religious rituals is not protected under the First Amendment of our Constitution. As long as a law is allegedly neutral and generally applicable, the Supreme Court need not determine whether a state has a "compelling interest" in restricting religious freedom. Accordingly, religious freedom for the NAC may be trampled whenever a majority of those in Congress, or in individual state legislatures, so desire. Because the vast majority of peyote used in America is consumed in religious rituals of the NAC, this Supreme Court decision seems more discriminatory than neutral on its face.

Some Americans think that all decisions reached by the Supreme Court are unaffected by "events in the street." Others believe that this particular ruling is directly but tacitly connected with our national anti-drug hysteria. Could the Native American Church's sacramental peyote use be confused with recreational use by non-Indians in the psychedelic movement? The virtual hysteria about drug abuse mitigates against rallying the political support needed to preserve the NAC's religious freedom. As 1993 begins, NAC sponsored efforts to legally protect their sacramental and medicinal use of peyote have met with little Congressional enthusiasm.

Anthropologists are among the few non-Indian organizations which affirm that the NAC's "solemn and controlled use of peyote as a sacrament is in no sense harmful . . . it is a scientific, ethical, and legal error to classify peyote used in the rituals of the NAC as a deleterious drug." On November 29, 1990, the American Anthropological Association accepted a "Resolution in Support of the Native American Church." In 1991 the resolution was approved by the membership. Ninety-six percent of those voting were in favor. The resolution states that

> there is no compelling interest that justifies restricting the first amendment rights of members of the NAC to practice their religion; therefore be it resolved that the American Anthropological Association supports NAC efforts to protect their sacramental use of peyote, and calls upon the federal and state governments to assure that NAC members have full legal protection for their way of worship.

James Mooney, Weston La Barre, Franz Boas, Omer C. Stewart, J.S. Slotkin, David Aberle and all other anthropologists who have studied peyote use among Indians have observed that members of the Native American Church regard peyote as a sacrament and use it in highly controlled religious rituals. Their reverent and sacramental use of peyote contrasts dramatically with non-Indian recreational use of peyote. Although anthropological "expert witness" testimony has helped protect the NAC before, this time is different.

Non-Indian advocates of psychedelics have constantly compared themselves to the NAC, demanding the same religious freedom that members of the NAC enjoy (Alpert and Cohen 1966: 61, 76; Stafford 1983: 120-121). They fail to understand how treaty rights and the federal trust responsibility to Indians have placed Indians in a special legal and political category. Perhaps the biggest obstacle to gaining full legal protection for NAC use of peyote in bona fide religious rituals is the widespread fear that exempting Indians from prosecution on religious grounds will encourage recreational or pseudo-religious use of peyote among non-Indians (the very problem La-Barre anticipated). For most members of Congress, if not most Americans, peyote was given a bad name during the frenzy of 1960s experimentation with chemical psychedelics; not peyote. Whether or not the non-ritual use of peyote by non-Indians *should* jeopardize legal protection of the NAC is immaterial. The fact is that publicity about non-Indian use of any psychedelic, including peyote, has and does make it more difficult to protect religious freedom of Indians who use peyote. The fact that relatively few non-Indians use peyote today may be irrelevant to policy-makers. Many of them assume that because peyote is classified as a Schedule 1 controlled substance it must be a dangerous drug. Senator Joseph Biden's comments on the 1990 Senate Bill, S. 3254, are illustrative. As Biden (1990) sees it, even if the "compelling state interest" test abandoned in *Smith* is restored by federal legislation, the Supreme Court would probably rule against the NAC.

Leaders of the NAC feel that their religious freedom is imperiled by the Peyote Way Church of God, Inc. After three members of this church were arrested for possession of peyote in 1980, they filed a lawsuit contending that the exemption for the NAC is unconstitutional for two reasons. According to Steve Moore, attorney for the Native American Rights Fund (personal communication October 30, 1990), they claimed a) they were entitled to equal protection – that the laws of the United States and of individual states should apply equally to all citizens; and b) that a specific exemption for the NAC "established" a religion, in violation of the establishment clause of the First Amendment of the Bill of Rights. In its decision of February 6, 1991, the U.S. Court of Appeals for the Fifth Circuit held that peyote use by members of the Peyote Way Church is illegal. Unlike members of the NAC, virtually all Peyote Way adherents have less than 25% Indian blood, and none are enrolled members of any federally recognized tribe. They are, therefore, ineligible for the legal exemption granted to NAC members. Granting such legal protection to the NAC does not violate the "establishment clause" because it applies to a special class of people with whom the federal government has established a special "trust responsibility". Protecting sacramental use of peyote in bona fide NAC rituals fulfills an obligation intrinsic to our federal government's trust responsibility with Native American nations. Exempting NAC peyote use from prosecution does not "establish" a religion, it simply recognizes the federal government's obligation to protect the culture shared by members of nations with whom it has a trust responsibility.

### Native Americans have Special Rights

Few non-Indians understand how our Constitution's provision for treaty-making with foreign nations, e.g.,

Native Americans, set them apart legally, politically, and culturally. Although this nation-to-nation relationship has been partially superseded (in a de facto way) by imposing citizenship and the "trust responsibility" on Native American societies which were fully sovereign, members of aboriginal American societies ("tribes") still enjoy special rights. To treat them as if they were only ordinary immigrant Americans is to ignore U.S. history and Constitutional law.

In addition to the legal and political differences hinted at above, there are profound differences in religious perspectives. Even today, after centuries of forced assimilation, Native Americans preserve an epistemology radically unlike the kind of cognition essential in science (Fikes 1978, 1985; La Barre 1969: xiv) and in monotheist religions developed in the Middle East (Fikes and Nix 1989). The inalienable right of Native Americans to persist as distinct nations, and to determine their own destinies, includes the right to use peyote as a sacrament. Anything short of full legal protection for NAC rituals is inexcusable. Penalizing them for using peyote as a sacrament would be tantamount to blaming them for the drug abuse epidemic plaguing our society.

## Postscript

The precedent set in *Smith* jeopardizes the religious freedom of all Americans. From 1963, in *Sherbert vs. Verner*, to 1990, in *Smith*, whenever compliance with state or federal law involved a restriction of religious freedom, the government was required to determine if it had a "compelling interest" (e.g., public health or safety). After a government tested whether there was a sufficient cause for curtailing religious freedom, it was obliged to seek the least restrictive method to make citizens comply with the state or federal law at issue. In *Smith*, the Supreme Court abandoned the compelling interest test. Today, if a law is allegedly neutral and generally applicable, the Supreme Court need not apply the compelling state interest test. In our post-*Smith* society there is no legal defense for exempting sacramental use of wine from prosecution under "neutral, generally applicable laws" outlawing alcohol. Since the *Smith* decision, the Amish in Minnesota have been forced to comply with state laws requiring them to place bright orange reflectors on their buggies. Jews in Michigan, and Laotian immigrants (of the Hmong faith) in Rhode Island, have been forced to allow autopsies to be done on their children. This gradual erosion of religious freedom will continue until national legislation restores the judicial standard discarded in *Smith*.

A broad coalition of religious denominations, led by Representative Steven Solarz (NY), gathered over 150 cosponsors for H.R. 2797, a bill to reinstate the "compelling interest" test for free-exercise claims against a federal, state or local authority. On October 1, 1992 the full House Judiciary Committee passed H.R. 2797. But neither it nor its companion bill in the Senate, S. 2969, went to the floor for a vote before the 102nd Congress ended. These bills were introduced again in the 103rd Congress as S. 578 and H.R. 1308.

Senator Daniel Inouye (HI) plans to introduce several amendments to the American Indian Religious Freedom Act of 1978 sometime in the spring of 1993. Included among these amendments are provisions to protect the religious freedom of Native Americans who revere and ingest peyote in *bona fide* religious rituals.

# APPENDIX B

## *HOW MAIZE WAS ACQUIRED BY* HUATÁCAME

The maize myth recited during the *Tatei Neixa* ritual (Serratos version):

Our ancestor *Huatácame* was working in his cornfield. He married a woman, or something resembling one. The ant people were toasting their corn kernels on a *xatü* [a round ceramic griddle called a *comal* in Spanish] when *Huatácame* spoke to them: "You always have corn to toast on the comal but I don't have any. I am hungry. Please tell me where to obtain the corn." The ant people promised to get it for him, provided that he bring a miniature comal, a bundle of coarse grass, a digging stick, and some ashes to a certain place on a particular day. He assembled these items and kept his date with the ant people.

Poor *Huatácame*; his eyebrows were eaten by the ant people. The ants started a fire and *Huatácame* fell asleep. When he woke up he discovered that the ants were gone and so were his eyebrows. He couldn't walk very well because his vision was impaired. He fumbled along slowly, holding his eyelids up with his hands. He shouted, "Listen, won't somebody come and guide me?" But nobody answered him. Then he heard a noise like something flying; perhaps a bird. It was flying and making a noise "huapopopo." As the bird rose from the ground, the whole world trembled. He opened his eyes and saw *cócoro* [the white-winged dove, *Zenaida asiatica*] perched in a large tree. The sound of its call caused him to ask, "Are you the *cócoro*? You are

225

definitely not a person because if you were you would tell me where to obtain the corn the ant people were going to get for me. They ate my eyebrows instead." The bird answered by moving its wings as if to take flight and then it said "*cócoro*" again. The instant the bird flew *Huatácame* began seeing things again.

The bird flew toward the west, to where there was a house with white walls and a thatched roof. The bird decided to go there and *Huatácame* followed, arriving at the house somewhat later. Inside the house was a woman weaving a bag. Next to the house was a *xiriqui* [god-house] and inside it *Huatácame* observed women with dresses of various colors: yellow, red, blue, spotted, black, white, and brown. The mother of these women gave *Huatácame* a chair and invited him to sit down. She told her daughters that their brother had arrived, but because he appeared so unkempt, they laughed at him. Nevertheless, they brought him the chair and he sat down in it. The mother left her weaving and went to the kitchen to bring him some food and water. She brought a little bit of water in a gourd bowl, five very tiny tortillas [i.e. *inütüritzi*], and a tiny bowl of beans. *Huatácame* thought to himself, with this tiny portion of food I'll never get full. Yet when he put one of the tiny tortillas in his mouth, it expanded tremendously. The second tortilla also grew enormously as did the beans he put in his mouth. He could only eat three tortillas. He returned the remaining food to the mother.

Although he had not verbalized his thought, the mother read his mind and asked him: "So you thought there would not be enough food to fill you up?" *Huatácame* replied, "Thanks very much. I'm quite full. Now I have a favor to ask of you. I asked my brothers the ants where I could obtain corn and we made a date. I brought all the items they requested of me: the miniature comal, the bundle of coarse grass, the digging stick, and the ashes. But they ate my eyebrows. I asked them where to get the corn, but they blinded me and left me behind. When I woke up, I walked a short distance before meeting the *cócoro* [dove]. I followed the dove to your house. It is the dove, isn't it? Will you sell me some corn?" The mother replied: "Let us see which of these maidens is interested in leaving with you." *Huatácame* thought to himself, I didn't come here to return with women but only to obtain maize. The mother knew what he was thinking again and asked: "Why do you think that way if you want maize?" Then she went to ask which of her daughters would be willing to go with *Huatácame*.

Feeling slightly bored he sat down to wait. The only one interested in going with him was *Tatzí Tehuiyari* [i.e., an inedible plant which resembles amaranth]. So the mother ordered *Huatácame* to construct, within five days, a god-house, a corn storehouse built on top of a boulder, and a large house. "If you have a mother, tell her to sweep the patio very well and to light a candle at midnight." Upon hearing this, all the women were willing to go with *Huatácame*. Their mother insisted that *Huatácame* comply with her orders before they would be allowed to leave. He agreed to fulfill her demands but commented that women were always after him. To this she replied: "It only has the appearance of a woman; in reality it is maize."

*Huatácame* left and after arriving at his house, told his mother what had to be done within five days. "If we do all this, we will have something to help us live better. We must build a god-house and a corn storehouse on top of a boulder." They completed the work and at midnight five days later *Huatácame* heard a noise like a whirlwind. The maize maidens had arrived at his house. A large *haicü*, which was really *Nihuetzica*, sat down on a shelf inside the god-house. He lighted a candle and offered copal incense to it. The next day *Huatácame* went to prepare his cornfield for planting. It was not long before *Huatácame*'s relatives came to marry the maize maidens. Roadrunner-Person married a sister of *Huatácame*'s spouse. Badger-Person married a sister of *Huatácame*'s spouse. Fox-Person married a sister of *Huatácame*'s spouse. Rat-Person married a sister of *Huatácame*'s spouse. Crow-Person married a sister of *Huatácame*'s spouse. Ground-Squirrel-Person married a sister of *Huatácame*'s spouse. Then they all went to work in their respective corn-fields.

Whereas *Huatácame* did not complain at all, his relatives complained bitterly about all the work they had to do in their cornfields. Their mother-in-law, *Tatei Nihuetzica*, noticed that only *Huatácame* was working without complaint. She visited *Huatácame* in his cornfield and observed many other people working there. The sun's rays reflected off their machetes. She soon returned to speak with *Huatácame*'s wife. "Why don't you take some water to those workers? You don't seem very concerned about your husband. You don't even take him food. Has he said something insulting to you?" Then *Huatácame*'s mother-in-law began grinding corn to take food to the workers. Upon returning to the cornfield with the tortillas she saw that the workers still had some work left to finish. She said to *Huatácame*: "I noticed that the workers were hard at work so I brought them some food." Being all alone he replied, "I don't know anything about other workers." Still his mother-in-law gave him cornmeal, chocolate, and water. *Huatácame* offered these liquids to the five cardinal directions, drinking nothing himself. He finished clearing his cornfield and then came back to burn it.

He never asked anyone for help. He worked alone.

He planted corn but his relatives did not. Consequently, Roadrunner-Person, Rat-Person, Fox-Person, Crow-Person, Badger-Person, and Ground-Squirrel-Person had to beg their mother-in-law to give them corn. They lied to her, claiming to have much land to plant. Even though he really had a lot of land to plant *Huatácame* didn't complain. The six animal people advised their mother-in-law to go inside the house while they were burning their cornfields. This was supposedly said to prevent her from being harmed by all the smoke. However, only a small amount of smoke was produced and when she saw it she realized they had lied to her. When *Huatácame* began burning his cornfield, his mother-in-law started complaining about all the smoke. Being lazy, the animal people hit their machetes against a boulder and broke them. They did not work at all. Their mother-in-law noticed that only *Huatácame* was truly working hard.

*Huatácame* harvested much maize, beans, and squashes. After exhausting the fruits of their own harvest, the animal people started eating the harvest of *Huatácame*. After eating their fill, Ground-Squirrel-Person went beneath a rock and Crow-Person flew far away. Roadrunner-Person, Rat-Person, and Badger-Person ate their fill and returned to their respective homes. *Huatácame* asked the Sun-Father for help and he responded by ordering the animals to go far away, to their present homes. Sun-Father ordered the badger to eat the white cactus apple (which grows in the canyons), wild tubers, and the fruit of the fig tree. He commanded the other animals to go to their respective homes. Then he placed the *haicü* snake as a guard in the south and north. He sent the red-tailed hawk to guard the cornfield against the ground squirrel. *Huatácame* has always been favored by the ancestor-deities. At the zenith, the great eagle [*cuixü huerica*]guards the cornfield as ordered by the Sun-Father. That is why the *cuixü* (red-tailed hawk) will eat squirrels which come to eat maize. Sun-Father also commanded the snakes to eat rats which invade the cornfield. Whenever he planted, *Huatácame* solicited aid from *Tatei Huerica Huimari*, the owner of the maize. She helped him and that's why the maize and squashes were abundant. Maize, squash, and beans were grown in truly great quantity. *Tatei Huerica Huimari* left the woodpecker to help the maize grow well. Ever since then, the animals have been prohibited from eating corn by the Sun-Father. He ordered them to eat other plants instead. The animals were fearful of the snakes and eagles guarding the cornfield. Thus the corn grew without their intruding.

At harvest time, *Huatácame* told his mother-in-law to go and fetch the maize, the beans, and the squashes now that they were ripe. Then he told the *cuixü* that his mother-in-law was coming to the cornfield and thanked him for having stood watch over the cornfield so long. Upon arriving at the cornfield, there were so many squashes that she tripped over one and fell down. Stepping on another one, she fell down again and then returned to the house. She advised *Huatácame* to check and see if badger was in the cornfield.

All this time the maize wife of *Huatácame* was inside the god-house (*xiriqui*) when *Huatácame*'s mother demanded to know:

"Why doesn't your wife work? You never order her to do anything. I am tired of working so hard while she does nothing! She doesn't even make *tortillas* or bring you water. I help you but she doesn't." Later, the mother of *Huatácame* grabbed the maize hanging inside the god-house and threw it inside the hot water of the *nixtamal* [Sp. a basin for soaking corn kernels]. Then she began to grind it on the *metate* [Sp. a large stone slab for grinding maize].

The *metate* was instantly covered with blood because the maize maiden had the form of a person. Blood spurted out from her body.

In the meantime, *Huatácame* had returned to work in his cornfield. Upon returning to his house he noticed that his wife was gone. Within five days the corn of seven colors that had been in the god-house and in the corn-storehouse had also disappeared. The disappearance of the maize was due to the misbehavior of *Huatácame*'s mother. When he saw that his wife was not inside the god-house, *Huatácame* asked, "Why did you make tortillas out of my wife? I acquired her with great difficulty and now you are to blame for the maize having left us. I am leaving to ask my mother-in-law why my wife left."

His mother-in-law was there at *Quitotometa* [the ancient temple]. Upon arriving at her house, he heard her say: "I cannot help you with your wife, the maize. I can only give you the husks of the maize now. Henceforth you must hunt and kill the deer, make another god-house, and fill it full of offerings. You must offer deer to the maize."

Within five days *Huatácame* had obtained a deer. As he examined the corn husks, he found five ears of corn, which he anointed with the blood of the deer. He performed the ritual with the deer to comply with the order of his mother-in-law. She also advised him, "If you kill cattle, you must also give their blood to the maize in addition to deer blood."

Because his mother had insulted and offended the maize, *Huatácame* was obligated to perform rituals for five consecutive years. At the end of the five years, the corn of seven colors appeared once more. Today we Huichols must always go the *Na'arihuame* [the shrine of a Rain-Mother] to obtain the sacred water we use to bless the maize. We must ask *Tatei Otoanaca* for her aid in promoting the growth of corn. For this reason, we Huichols perform our rituals the way we do, today and in the future. Because of the precedents set by our ancestors, the rituals must be performed. Because of the sacrifices made by *Huatácame*, the rituals must be performed.

# APPENDIX C

## *PEYOTE SONG*

The peyote song learned by Bonales:

Like this, like this, the song I am listening to is composed. Like this, like this, the words of this song appear at the same time as the many-colored flowers of peyote. The ancestor-deities appear like the flowers of peyote, speaking in this way. Their song is like this. The letters of diverse languages are being formed here. What do the letters mean? What person can fathom their meaning? The different letters being formed are of a blue color, dedicated exclusively to *moco yoahui* [blue peyote] and *toto maraiyari*. A blue letter written in a book has appeared. It is the word-flower of the peyote. It is formed like the deer.

*Maxa Tehuiyari* [Deer-Person], the *mara'acame* [shaman], lives in *Huíricüta*. He is teaching the song. Now peyote exists and is teaching this song. The peyote is the *nierica* [mirror] of the ancestor-deities. The peyote dwells in *Huíricüta*. It teaches the amaranth song and many others. Under the influence of peyote, *Iromari* and *Caoyomari* are working together. The peyote's song is transported by the wind. The wind is circling around the mountain. The rose-colored flower grows on the head of the peyote. The peyote continues singing. *Maxa Tehuiyari* [Deer-Person], my elder brother, is moving now. This is the tune of the peyote's song. *Yoz Ipana* is mentioned in the song. During the rainy season [*tocárita*] my Rain-Mothers are present. The countenance of the ancestor-deities is really visible. This song is heard at *Yoz Ipana*. Likewise, it is heard at all

233

the *ranchos* [villages].

At the place of the ceremonial candle [i.e., *Haori-yapa*], the ancestor-deities light the candle as is customary in the rainy season. Peyote, I learned your song while under the influence. My Rain-Mothers you are here now as is your custom during the rainy season. All the colors appear and disappear speaking in this way. The peyote flower is a *nierica* [mirror]. At last I am beholding you, peyote. You are composing this song by yourself. You say you will teach me the peyote song. Peyote, you teach all things, especially songs.

[Peyote speaks through the singer]. "I, *Maxa Tehuiyari*, am the peyote. I, *Maxa Tehuiyari*, am the peyote. I have a *matzua* [wristguard]. I am truly *Eacá Tehuari* [Grandfather-Wind], the *matzua*, *Caoyomari*, and the *mara'acame* [shaman]." [Bonales speaks.] "Peyote, your flower is very beautiful." [Peyote answers.] "I have been like this from the beginning. Some say that my flower is very bitter. But I am *Eacá Tehuari* [Grandfather-Wind]. I am *Maxa Tehuiyari* [Deer-Person]. I am the dwelling where all the ancestor-deities rest [i.e., *Pariteciia*]. *Toto maraiyari* lives at *Pariteciia*. I am a *mara'acame* and I am speaking. In my hand I carry a flowering book. It is I who am pronouncing, so do not be afraid my younger brothers [i.e., Huichols]. Do not make yourselves foolish by committing sexual infractions in my presence. Be careful because I can erase your mind. Keep your thoughts focused only on me. Why did you come here to study if you weren't interested in knowing me? My tests are difficult. I have many songs to teach you. I am your elder brother with my head full of flowers [hair]. You may continue learning from me if you desire. I am always like this. Your tests will last five years. You Huichols are my younger sisters and younger brothers. Although you don't see me, I am always like this. Pardon me, but if you come to know me intimately, you shall be like me and feel like I do. Although you may not see me, I shall always be your elder brother. I am called *toto maraiyari*. Have no fear for I shall always be the flower of God. I live at *Yoz Ipana*, where the ancestor-deities rest." Amen.

# HUICHOL GLOSSARY

**ahuatámete**, those who obtain antlers. This word designates a category of tutelary animals including pumas, jaguars, wolves, river otters, kingfishers, cormorants, and Forster's terns which are credited with establishing precedents in fishing, rabbit, deer, and peyote hunting. Also considered *ahuatámete* are those Huichols temporarily representing such tutelary animals as well as the five wolf constellations known as *Huahuatzarí, Ototahue, Xipo Xahui, Toto Haoqui,* and *Pitziteca.* According to Serratos, these celestial wolves send the deer when implored by the singing shaman.

**Aitzárica**, the shrine of the Rain-Mother (*Tatei Aitzárica*) dwelling in the intersection. This Rain-Mother, also called *Yorienaca Matinyeri,* has her shrine near *Teacata* and after the ritual of *Tatei Neixa* a replica of *Tacützi's* cane and a "god's eye" (*tzicori*) are deposited there. The word also signifies the place where all Rain-Mothers convene. Accordingly, sacred water is obtained for use in ritual by the temple officers.

**Aiyoahuicüta**, the blue cliff where the sun, rain, and deer were born. Also known as *Paritecüa,* this is the place where the *Namahuita Neixa* ritual was first performed.

**cacaomama**, a general term for male ancestor-deities and their petrified remains (i.e., rocks).

**cahuitero**, the foremost ritual orator within a Huichol temple district.

**cahuito**, a "myth," text, or narrative which is recited during ritual. This form of ritual oratory is distinguished from a *nenehuieri,* a term best translated as prayer or oration.

**Camóquime**, an ancestor-deity represented by a temple

officer and acclaimed as the Father of the Wolves. In the primordial world of *Huatetoapa* people and animals had interchangeable forms and *Camóquime* was both wolf and human. He can, like *Caoyomari*, teach Huichols to sing and cure. According to Negrín (personal communication), he was the chief singer in *Huatetoapa* and he became a *cacaoma*. Similarly, Zingg identified *"Kumúkame"* as the man appointed by *Tacútzi* (Great-grandmother-Germination) as the chief singing shaman of the wet season gods (Zingg 1938: 348, n.d.: 42, 47-48). Benítez reports that among the peyote pilgrims he is fifth in line (1968b: 260).

**Camoquite**, the immortal ones, or wolves. *Ca*, the prefix, means "strongly negative" (Grimes 1964: 89), *moqui* means dead, and *te* is a plural morpheme.

**Caoyomari**, the male ancestor-deity who originally organized and still maintains ecological order. He is omniscient, omnipresent, and incarnate in various zoomorphic forms. Although his mother is the Rain Mother, he is closely connected with dawn or daylight. His nocturnal counterpart, *Iromari*, is said to depart at sunrise. He is represented by a temple officer and was present at the birth of the Sun-Father. He is the culture hero of the Chapalagana Huichols and the tutelary spirit of singers. His *iyari* (heart-soul-memory) is peyote, and, in harmony with *Camóquime*, he works to promote terrestrial order and health. He teaches Huichols how to sing and heal.

**cócoro**, the white-winged dove (*Zenaida asiatica*) which *Huatácame* followed to the temple where he obtained maize. This dove incarnates the "earth and corn goddess" called *Tatei Cócoro Huimari* (Preuss 1907: 190).

**Cohuaoriyapa**, an archaic name for *Toapori* or Santa Catarina. The word literally means "place of the burning ember," a term which recalls the fire placed in the temple by Grandfather-Fire. A fire burning at the center of the temple is still required in Huichol rituals.

**Cuanameyapa**, the final destination of the children led by the singing shaman in the *Tatei Neixa* ritual. The Rain-Mothers residing there are visited and given offerings by the children.

**Cuixü**, a red-tailed hawk species; either *Buteo jamaicensis* or *Buteo borealis*.

**Cuixü Huerica**, an unidentified species of the genus *Buteo*.

**Eacá Tehuari**, Grandfather-Wind, a male ancestor-deity represented by a temple officer. He can travel everywhere and is related to singing shamans, peyote, deer, and maize.

**haicü**, literally means cloud snake. It is a large black serpent (of unknown species) which dwells near water. These serpents are said to be messengers controlled by the Sun-Father and Great-grandmother-Germination. The Sun-Father may order them to eat Huichols who have committed sexual misdeeds. They are considered to be the Mother of the Fish and an equivalent of the corn deity called *Nihuetzica*.

**Haori**, a category which includes the ceremonial candle, the deer's antlers, and the bundle of pitch pine lighted during the *Namahuita Neixa* ritual.

**Haoriyapa**, the place of the ceremonial candle as identified by Benítez (1968b: 228).

**hicüri**, peyote, a species of spineless cactus known as *Lophophora williamsii*.

**Hicüri Neixa**, the Dance of Peyote performed at the end of the dry season.

**hixüapa**, the intersection, world navel, or fifth direction named in ritual.

**hixüata**, the east or fourth direction named in ritual.

**Huahuatzari**, a master of deer associated with the south or right side. Also identified as a wolf constellation called upon for assistance in rabbit and deer hunting rituals.

**huahuahuüte**, aboriginal Huichol temple officers who serve (represent) various ancestor-deities during a five-year cycle.

**huahua mota cuica**, a Huichol publicly recognized as a singing shaman by virtue of having served as a temple officer for ten years.

**Huatácame**, the ancestor-deity who survived the great flood by building a canoe as ordered by Great-grand-mother-Germination. Considered the father of the post-deluge Huichols, he is credited with obtaining maize maidens at the ancient temple of *Quitotometa*. He is served by a temple officer and represented by one of two singers who provide a chorus for the lead singer in rituals.

**Huatetoapa**, the primordial underworld, or ocean, in which the Sun-Father travels at night.

**huehuiya**, a graphic representation of some benefit solicited from the ancestor-deities. Called "hawime itali" by Zingg (1938: 628), this graphic prayer is the matrix from which the tourist phenomenon of yarn paintings evolved.

**Huerica**, a large black bird, possibly a buzzard or eagle, assumed to represent or incarnate the celestial mother known as *Tatei Huerica Huimari*.

**Huíricüta**, a sacred high desert plateau, located between *Tatei Matinyeri* and *Paritecüa*, where peyote is hunted.

**Huixárica**, a native of the Chapalagana River region; a Huichol Indian.

**Huixáritari**, a plural of *Huixárica*; i.e., Huichols.

**icuahua**, a Huichol healer who has served at least five years as a temple officer before beginning to heal.

**inütüritzi**, minature tortillas used as offerings for ancestor-deities.

**Iromari**, a male ancestor-deity and tutelary spirit of singers. He is the nocturnal deity of wisdom and the counterpart of *Caoyomari*. In the primordial world which existed before the great flood the blue *Iromari*, call *Tehuari Yoahui*, was the *ne'acame* (guardian) of the world. *Iromari* is still indispensable in fishing and funeral rituals and for delivering food to the Sun-Father and other ancestor-deities. Residing with the Sun-Father at *Parítzica, Iromari* is active only at night, departing at sunrise. Singers identify with him and strive to merge in trance with him as well as *Caoyomari*.

**iyari**, the mind or soul located in the heart; a synonym for memory and that which survives physical death. The *iyari* has wings and during sleep may travel to the Pacific Coast or the peyote country.

**mara'acame**, an animal, plant, or person credited with "supernatural" power.

**mara'acate**, plural of *mara'acame*.

**matzimama**, elder brothers, a term applied to wolves and other tutelary animals.

**matzua**, the wristguard used by archers. By extension it refers to a bracelet and to the pulse.

**maxa**, the white-tailed deer (*Odocoileus virginianus*) whose importance to the Huichols is well summarized in Benítez (1968b: 274-285).

**maxa haori**, deer candle is the literal meaning. The deer is assumed to carry a ceremonial candle (*haori*) above or within its antlers.

**Maxa Tecüa**, a peak, possibly *Pariteciia*, which has a godhouse dedicated to *Maxa Tehuiyari* (Deer-Person). This shrine is where *Nihuetzica* is offered to the Sun-Father in the first fruits ritual song.

**Maxa Tehuiyari**, the ancestor-deity known as Deer-Person. Although his inner form is human, he was in deer form when killed by the immortal wolves. His heart or memory is in the peyote and he teaches Huichols how to sing and heal. He is the offering for *Nihuetzica* and is incarnate in maize, deer, peyote, fish and rabbits.

**Maxayapa**, the place of the deer, presumably a shrine located near the town of Real de Catorce.

**Maxa Yoahui**, the Blue-Deer, the quintessential sacrificial animal. Equated with *Caoyomari*, with the wind deity, and with ears of corn, the Blue-Deer is called the altar (*itari*) for all the gods (Benítez 1975: 103-104). Similarly, for Benítez Sánchez, the Blue-Deer represents the life of all the ancestor-deities. Because the Blue-Deer was created from the body of Deer-Tail in order to lend vital energy to ritual offerings, each time a deer is sacrificed, it is his blood which feeds them. Significantly, the blood of the Blue-Deer is the special offering of the maize deity, *Nihuetzica* (Negrín 1977: 116-117, 124). Another of Negrín's informants (1977: 140) calls the Blue-Deer the ancestor of all deer and believes his spirit is still present in peyote.

**Moco Yoahui**, the place of blue water mentioned in the *cahuitero*'s ritual rabbit hunting song. This name is also given to an extremely potent type of "blue peyote."

**Na' arihuame**, a Rain-Mother represented by a temple officer and assumed to have witnessed the birth of the Sun-Father. This Rain-Mother is identified with the first rains to arrive in the sierra each rainy season, rain believed to come from the east. Like *Tatei Matinyeri*, water from her shrine is used in rituals to solicit rain. Lumholtz noted (1900: 13) that she brings rain and lightning from the east and called her "Mother East-Water." She is also an owner or mother of maize.

**nierica**, derived from the verb "to see" (*nieriya*), the *nierica* signifies a visionary ability facilitated by a small round mirror, or formerly, by water. With the *nierica*, a shaman can see whether a patient will live or die, and visualize both ancestor-deities and deceased Huichols. The *nierica* facilitates a trance or altered state of consciousness in which clairvoyance and other paranormal abilites are allegedly manifested. Lumholtz's definition of the *nierica* is short but accurate (1900: 122) and Zingg noted that Huichol men commonly wear small round mirrors around their necks. "The mirror is symbolic of the Sun-Father, whose rays it reflects . . . It was the splendor of this addition to the full festal array of the Huichol man, that enabled the Sun-Father to shine in the first times. Fire also appeared first as a mirror" (Zingg 1938: 702).

**Nihuetari Matahani**, a synonym for *Paritecüa*.

**Nihuetzica**, the ears of maize used in ritual, the maize personified as a corn boy (*Nihuetzica nonotzi*) and as a mother (*Tatei Nihuetzica*). The *haicü* snake is considered an equivalent of *Nihuetzica*.

**noihuari**, one's family or relatives.

**ohueni**, a bamboo chair used by singers and illustrated in Lumholtz (1900: 69-70).

**Otoanaca**, see *Tatei Otoanaca*.

**Ototahue**, a master of deer and rabbits associated with the north or left side. Like *Huahuatzari*, he sings with antlers and orders the wolves to kill the deer.

**Parietzie**, the place where light first appeared on earth, i.e., the peyote country beginning in *Tatei Matinyeri* and extending to *Paritecüa*.

**Paritecüa**, the place where the Sun-Father was born and where the singing shaman presents the children, their offerings, and the ripe maize to the Sun-Father in the *Tatei Neixa* ritual. *Paritecüa* is a peak located near the town of Real de Catorce and believed to be the home of deer. The temple officers take offerings there and ask for various benefits including rain. This "world navel" is also called *Yoz Tecüa, Yoz Yapa, Maxa Tecüa, Tei Yoahuicuta, Nihuetari Matahani, Reunar*, and, in Spanish, "Cerro Quemado" (burnt hill).

**Pitziteca**, see *ahuatámete*.

**pohoari**, a species of marigold (*Tagetes erecta*) whose orange-red flowers are used in the *Tatei Neixa* ritual. According to Lumholtz (1900: 187) the marigold flowers were offered to the maize mother.

**potzi**, an incised ceramic tripod vessel for burning copal incense illustrated in Weigand (1969a: 12-15).

**quieri**, an atropine bearing plant in the genus *Solandra*. Its pollen is used in deer hunting and is said to be wind-borne until it lands on a rock where it begins to germinate. Although it is also derived from Deer-Person, some Huichols consider it less powerful than peyote. Nevertheless, offerings are made and children consecrated to it.

**Quitotometa**, the literal meaning is "inside the house of ancient customs" or "inside the house of flowers." This large temple was located somewhere near the Pacific Coast and had drawings on the outside walls. It is regarded as the home of Great-grandmother-Germination and the place where the white-winged dove led *Huatácame*. It was there that he obtained the maize maidens.

**Reunar**, a synonym for *Paritecüa*, the peak called Cerro Quemado in Spanish.

**Tacützi Yürameca**, "Our Great-grandmother-Germination," an ancestor-deity represented by a temple officer. Also known as *Tacützi Xaorima* or *Tacützi Nacahué*, this goddess of germination is credited with having warned *Huatácame* about the impending deluge. Women may obtain healing and singing ability from her. Her power reaches its peak in the rainy season, the interval between *Namahuita Neixa* and *Tatei Neixa*.

**Tao**, "Our Father" (the sun), a contraction of *ta* (our) **Yao** (Father). The sun is represented by a temple officer and acknowledged as the supreme source of life. The Sun-Father is believed to send rain and clouds from his heart. A god-house dedicated to the Sun-Father is located at the summit of a hill east of Santa Catarina. From there a notch, or "window," where the sun appears at the winter and summer solstices, is visible in the mountain range on the eastern horizon. Huichols believe the Sun-Father is tired and hungry at these points in his journey. Consequently, the blood of deer and rabbits is needed to feed him. The Sun-Father or one of his representatives may send sickness or death as a punishment for misdeeds. Huichols who live a moral life may dwell with the Sun-Father after death.

**taocari**, a reciprocal kinship term used by grandparents and grandchildren. This term also applies to ritual name givers and name takers (i.e., children). It refers to "parent's parent" or "child's child" and, by extension, to secondary consanguineals two generations above Ego (Grimes 1962: 109).

**Tatei Huerica Huimari**, the all-seeing celestial Mother who is represented by a temple officer and assumed to have witnessed the birth of the Sun-Father. She is symbolized by the two-headed eagle and regarded as the mother of maize and children. She is closely connected with women, children, maguey, the cornfield, and the moon. Her double, *Tatei Huetócame,* is presumably the lunar deity. The moon is said to travel above and below (within) the earth, to call the rain clouds, and to receive offerings from Huichols at the hole in the center of the dance plaza located immediately outside (east) of the temple.

**Tatei Matinyeri**, a Rain-Mother identified as the goddess of children and animals by Benítez (1968a: 104-109) and Zingg (1938: 333-336). Following the first fruits ritual (*Tatei Neixa*) a *tzicori* (god's eye) is left at her shrine in the peyote country.

**Tatei Neixa**, Dance of our Mother, the first fruits ritual celebrated in early October as the Pleiades and new corn appear. This ritual is called "yuimacuari" by informants of Grimes, Lumholtz, and Negrín.

**Tatei Nihuetzica**, the maize mother present at the birth of the sun. She is also identified as *Tatei Otoanaca*.

**Tatei Otoanaca**, a female ancestor-deity represented by a temple officer and assumed to have witnessed the birth of the sun. She is regarded as the Mother of fish and maize, i.e., the Mother of the *haicü* and *Nihuetzica*. She is the daughter of Great-grandmother-Germination and the maize-wife of *Huatácame*. In the rituals of *Namahuita Neixa* and *Tatei Neixa* she is represented by a human-size doll composed of corn husks. She has a shrine on the Mesa de Nayarit and is said by Benítez (1975: 168) to live at the "Hill of Paritsika."

**Tatei Yoahuima**, Our Mother Blue Maize, the prototype of maize. She was the first of the maize maidens to reappear after *Huatácame* obtained the blood of the deer to atone for the offense his mother committed.

**taxáricü**, the dry season which begins in October and ends in early June.

**Teacata**, a shrine with various god-houses photographed and described by Lumholtz (1902: 165-173).

**Teiteima**, Rain-Mothers or female ancestor-deities as a group. My informants use *Tei* as a term for Mother and thus I translate this word as Rain-Mothers, acknowledging that it is translated as our aunts – the rain deities – by Grimes and Grimes (1962: 111).

**Teiyoahuicüta**, the place of the Blue-Mother. A synonym for *Aiyoahuicüta* or *Paritecüa*. My informants regard this as the place where deer and Rain-Mothers were born.

**Toapori**, is the name of two small mountains which rise above Santa Catarina (Lumholtz 1900: 9). I use this term to designate the temple district surrounding Santa Catarina.

**Toaporitari**, the inhabitants of the temple district centered at Santa Catarina.

**tocáripa**, the literal meaning is immersed in life, night, and rainy season. *Tocari* and *tocarita* are synonymous.

**toqui**, the aboriginal Huichol temple, round in shape, with walls of adobe and rock, and a thatched roof which is replaced every five years.

**Toto Haoqui**, a wolf constellation, see *ahuatámete*.

**toto maraiyari**, a synonym for Deer-Person's heart and a huge type of peyote which lives at *Pariteciia*.

**tuhuaino**, the child who travels to *Pariteciia* in the song of the first fruits ritual. Huichol children under ten years of age should not eat ears of corn, beans, squash, venison, fish, or peyote until after this first fruits ritual is performed. *Tühuainorixi* is the plural of *tühuaino*.

**tzicori**, the "god's eye" or sacred part of a deer's intestine which must be given to Grandfather-Fire after skinning the deer. A textile *tzicori* is carried by children in the first fruits ritual and used to mark the first five years of their lives. I have seen this geometrical symbol in Mimbres and Chupicuaro ceramics. Lumholtz noted that this design is found in burials in Peru (1900: 160) and reported that both the moon and male squash flowers are called *tzicori* (1900: 154). Lumholtz (1900: 73, 97-98, 155) and Negrín (1977: 32) suggest that the *tzicori* is a *nierica* which the Rain-Mothers use to watch over children dependent upon them.

**Tzicoritari**, like *tühuainorixi*, this name is given to children participating in the first fruits ritual.

**Tzimanixi**, the constellation we identify as the Pleiades.

**Xipo Xahui**, a wolf constellation, see *ahuatámete*.

**xiriqui**, the god-house used for *rancho*-based rituals. At ceremonial centers such god-houses are consecrated to specific ancestor-deities served by the temple officers. The god-house is virtually identical to the Huichol house (*qui*) in size, shape, and construction. Pine timbers were used as the frame for the thatched roof of the archaic god-house called *pariya*.

**Yocáhuima**, the daughter of Great-grandmother-Germination and the black dog who married *Huatácame* after assuming human form. She is regarded as the Mother of rabbits and deer and is assumed to dwell in the middle of the Pacific Ocean. She is said to receive the dead deer and its antlers and is represented by Huichol women in temple rituals. She is also identified as the dog which helps chase deer.

**Yocáhuita**, the plural of *Yocáhuima*.

**Yozyapa**, the place of God. *Yoz* is a mispronunciation of the Spanish word for God (*Dios*). The pilgrimage to this sacred peak, also known as *Pariteciia*, is, in effect, sanctified by being associated with the Spanish God.

**Yoz Ipana**, a synonym for *Pariteciia*.

**Yoz Teciia**, a synonym for *Pariteciia*.

# BIBLIOGRAPHY

Aberle, D.F. *The Peyote Religion Among the Navajo.* Chicago: Aldine Publishing Co., 1966.

Abrams, Ira. Personal communication, 29 November 1987.

Adovasio, J. M., and G.F. Fry. "Prehistoric Psychotropic Drug Use in Northeastern Mexico and Trans-Pecos Texas." *Economic Botany* Vol. 30, No. 1: 94-96, 1976.

Alpert, Richard, and Sidney Cohen. *LSD.* New York: New American Library, 1966.

American Indian Science and Engineering Society. "Our Voices, Our Vision: American Indians Speak Out for Educational Excellence." New York: College Entrance Examination Board, 1989.

Anderson, Edward F. *Peyote: The Divine Cactus.* Tucson: University of Arizona Press, 1980.

Anonymous. *Freedom,* "Mind Control Activities." Vol. 22, No. 2: 29, 1990.

Applegate, R.B. "The Datura Cult Among the Chumash." *Journal of California Anthropology* Vol. 2, No. 1: 7-17, 1975.

Baigent, Michael Richard Leigh and Henry Lincoln. *Holy*

*Blood, Holy Grail.* New York: Dell Publishing Co., 1983.

_____.*The Messianic Legacy.* New York: Dell Publishing Co., 1986.

Baker, Deborah. "Huichol Indians dance to the past." *Santa Fe New Mexican*, 22 September, 1989, C-1.

Bateson, Gregory. *Steps to an Ecology of Mind.* New York: Ballantine Books, 1972.

Beals, Ralph. "Sonoran Fantasy or Coming of Age?" *American Anthropologist* 80(2): 355-362 (June 1978).

Bebb, Bruce. "Carlos Castaneda's Questionable Teachings." *Los Angeles Reader* 6(43): 18-19 (17 August 1984).

Bedford, Sybille. *Aldous Huxley A Biography.* New York: Alfred Knopf, 1974.

Bell, Betty. Letter to Warren Snyder, 6 April 1970.

Benítez, Fernando. *Los Indios de México*, Vol. 2. México: Biblioteca Era, 1968a.
_____. *En la Tierra Mágica de Peyote.* México: Biblioteca Era, 1968b.
_____. *In the Magic Land of Peyote.* Translated by John Upton. New York: Warner Books, 1975.

Berrin, Kathleen, ed. *Art of the Huichol Indians.* New

York: Harry N. Abrams, Inc., 1978.

Biden, Senator Joseph. *Congressional Record* S17330-S17331, October 26, 1990.

Borhegyi, S.A. De. "Miniature Mushroom Stones from Guatemala." *American Antiquity* 26: 498-504, 1961.
_____. "Pre-Columbian Pottery Mushrooms from Mesoamerica." *American Antiquity* 28: 328-38, 1963.
_____. "Archaeological Synthesis of the Guatemalan Highlands." In *The Handbook of Middle American Indians.* Vol. 2 Edited by R. Wauchope. Austin: University of Texas Press, 1965.

Burns, Mary Ellen. "Diego Delgado, man without a country." *The State Hornet,* 15 March 1972: 2, 8.

Bye, Robert. "Short Communications." *Journal of Ethnobiology* Vol. 7, No. 1: 121-122 (Summer 1987).

Campbell, Joseph. *Historical Atlas of World Mythology.* Vol. 2, *The Way of the Seeded Earth,* Part 3: *Mythologies of the Primitive Planters: The Middle and Southern Americas.* New York: Harper and Row, 1989.

Carrasco, Pedro. Letter to author, 3 March 1989.

Castancda, Carlos. *The Teachings of Don Juan: A Yaqui Way of Knowledge.* New York: Ballantine Books, 1969. First edition published 27 June 1968 by the University of California Press (according to deMille 1990).

_____. *A Separate Reality: Further Conversations with Don Juan*. New York: Simon and Schuster, 1971.

_____. *Journey to Ixtlan: The Lessons of Don Juan*. New York: Simon and Schuster, 1972.

_____. *Sorcery: A Description of the World*. Doctoral dissertation: University of California, Los Angeles, 1973.

_____. *The Power of Silence*. New York: Simon and Schuster, 1987.

Castaneda, Carlos, and Theodore Roszak. *"Don Juan: The Sorcerer."* Cassette tape 38 minutes, recorded at KPFA Berkeley, 1968. Available from Audio-Forum 96 Broad Street Guilford, CT 06437.

Castaneda, Margaret Runyan, as told to Wanda Sue Parrott. "My Husband Carlos Castaneda." *Fate*, 28 (2/299): 70-78 (February 1975).

Chagnon, Napoleon A. *Yanomamo: The Fierce People.* 2d ed. New York: Holt, Rinehart and Winston, 1977.

Chickering, A. Lawrence. "The Shaman of Ruthlessness." Review of *The Power of Silence* by Carlos Castaneda. in the *Los Angeles Times* Book Review, 1:8, (January 17, 1988).

Churchill, Ward. "A Little Matter of Genocide: Native American Spirituality and New Age Hucksterism." *The Bloomsbury Review*, 23-24 (Sept./Oct. 1988).
_____. "Spiritual Hucksterism." *Z Magazine*. Vol. 3, No. 12: 94-98 (December 1990).

Clapham, W.B. *Natural Ecosystems*. New York: Macmillan Publishing Company, 1973.

Clare, Ray. "The Breaching of Don Juan's Teaching: A Twenty Year Review of Carlos Castaneda's *The Teachings of Don Juan: A Yaqui Way of Knowledge*, (1968)." *Psychedelic Monographs and Essays,* Vol. 4: 43-63 (Summer, 1988).

Clastres, Pierre. *Society Against the State.* Translated by Robert Hurley and Abe Stein. New York: Urizen Books, 1977.

Clifford, James. *The Predicament of Culture.* Cambridge: Harvard University Press, 1988.

Clifford, James, and George E. Marcus. *Writing Culture: The Poetics and Politics of Ethnography.* Berkeley: University of California Press, 1986.

Clifton, J. A. ed. *The Invented Indian.* New Brunswick, N.J.: Transaction, 1990.

Cohen, Maimon M., and M.J. Marmillo. "Chromosomal damage in human leukocytes induced by lysergic acid diethylamide." *Science* 155: 1417-1419, 1967.

Cohen, Sidney. "Lysergic Acid Diethylamide: Side Effects and Complications." *Journal of Nervous and Mental Diseases.* 130: 30-40, 1960 .

Cox, Harvey. *Turning East.* New York: Simon and Schuster Touchstone Books, 1977.

Däniken, Erich von. *Chariots of the Gods?* London:

Souvenir, 1969.

_____. *The Gold of the Gods*. New York: Putnam, 1973.

Dedrick, John. Letters to author, 23 May 1989 and 17 January 1990.

Delgado-Vega, Diego W. *Arquitectura Funeraria Precolombina en el Estado de Jalisco*. Master's thesis, Latin American Studies, UCLA, 1969.

DeLoria, Vine Jr. *Custer Died For Your Sins*. New York: Avon Books, 1969.

deMille, Richard. *Castaneda's Journey: The Power and the Allegory*. Santa Barbara: Capra Press, 1976.

_____. (2d ed.) *Castaneda's Journey: The Power and the Allegory*. Santa Barbara: Capra Press, 1978.

_____. "Explicating Anomalistic Anthropology with Help from Castaneda." Paper presented at the 77th annual meeting of the American Anthropological Association, Los Angeles, November 1978 (1978b).

_____. "Occultism is not Science: A Reply to Kootte." *The Journal of Mind and Behavior,* Vol. 5, No. 2: 223-226 (Spring 1984).

_____. *The Don Juan Papers: Further Castaneda Controversies*. Belmont, Calif.: Wadsworth Publishing Company, 1990.

_____. "Validity is not Authenticity." In *The Invented Indian*, edited by J.A. Clifton. New Brunswick, N.J.: Transaction, 1990.

Dibble, Charles E., and Arthur J. O. Anderson. *Florentine Codex, Book 10: The People*. Santa Fe, New Mexico: The School of American Research and the University of Utah, 1961.

Dobkin de Rios, Marlene. *Hallucinogens: Cross-Cultural Perspectives.* Albuquerque: University of New Mexico, 1984.

Dreben, Steve. *Huichole: People of the Peyote.* Film distributed by Perry/Dreben Productions 1911 Hillcrest Road Los Angeles, CA 90068, 1986.

Duerr, Hans Peter. *Dreamtime: Concerning the Boundary between Wilderness and Civilization.* Translated by Felicitas Goodman. London/New York: Basil Blackwell, 1985.

Eger, Susan, in collaboration with Peter Collings. "Huichol Women's Art." In *Art of the Huichol Indians.* Edited by Kathleen Berrin, New York: Harry N. Abrams, Inc., 1978.

Eliade, Mircea. *Shamanism: Archaic Techniques of Ecstasy.* Translated by Willard Trask. New York: Pantheon Books, 1964.

Fabila, Alfonso. *Los Huicholes de Jalisco.* México, D.F.: Instituto Nacionál Indigenista, 1959.

Faber, Mel D. "Don Juan and Castaneda: The Psychology of Altered Awareness." *The Psychoanalytic Review,* Vol. 64, No. 3: 323-379, 1977.

Faris, J.C. *The Nightway: A History and a History of Documentation of a Navajo Ceremonial.* Albuquerque: University of New Mexico Press, 1990.

256      **Bibliography**

Fetterman, D. M. *Ethnography.* Newbury Park, Calif.: Sage Publications, 1989.

Fikes, J.C. "Native American Education: Cognitive Styles, Cultural Conflict, and Contract Schools." *Michigan Discussions in Anthropology,* Vol. 4:31-51 (Fall 1978).

_____. *Huichol Indian Identity and Adaptation.* Ph. D. dissertation, University of Michigan, 1985.

Fikes, J.C., and Nelleke Nix. *Step Inside the Sacred Circle.* Bristol, Ind: Wyndham Hall Press, 1989.

Fontana, Bernard. Review of *Art of the Huichol Indians. American Indian Art* Vol. 5:72-73 (November 1979).

Foote, Shelby. *The Civil War* (Vol. 1). New York: Vintage Books, 1990.

Foster, G.M. "Nagualism in Mexico and Guatemala." *Acta Americana* 2 (102): 85-103, 1944.

Frankfurt, Harry. "On Bullshit." *Raritan,* Vol. 6, No. 2: 81-100, 1986.

Furst, Peter T. "West Mexican Tomb Sculpture as Evidence for Shamanism in Prehispanic Meso-America." *Anthropologica* No. 15: 29-60 (December 1965).

_____. *Shaft Tombs, Shell Trumpets and Shamanism: A Culture-Historical Approach to Problems in West Mexican Archaeology.* Ph. D. dissertation, University of California at Los Angeles, 1966.

_____. "The Olmec Were-jaguar Motif in the Light of Ethnographic Reality." Reprinted from the Dumbarton Oaks Conference on the Olmec. Trustees for Harvard University. Washington, DC, 1968a.

_____. "Myth in Art: A Huichol Depicts His Reality. *Los Angeles County Museum of Natural History Quarterly* 7:3 (Winter 68/69): 16-25, 1968b.

_____. *To Find Our Life: The Peyote Hunt of the Huichols of Mexico.* 1969. Film distributed through the University of California, Berkeley Media Center. 2176 Shattuck Ave., Berkeley, Calif. 94704.

_____. *To Find Our Life: Peyote Among the Huichol Indians of Mexico.* In *Flesh of the Gods: The Ritual Uses of Hallucinogens.* Edited by Peter T. Furst. New York: Praeger, 1972a.

_____. "Hallucinogenic Rituals and Therapy: A discussion of ancient peyote rituals and modern LSD psychotherapy." Cassette distributed by the Center for Cassette Studies, Inc. 8110 Webb Ave., N. Hollywood, Calif. 91605, 1972b.

_____. "Morning Glory and Mother Goddess at Tepantitla, Teotihuacan: iconography and analogy in pre-Columbian Art." In *Mesoamerican Archaeology: New Approaches.* Edited by N. Hammond. Austin, Texas: University of Texas Press, 1972c.

_____. "An Indian Journey to Life's Source," *Natural History* Vol. 82, No. 4 (April, 1973). Reprinted in *Shaman's Drum*, No. 8: 33-39, 1989.

_____. "The Roots and Continuities of Shamanism." *ArtsCanada.* Vol. 30, Nos. 5 and 6:33-60 (Dec. 1973-Jan. 1974) . Reprinted in *Stones, Bones, and Skin: Ritual and Shamanic Art.* Edited by Brodsky, Danesewich, and Johnson. Toronto: The Society for Art Publication, 1974.

_____. "Introduction" in *The Magic Land of Peyote*. Translated by John Upton. New York: Warner Books, 1975.

_____. "Drugs, chants and magic mushrooms." *Natural History* 84(10): 74-79, 1975b.

_____. *Hallucinogens and Culture*. San Francisco: Chandler and Sharp, 1976.

_____. "The Art of Being Huichol." In *Art of the Huichol Indians*, 18-34. See Berrin, 1978.

_____. Letter to Richard deMille, July 25, 1981, with copies to Barbara Myerhoff and Jay Fikes, 1981.

_____. *Mushrooms: Psychedelic Fungi*. New York: Chelsea House, 1986.

_____. 1989. Reprint. See 1973 entry.

_____. "Vistas Beyond the Horizon of this Life: Encounters with R. Gordon Wasson." In *The Sacred Mushroom Seeker*, Portland, Oregon: Dioscorides Press, 1990.

Furst, Peter T., and Marina Anguiano. "Myth and Ritual Among the Huichol Indians." In *Enculturation in Latin America: An Anthology*. Edited by Johannes Wilbert. Los Angeles: U.C.L.A. Latin American Center Publications, 1977.

Furst, Peter T., and Michael D. Coe. "Ritual Enemas." *Natural History* 86 (8): 88-91, 1977.

Furst, Peter T., and B.G. Myerhoff. "Myth as History: The Jimson Weed Cycle of the Huichols of Mexico." *Anthropologica*, (17): 3-39, (June 1966). Reprinted in 1972 as "El Mito Como Historia: El Ciclo del Peyote y la Datura Entre los Huicholes." In *El Peyote y los Huicholes*. Edited by S. Nahmad. México:

SepSetentas #29.

Garrett, L., B. Miskin, and P. Woolf. "Why Do Scientists Cheat?" American Academy for the Advancement of Science *Observer* Vol. 7: 8-9, 1989.

Gayton, A.H. *The Narcotic Plant Datura in Aboriginal American Culture.* Ph. D. dissertation, University of California, Berkeley, 1928.

Grimes, Joseph E. *Huichol Syntax.* The Hague: Mouton, 1964.

Grimes, Joseph E., et al. *El Huichol: Apuntes Sobre el Lexico.* Technical Report to NSF distributed by the Department of Modern Languages and Linguistics, Cornell University, 1981.

Grimes, Joseph E., and Barbara F. Grimes. "Semantic Distinctions in Huichol (Uto-Aztecan) Kinship." *American Anthropologist* 64: 104-112, 1962.

Grinspoon, Lester, and J.B. Bakalar. *Psychedelic Drugs Reconsidered.* New York: Basic Books, 1979.

Gutiérrez-López, Gregorio. *El Mundo de los Huicholes.* México, D.F.: B. Costa-Amic, 1968.

Halifax, Joan. *Shamanic Voices.* New York: Dutton, 1979.

Harner, Michael J. "Jivaro Souls" *American Anthropologist* 64(2): 258-272, (April 1962).
_____. *The Jivaro: People of the Sacred Waterfall.* 1972. Reprint. Berkeley: University of California Press,

1984.

———. "The Ancient Wisdom in Shamanic Cultures." In *Shamanism*. Edited by Shirley Nicholson. Wheaton, Illinois: Theosophical Publishing House, 1987.

Henderson, Jim. "When Scientists Fake It." *American Way Magazine* March 1, 1990: 56-62, 100-101.

Henry, Jules. *Culture Against Man*. New York: Vintage Books, 1965.

Hernandez, Luis. "Professor Explores Unlimited World." *United States International University News*, November 10, 1972: 5.

Hers, Dr. Marie Areti. Interview with Dr. Celia Weigand (on cassette tape), August 10, 1990 .

Hughes, Robert, Sandra Burton, Tomas A. Loayza and others. "Don Juan and the sorcerer's apprentice." *Time*, March 5, 1973, 101 (10): 30-35.

Hultkrantz, Ake. *Conceptions of the Soul Among North American Indians*. Stockholm: The Ethnographical Museum of Sweden, 1953.

———. *The Religions of the American Indians*. Translated by Monica Setterwall. Berkeley: University of California Press, 1979.

Huxley, Aldous. *Doors of Perception*. New York: Harper, 1954.

———. "Mescaline and the Other World." In *Lysergic acid diethylamide and Mescaline in Experimental Psychiatry*. Edited by L. Chadden. New York/London: Grune and Stratton, 1956.

———. "Drugs That Shape Men's Minds." *Saturday Evening Post* October 18, 1958, 231 (16): 28-29, 108, 110-111, 113.

———. *Island.* New York: Harper, 1962.

Huxley, Laura A. *This Timeless Moment.* New York: Farrar, Straus and Giroux, 1968.

Illich, Ivan *Deschooling Society.* New York: Harrow Books, 1972.

Iltis, H. H. "From Teosinte to Maize: The Catastrophic Sexual Transmutation." *Science*, Vol. 222, No. 4626: 886-894, 1983.

Jolly, C.J., and F. Plog. *Physical Anthropology and Archaeology.* New York: Alfred A. Knopf, Inc., 1976.

Joralemon, Donald. "The Selling of the Shaman and the Problem of Informant Legitimacy." *Journal of Anthropological Research.* Vol. 26, No. 2: 105-118 (Summer, 1990).

Jorgensen, D.L. *Participant Observation: A Methodology for Human Studies.* Newbury Park, Calif.: Sage Publications, 1989.

Kesey, Ken. *One Flew Over the Cuckoo's Nest.* New York: Viking Press, 1962.

Kelley, Jane H. Letters to author, 20 May 1988 and 16 June 1988.

Kelley, J.H., W.C. Holden, and Rosalio Moisés. *The Tall Candle.* Lincoln: University of Nebraska Press, 1971.

Klineberg, Otto. "Notes on the Huichol." *American Anthropologist* NS 36: 446-460, 1934 .

Kluckhohn, Clyde. 1944. Reprint. *Navajo Witchcraft.* Boston: Beacon Press, 1967.

Knab, Tim. "Notes Concerning Use of Solandra among the Huichol." *Economic Botany* 31: 80-86, 1977.

Kobler, John. "The Dangerous Magic of LSD." *Saturday Evening Post,* November 2, 1963, 236 (38): 30-32, 35-36, 39-40.

Kramer, Kenneth. *The Sacred Art of Dying.* New York: Paulist Press, 1988.

Krickeberg, Walter. *Las Antiguas Culturas Mexicanas.* México, D.F.: Fondo de Cultura Economica, 1961.

LaBarre, Weston. *The Peyote Cult.* New York: Schocken Books, 1969. Reprint. Norman: University of Oklahoma Press, 1989.
_____. Film review of Furst's "To Find Our Life: The Peyote Hunt of the Huichols of Mexico." *American Anthropologist,* Vol. LXXII, 5: 1201, 1970.
_____. "Stinging Criticism from the author of *The Peyote Cult.*" In *Seeing Castaneda.* Edited by Daniel Noel. New York: G.P. Putnam's Sons, 1976.

Leary, Timothy. *Playboy* interviews Tim Leary, *Playboy,*

Vol. 13 (9) (September 1966).

_____. *High Priest*. New York: World Publishing Co., 1968.

_____ *Politics of Ecstasy*. New York: Putnam, 1968.

_____. *Flashbacks: An Autobiography*. Los Angeles: J.P. Tarcher, 1983.

Leon-Portilla, Miguel. *Aztec Thought and Culture*. Norman: University of Oklahoma Press, 1963.

Linkletter, Art. *Drugs at my door step*. Waco, Tex: Word Books, 1973.

Lumholtz, Carl. *Symbolism of the Huichol Indians*. New York: American Museum of Natural History, Memoirs 1 (2), 1900.

_____. 1902. Reprint. *Unknown Mexico, Vols. 1 and 2*. Glorieta, New Mexico: Rio Grande Press, 1973.

Mandell, Arnold J. "The Neurochemistry of Religious Insight and Ecstasy." In *Art of the Huichol Indians*, 71-81. *See* Berrin, 1978.

Mangelsdorf, P.C. *Corn: Its Origin, Evolution, and Improvement*. Cambridge, Mass.: Belknap, 1974.

Marcus, George, and Michael Fisher. *Anthropology as Cultural Critique: An Experimental Moment in the Human Sciences*. Chicago: University of Chicago Press, 1986.

Marks, John. *The Search for the Manchurian Candidate*. New York: Times Books, 1979.

Mason, J. Alden. "Tepecano Prayers." *International Journal of American Linguistics*, Vol. 1: 91-153, 1918.

Mata Torres, Ramón. *Peregrinación del Peyote.* Guadalajara: Edición de la Casa de las Artesanías del Gobierno de Jalisco, n.d..

_____. *Vida y Arte de los Huicholes.* Primera Parte (La Vida). No 160 Año XIX. México: Artes de México, 1974.

McCarty, Kieran, and Dan S. Matson. "Franciscan Report on the Indians of Nayarit, 1673." *Ethnohistory* 22 (3): 193-222, 1975.

Millón, Rene. Letter to author, 28 January 1988.

Montagu, Ashley. "Wolf Children." In *Culture and Human Development: Insights into Growing Human.* Edited by A. Montagu. Englewood Cliffs, N.J. : Prentice-Hall, Inc., 1974.

Moore, Steve. Personal communication, including "Fact Sheet on Peyote Way Church of God, Inc.," 1990.

Morotti, Alan. Interviews with Diego Delgado-Vega, 15 and 27 May 1970.

Moyers, Bill. *The Secret Government: The Constitution in Crisis.* Cabin John, Md: Seven Locks Press, 1988.

Myerhoff, Barbara G. *The Deer-Maize-Peyote Complex among the Huichol Indians of Mexico.* Ph. D. dissertation, University of California at Los Angeles, 1968.

———. *Peyote Hunt: The Sacred Journey of the Huichol Indians*. Ithaca, New York: Cornell University Press, 1974.

———. "Shamanic Equilibrium: Balance and Mediation in Known and Unknown Worlds." *American Folk Medicine: A Symposium*. Edited by W. Hand. Berkeley: University of California Press, 1976.

———. "Peyote and the Mystic Vision." In *Art of the Huichol Indians*, 56-70. *See* Berrin, 1978.

———. *Number Our Days*. New York: Simon and Schuster Touchstone Books, 1980.

Nash, Jesse. "Bob Weir of the Grateful Dead." *High Times* No. 180: 39-41, 54-56, August 1990.

National Institute on Drug Abuse. *Annual Data 1989* Statistical Series 1, Number 8. Rockville, Md: U.S. Department of Health and Human Services, 1989.

Negrín, Juan. *The Huichol Creation of the World*. Sacramento: E.B. Crocker Art Gallery, 1975.

———. *El Arte Contemporáneo de los Huicholes*. Guadalajara: Universidad de Guadalajara, 1977.

———. *Acercamiento histórico y subjetivo al Huichol*. Guadalajara: Universidad de Guadalajara, 1985.

Nova. PBS documentary program, "Do Scientists Cheat?" 1988.

Ortega, José *Conquista del Nayarit*. 1754. Reprint. México, D.F.: Editorial Layac, 1944.

Ortiz, Alfonso. *The Tewa World*. Chicago: University of Chicago Press, 1969.

Palafox-Vargas, Miguel. *La Llave del Huichol.* México: Instituto Nacionál de Antropología e Historia, 1978.

Parrott, Wanda Sue. "I Remember Castaneda." *Fate* 28 (2/ 299): 79-81 (February 1975).

Pelto, P.J., and G.H. Pelto. *Anthropological Research.* London: Cambridge University Press, 1978.

Pollack, Steven H. "The psilocybin mushroom pandemic." *Journal of Psychedelic Drugs* Vol. 7 (1):73-84 (Jan.- Mar. 1975).

Philips, S.U. "Participant Structures and Communicative Competence: Warm Springs Children in Community and Classroom." In *The Nacirema.* Edited by J.P. Spradley and M.A. Rynkewich. Boston: Little, Brown, and Co., 1972.

Prem Das. "Initiation by a Huichol Shaman." In *Art of the Huichol Indians,* 129-141. *See* Berrin, 1978.
_____. "The House of Dreams." In *Shamanic Voices.* Edited by Joan Halifax. New York: Dutton, 1979.

Preuss, Konrad T. "Die Hochzeit des Maises und andere Geschichten der Huichol-Indianer." *Globus* 91: 185-192, 1907.
_____. " Un Viaje a la Sierra Madre Occidental de México." *Boletín de la Sociedad Mexicana de Geografía y Estadistica.* Vol. 3, part 4, 187-214, 1909.

Puharich, Andrija. *The Sacred Mushroom.* New York: Doubleday, 1959.

Rappaport, Roy. *Ecology, Meaning, and Religion.* Richmond, Calif: North Atlantic Books, 1979.

Razo-Zaragoza, José Luis. Letters to Gordon J. Dugan, et al. 3 August and 10 September 1970.

Rios, Guadalupe de la Cruz. Taped Interviews, 3 May and 14 May 1988, 22-23 March 1991.

Rohner, Ronald P. "Franz Boas: Ethnographer on the Northwest Coast." In *Pioneers of American Anthropology.* Edited by June Helm. Seattle: University of Washington Press, 1966.

Root-Bernstein, Robert. "Breaking Faith." *The Sciences* Vol. 30(1): 8-11, 1989.

Roszak, Theodore. *The Making of a Counter Culture.* Garden City, N.Y.: Doubleday, 1969.

Safford, W.E. "Daturas of the Old World and New: An Account of Their Narcotic Properties and Their Use in Oracular and Initiatory Ceremonies." *Annual Report of the Board of Regents of the Smithsonian Institution,* 537-567, 1920.

Santoscoy, Alberto. *Nayarit, Colección de Documentos Inéditos, Históricos, Y Etnográficos Acerca de la Sierra de Ese Nombre.* Guadalajara: Yguinez, 1899.

Schultes, R.E. "Teonanacatl: The Narcotic Mushroom of the Aztecs." *American Anthropologist,* N.S. 42 : 429-443, 1940.

_____. "A Contribution to our Knowledge of Rivea

Corymbosa: The Narcotic Ololiuqui of the Aztecs." *Botanical Museum of Harvard,* Cambridge, Mass., 1941.

_____. "The Botanical and Chemical Distribution of Hallucinogens." *Annual Review of Plant Physiology* *21*: 571-98, 1970.

_____. "An Overview of Hallucinogens in the Western Hemisphere." In *Flesh of the Gods.* Edited by P.T. Furst. 3-54. *See* Furst 1972a.

Seldes, George. *Witness to a Century.* New York: Ballantine Books, 1988.

Shults, Frank. "Peyote Seizures, 1980-1989." Washington, D.C.: Drug Enforcement Agency Public Affairs Office, 1990.

Siegel, Ronald K. "Inside Castaneda's Pharmacy." *Journal of Psychoactive Drugs.* 13: 325-331, 1981.

_____. *Intoxication. Life in Pursuit of Artificial Paradise.* New York: Dutton, 1989.

Slotkin, J.S. *The Peyote Religion: A Study in Indian-White Relations.* Glencoe, Ill.: Free Press, 1956.

Spicer, Ed. *Pascua: A Yaqui Village in Arizona.* 1940. Reprint. Tucson: University of Arizona Press, 1984.

_____. *Cycles of Conquest.* Tucson: University of Arizona Press, 1962.

Spradley, J.P. *The Ethnographic Interview.* New York: Holt, Rinehart, and Winston, 1979.

Stafford, Peter. *Psychedelics Encyclopedia.* Berkeley,

Calif.: And/Or Press, 1977.

_____. 2d ed. *Psychedelics Encyclopedia.* Los Angeles: J.P. Tarcher, 1983.

Stanley, James. *Larry King Live.* Interview on December 5, 1990.

Steinmetz, P.B. *Pipe, Bible, and Peyote Among the Oglala Lakota.* Knoxville, Tenn.: University of Tennessee Press, 1990.

Stewart, Omer C. *Peyote Religion: A History.* Norman, Okla.: University of Oklahoma Press, 1987.

Sykes, Charles J. *Profscam.* New York: St. Martin's Press, 1988.

Taylor, R. E. "The Shaft Tombs of Western Mexico: Problems in the Interpretation of Religious Function in Nonhistoric Archaeological Contexts." *American Antiquity,* Vol. 27: 71-81, 1970.

Taylor, W.W. "Archaic Cultures Adjacent to the Northeas tern Frontiers of Mesoamerica." In Archaeological Frontiers and External Connections. Edited by G.F. Ekholm and G.R. Willey. *Handbook of Middle American Indians,* Vol. 4, 1966.

_____. "The hunter-gatherer nomads of northern Mexico: a comparison of the archival and archaeological records." *World Archaeology* 4(2): 167-178, 1972.

Thompson, J. Eric S. "The Moon Goddess in Middle America." *Contributions to American Anthropology and History,* No. 29. Reprinted by the *Carnegie In-*

*stitution of Washington*, Publication No. 509, June, 1939: 121-173.

Time 1973. *See* Hughes, Robert.

Traditional Circle of Elders. *Communique No. 9.* Unpublished report of the Tenth Meeting of the Traditional Elders Circle Loneman School, White Clay District Pine Ridge, Lakota Nation, South Dakota. June 21, 1986.

Trebay, Guy. "Mexican Standoff: Carlo McCormick's Bad Trip." *Voice,* July 10, 1990: 19.

Valadez, Susan. "Mirrors of the Gods: The Huichol Shaman's Path of Completion." *Shaman's Drum,* No. 6: 28-40 (Fall 1986).
_____. "Guided Tour Spirituality: Cosmic Way or Cosmic Rip-off?" *Shaman's Drum* No. 6: 4-6 (Fall 1986).

Wasson, R. Gordon. "Seeking the Magic Mushroom." *Life,* May 13, 1957.
_____. "The Divine Mushroom of Immortality." In *Flesh of the Gods*, 185-200. *See* Furst, 1972a.
_____. *The Wondrous Mushroom: Mycolatry in MesoAmerica.* New York: McGraw-Hill, 1980.

Weigand, Phil C. "Modern Huichol Ceramics." *Mesoamerican Studies* No. 3. Carbondale: Southern Illinois University Museum, 1969a.
_____. "The Role of an Indianized Mestizo in the 1950 Huichol Revolt." *Specialia Inter-americana* No. 1. Carbondale: Latin American Institute, Southern Illi-

nois University, 1969b.

_____. "Contemporary Social and Economic Structure."
In *Art of the Huichol Indians*, 101-115. *See* Berrin
1978.

_____. "The Role of the Huichol Indians in the Revolu-
tions of Western Mexico." *Proceedings of the
Coast on Latin American Studies*, Vol. 6: 167-176.
Tempe: Arizona State University, Center for Latin
American Studies, 1979a.

_____. "Consideraciones Acerca de la Arqueologia y la
Etnohistoria de los Tepecanos, Huicholes, Coras, Tequales y Mexicaneros; con notas sobre los
Caxcanes." In *Zacatecas, Anuario de Historia*, #2,
169-217. Edited by Cuahtemoc Esparza. Zacatecas
Universidad Autónoma de Zacatecas, 169-217,
1979b.

_____. "Differential Acculturation Among the Huichol
Indians." In *Themes of Indigenous Acculturation in
Northwest Mexico*. Edited by P.C. Weigand and
Thomas B Hinton. Tucson: University of Arizona
Press, 1981.

_____. "Considerations on the Archaeology and Eth-
nohistory of the Mexicaneros, Tequales, Coras,
Huicholes, and Caxcanes of Nayarit, Jalisco, and
Zacatecas." In *Contributions to the Archaeology
and Ethnohistory of GreaterMesoAmerica*, 126-187.
Edited by William J. Folan. Carbondale: Southern
Illinois University Press, 1985.

_____. "Mexicaneros, Tecuales, Coras, Huicholes y
Caxcancs de Nayarit, Jalisco y Zacatecas: Algunas
consideraciones sobre su arquelogia y etnohistoria."
*Trace*, #15, 5-21 (June 1989) . Centro de Estudios
Mexicanos y Centroamericanos, 1989a.

_____. Weigand quoted in Avila-Palafox, Ricardo. *El*

*Occidente de Mexico: arqueologia, historia, an tropologia.* Guadalajara: Editorial Universidad de Guadalajara, 1989b.

Weigand, Phil C. and Celia Garcia Weigand. "Death and Mourning Among the Huicholes of Western Mexico." In *Coping with the Final Tragedy: Cultural Variation in Dying and Grieving*, 53-69. Edited by David Counts and Dorothy Counts. Amityville, New York: Baywood Publishing, 1991.

Weil, Andrew. "The Strange Case of the Harvard Drug Scandal." *Look*, November 5, 1963, Vol. 27 (22): 38, 43-44, 46, 48.

_____. "Some Notes on Datura." *Journal of Psychedelic Drugs,* 9(2): 165-169 (April-June, 1977).

Weinstein, Harvey. *Psychiatry and the CIA: Victims of Mind Control.* Washington, D.C.: American Psychiatric Press, 1990.

Werner, Oswald, and G.M. Schoepfle. *Systematic Fieldwork.* Newbury Park, Calif.: Sage Publications, 1987.

Wolfe, Tom. *The Electric Kool-Aid Acid Test.* New York: Farrar, Straus and Giroux, 1968.

Zerries, Otto, et al. *Pre-Columbian American Religions.* New York: Holt, Rinehart, and Winston, 1968.

Zingg, Robert M. *The Huichols: Primitive Artists.* New York: G.G. Stechert, 1938.

_____. *Huichol Mythology.* Manuscript on file at the

Laboratory of Anthropology, Santa Fe, New Mexico, n.d.

# INDEX

# ABOUT THE AUTHOR

Jay Courtney Fikes enjoyed caring for California King Snakes and hunting rabbits, quail, and doves in southern California before radical political and counter-cultural currents of the late 1960's attracted him. He graduated *cum laude* from the University of California at Irvine in 1973, obtained a master's degree (with honors) in bilingual education from the University of San Diego in 1974, and completed his doctorate in cultural anthropology at the University of Michigan in 1984. Since 1985 he has taught courses in cultural anthropology, policy research, and social science research methods at the United States International University, Marmara University in Istanbul, Turkey, and New Mexico Highlands University.

Dr. Fikes is presently researching Native American Church rituals and completing a documentary film on Huichol Indians. In 1991-92 he was a Postdoctoral Fellow at the Smithsonian Institution. In 1990 he began lobbying for beneficial national Native American legislation as a Legislative Secretary at the Friends Committee on National Legislation. He is an active participant in a national coalition working to pass legislation protecting Native American religious freedom, including sacramental peyote use and worship at sacred sites currently located on federal lands.

He has published numerous scholarly, popular, and technical articles. He reviews books on Native American religion for *Choice* and belongs to the International Platform Association, the New York Academy of Sciences, the American Anthropological Association, and the Religious Society of Friends. He is married and has a daughter.

# ORDER FORM

## CARLOS CASTANEDA,
## ACADEMIC OPPORTUNISM AND THE
## PSYCHEDELIC SIXTIES

by Jay C. Fikes, Ph.D.
Foreword by Professor Phil C. Weigand

**Cost**: $19.95 US          $22.95 CDN

<table>
<tr><td>

TO ORDER BY PHONE:
**1-800-667-8398**
Call 9 am to 5 pm, Western Standard Time,
Monday through Friday
Please have your VISA and this form at hand.

</td><td>

TO ORDER BY MAIL:
Mail Order Form to:
**MILLENIA PRESS**
#207-1005 View Street
Victoria, B.C. V8V 3L7
Canada

</td></tr>
</table>

**ORDERED BY:**

NAME _____

INSTITUTION _____

ADDRESS _____

CITY _____ STATE/PROV. _____

Telephone number _____

| ISBN | AUTHOR/TITLE | QTY | PRICE |
|------|--------------|-----|-------|
|      |              |     |       |
|      |              |     |       |
|      |              |     |       |
|      |              |     |       |

**METHOD OF PAYMENT:**

___ Check or Money Order (make payable to Millenia Press)

___ VISA

| | |
|---|---|
| Subtotal | |
| B.C. Residents add 7% G.S.T. Sales tax | |
| Postage & Handling ($2.50 for the first book; 50¢ for each add'l book) | |
| **TOTAL** | |

Account # ⬜⬜⬜⬜⬜⬜⬜⬜⬜⬜⬜⬜⬜⬜⬜⬜

Exp. Date _____

Signature _____